D1495238

The New York City Audubon Society
Guide to Finding Birds
in the
Metropolitan Area

The New York City Audubon Society will:

Protect and conserve wildlife
and wildlife habitats in New York City.

Educate and inform members and
the general public about environmental
issues, especially as they affect New York City.

Study and enjoy birds and other wildlife,
and foster appreciation of the natural world.

Cooperate with the National Audubon
Society and other conservation organizations
in furthering sound environmental practices.

Serve as a resource and advisor to
other groups concerned
with specific environmental issues.

Defend and improve the quality of green
spaces and the environment in New York City
for both wildlife and human beings.

Marcia T. Fowle and Paul Kerlinger
With a foreword by William Conway

The New York City Audubon Society
Guide to
Finding Birds
in the
Metropolitan Area

Maps by Mark Stein
Illustrations by Louise Zemaitis

Comstock Publishing Associates,
a division of
Cornell University Press
Ithaca and London

First published 2001 by Cornell University Press
First printing, Cornell Paperbacks, 2001

Printed in the United States of America

Library of Congress Cataloging-in-Publication Data

Fowle, Marcia T., 1935–
    New York City Audubon Society guide to finding birds in the metropolitan area/by Marcia T. Fowle and Paul Kerlinger ; maps by Mark Stein ; illustrations by Louise Zemaitis.
        p. cm.
    ISBN 0-8014-8565-7 (paperback : alk. paper)
    1. Bird watching—New York Metropolitan Area—Guidebooks.
    2. Birding sites—New York Metropolitan Area—Guidebooks.
    3. Birds—New York Metropolitan Area. I. Title: Guide to finding birds in the metropolitan area. II. Kerlinger, Paul. III. New York City Audubon Society. IV. Title.
    QL684.N7 F69 2001
    598'.07'2347471—dc21

                                                    00-012060

Cornell University Press strives to use environmentally responsible suppliers and materials to the fullest extent possible in the publishing of its books. Such materials include vegetable-based, low-VOC inks and acid-free papers that are recycled, totally chlorine-free, or partly composed of nonwood fibers. Books that bear the logo of the FSC (Forest Stewardship Council) use paper taken from forests that have been inspected and certified as meeting the highest standards for environmental and social responsibility. For further information, visit our website at www.cornellpress.cornell.edu.

Paperback printing   10   9   8   7   6   5   4   3   2   1

*To Bruce,
Margaret, Suzanne, and Abigail
and to Jane*

Contents

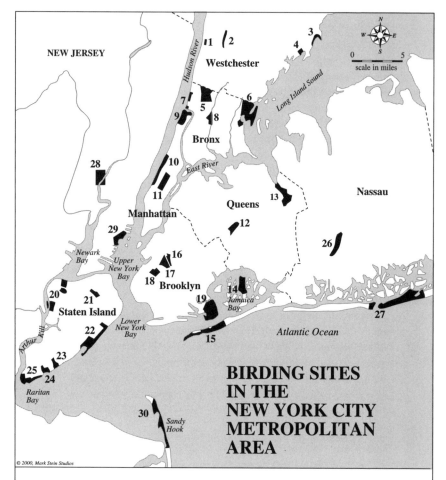

BIRDING SITES IN THE NEW YORK CITY METROPOLITAN AREA

© 2000, Mark Stein Studios

WESTCHESTER
1. Lenoir Preserve
2. Sprain Ridge Park
3. Edith G. Read Wildlife Sanctuary at Playland Park
4. Marshlands Conservancy

BRONX
5. Van Cortlandt Park
6. Pelham Bay Park
7. Spuyten Duyvil Shorefront Park, Riverdale Park, and Wave Hill
8. New York Botanical Garden

MANHATTAN
9. Inwood Hill Park
10. Riverside Park
11. Central Park

QUEENS
12. Forest Park
13. Alley Pond Park
14. Jamaica Bay Wildlife Refuge
15. Jacob Riis Park, Fort Tilden, and Breezy Point

BROOKLYN
16. Brooklyn Botanic Garden
17. Prospect Park
18. Green-Wood Cemetery
19. Floyd Bennett Field and Dead Horse Bay

STATEN ISLAND
20. Northwest Corridor: Arlington Marsh, Mariners Marsh Preserve, Goethals Pond, Saw Mill Creek Park/Prall's Island
21. Clove Lakes Park
22. Great Kills Park
23. Wolfe's Pond Park
24. Mount Loretto Nature Preserve and Long Pond Park
25. Conference House Park

NASSAU
26. Hempstead Lake State Park
27. Jones Beach State Park and Point Lookout

NEW JERSEY
28. Hackensack Meadowlands/Richard W. DeKorte Park
29. Liberty State Park
30. Sandy Hook

Maps

Foreword

A good guide to finding birds offers specific, immediate detail about bird locality plus a world of background information putting it in context. Of the many such guides to the New York City metropolitan area, the book in your hands is the best one yet. It has been developed through collaboration with scores of dedicated enthusiasts, compiled and vetted by experts, and now is available to the rest of us. In the section on Hunter Island in the Bronx, for example, the authors offer gems such as this: "In the vicinity of this intersection, look right (northeast) to a large northern red oak with a cavity at the top of its trunk. Here, from the end of January to April, is an active Great Horned Owl nest." This book widens our options, expands and enriches our experience with unique insights, and makes finding our way around much easier with the support of clear maps.

More than 350 species of birds are to be found in the New York City metropolitan area today. The first curator of ornithology of the Wildlife Conservation Society's Bronx Zoo, the famous naturalist William Beebe, birded the zoo's 265 acres from 1899 until the late 1940s but never saw there a cardinal, Tufted Titmouse, mockingbird, or House Finch. These are now among the 24 bird species that breed there more or less regularly. And they are among the most common of the more than 215 bird species fairly regularly recorded on the zoo's grounds, along with such mammalian immigrants as an occasional coyote.

The zoos, five in our area (Bronx, Central Park, Prospect Park, Queens, and Staten Island) and the aquarium on Coney Island comprise the largest system of living collections in any city in the world and are a great place to sharpen one's understanding and animal-watching skills. So too is the American Museum of Natural History, just west of Central

Park, where the long gone Passenger Pigeon and Carolina Parakeet and many extant species are the subject of permanent exhibits.

It is the variety of habitat in the metropolitan area, especially its wonderful parks, that accounts for the high numbers of birds seen here—and the high number of sharp-eyed birders! The parks are special places, oases of water and vegetation, where harried migrants can pause, rest, and find fuel to carry on their seasonal journeys. The excitement of birding in Central Park in spring, so improbably bordered by tall buildings, is a quintessential New York experience.

Nevertheless, to get to the parks and the city's few undeveloped areas, birds must run a gauntlet of killer skyscrapers, reflecting glass windows, confusing lights, foodless deserts of concrete and blacktop, dangerous airports, and murderous communications towers. It is conservatively estimated that two to four million songbirds die each year in the eastern United States from colliding with lighted communication towers, usually at night when many birds are migrating. Worse yet, the rapid growth of mobile phone use means that these towers will double in number in the next few years. The advent of digital television is expected in the next five years to add as many as one thousand new towers, each greater than a thousand feet tall, around the nation.

As wilderness areas continue to disappear, the number of individuals in the species populations in our area will inevitably decline. With each decline, local populations slide closer to extinction. Returning from their devastated condition of half a century ago or more, the forests north of our area are reclaiming the land from abandoned farms and timbering concessions. Their potential for supporting migratory birdlife may be increasing. In this context, however, migratory is a trouble-filled word, for the vast majority of songbirds that make New York birding so fascinating are dependent also on wintering areas in Latin America where deforestation is proceeding unabated.

In years past, following a strong tradition and supported still by rich bird migrations, the New York City metropolitan area has been the beneficiary of a series of almost uniquely excellent bird accounts and guides. Their genesis dates from 1900 with the Audubon Society's Christmas Bird Count, the first systematic effort to maintain records on local bird populations. Frank Chapman and Charles Rogers were the originators, and Chapman's 1906 *Birds of the Vicinity of New York* was the first real guide. It was followed by Ludlow Griscom's *Birds of the New York City Region* (1923), Allan Cruikshank's *Birds around New York City* (1942) and then John Bull's monumental *Birds of the New York Area* (1964). Together, these books provide a window on the changes in our region as well as in its birdlife and also on its distinguished culture of birding.

Today, Christmas counts are national and engage thousands of participants. They are highly competitive, with regional teams counting in defined areas and trying to see how many birds they can find—and to beat other teams. For a truly delightful account of such a challenging event, an early one featuring the Bronx County Bird Club, look up the late Roger Tory Peterson's *Birds Over America* (1948) and read the chapter "Census at Christmas"; indeed, read the whole book! It is not only refreshing but offers a fascinating view of birding half a century ago by one of the best and most eloquent birders there ever was.

Although each of these early publications was, at some level, a guide to finding birds in our region, the model for bird-finding publications was most extensively developed by Olin Sewall Pettingill and called *A Guide to Bird Finding East of the Mississippi* (1951). When the second edition of this volume came out in 1976, Pettingill wrote, "in the quarter century since its [earlier] publication, the changes in the twenty-six states I have found staggering." He noted that the Peregrine Falcon no longer bred east of the Mississippi. (They are now mating in New York City!) The Cattle Egret had become widespread, and the Snowy Egret and Glossy Ibis, "so commonly associated in our memory with southern swamps and bayous, are nesting on the coast of Maine." (And now nest on islands in Jamaica Bay and New York Harbor.) While citing Pettingill, New York City birders must not overlook Robert S. Arbib, Jr., lead author of *Enjoying Birds Around New York City*, who provided most of the information Pettingill found for the second edition of his famous guide.

Present-day birders will never see the Passenger Pigeon, whose vast flocks once roared through our region, nor the Heath Hen or lovely Carolina Parakeet. Nor will they list the Great Auk, probably a casual visitor to New York City's bays, or the Labrador Duck, which used to show up mainly in city markets. (The last was shot on Long Island in 1875.) However, ongoing changes are no less instructive, and many that occurred between 1942 and 1964 were compiled in John Bull's book (succeeded in 1998 by Emanuel Levine's *Bull's Birds of New York State*, Cornell University Press). Bull included the Red-bellied Woodpecker as a recent non-breeding arrival, which today nests in the metropolitan area. And he detailed the extraordinary reintroduction program and the control of some pesticides, which affect avian reproduction and have restored the Peregrine Falcon.

Birdwatching provides us with a personal window on the changing relationships between humans and wildlife and on what is happening to Earth's fauna in general. If done in an organized way, it can make us participants in the growing conservation struggle whose course will determine the livability of our environment. Tracking the local fauna, involving uninvolved friends, and providing data are all contributions that birdwatchers can make to effective wildlife advocacy through the Audubon Society. And such tracking is a door to rewarding friendships and associations. Besides, it is great fun.

William Conway
Senior Conservationist and former President of the
Wildlife Conservation Society, Bronx, New York

Preface

The New York City metropolitan region is dotted with remarkable natural areas, from the grasslands at Floyd Bennett Field, the woodlands of Pelham Bay Park, the Ramble in Central Park, the oceanfront of the Rockaway Peninsula, to the Greenbelt on Staten Island. Migratory and resident birdlife thrives in these habitats.

The New York City Audubon Society Guide to Finding Birds in the Metropolitan Area is a natural outgrowth of the chapter's twenty years of programming, which promotes awareness of and protection for avian species in the urban area. The Field Trip Committee organizes and leads birdwalks for thousands of participants to sites that are described in this book. The Program Committee arranges monthly programs that offer insights into bird (and other wildlife) behavior. The Education Committee introduces young New Yorkers to the joys of birding through such materials as the "Birds of New York City" slide show.

Chapter leaders David L. Burg and Peter Rhoades Mott enthusiastically endorsed the guidebook project as proposed by Paul Kerlinger. Longtime member and former President Norman I. Stotz provided significant and crucial support along with seasoned naturalists who know where, when, and how best to go birding. I congratulate these contributors and the authors, former Executive Director Marcia T. Fowle and Paul Kerlinger, Ph.D., for their dedication to the project. We take pride in the spirited way each of them has followed the Audubon tradition of volunteerism, education, and commitment to conservation.

Ten years ago founding President Emily Jones and former Education Committee Chairperson Naola Gersten-Woolf produced the forerunner to this guidebook, *Birding Without a Car*, a pamphlet describing birding sites in New York City that are accessible by public transportation. Without the assistance of Cornell University Press and the encouragement of science editor Peter J. Prescott, this guidebook would never have been realized. We are deeply grateful also to Furthermore, the publication program of The J. M. Kaplan Fund, for financial support and interest. This chapter is confident that *The New York City Audubon Society Guide to Finding Birds in the Metropolitan Area* will lead both the novice and the experienced birder to unusual adventures. I trust that these birding episodes will encourage citizens to join the chapter in its efforts to protect urban natural areas, and I look forward to seeing thumb-worn and weathered copies in the hands of birders throughout New York City.

Lynn Rollins, President, New York City Audubon Society

Acknowledgments

The New York City Audubon Society and the authors are grateful to all who assisted in the compilation of this special guidebook.

First and foremost, we heartily thank each resource person—47 ardent birders in the metropolitan area. Special thanks go to Carl Alderson, Natural Resources Group, City of New York/Parks and Recreation; Peter Bacinski, Sanctuary Director, Sandy Hook Nature Center, New Jersey Audubon Society; James Bangma, New Jersey Audubon Society; Scott Barnes, teacher-naturalist, Sandy Hook Nature Center, New Jersey Audubon Society; Catherine Barron, Treasurer, Mariners Marsh Conservancy; Alison Beall, Curator, Marshlands Conservancy; Robbin Bergfors, Natural Resources Group, City of New York/Parks and Recreation; Michael Bochnik, Hudson River Audubon Society of Westchester; Ronald V. Bourque, Board of Directors and former President, New York City Audubon Society; Thomas W. Burke, Greenwich Audubon Society; Robert V. DeCandido, Urban Park Ranger, City of New York/Parks and Recreation; Joseph DiCostanzo, President, Linnaean Society of New York, and Research Assistant, Great Gull Island Project, American Museum of Natural History; Sarah M. Elliott, teacher of nature classes in Central Park and Battery Park City and publisher of *The Elliott Newsletter: Nature Notes from Central Park*; Aline Euler, Board of Directors, New York City Audubon Society, and Education Director, Alley Pond Environmental Center; Mike Feller, Natural Resources Group, City of New York/Parks and Recreation; Tom Fiore; Howie Fischer; Robert Gochfeld, editor of Brooklyn Bird Club's *The Clapper Rail*; Adele Gotlib; Elizabeth Herland, Refuge Manager, Wallkill National Wildlife Refuge; Carl Jaslowitz; Scottie Jenkins; Edward W. Johnson, Curator of Science, Staten Island Institute of Arts and Sciences; Richard Kane, Vice President, New Jersey Audubon Society; George Karsch; Paul Keim, President, Brooklyn Bird Club; David S. Künstler, Wildlife Manager, Van Cortlandt and Pelham Bay Parks, City of New York/Parks and Recreation; Jeff Main, Curator, Read Wildlife Sanctuary; Annie McIntyre, Environmental Educator, Theodore Roosevelt Nature Center, Jones Beach State Park; Peter Rhoades Mott, Board of Directors and former President, New York City Audubon Society; Christopher A. Nadareski, wildlife biologist, New York City Department of Environmental Protection, and Peregrine Project Manager for New York City; Geoffrey Nulle, volunteer, Riverside Park Fund, and Park Tender, Riverside Park Bird Sanctuary; Roger Pasquier, Environmental Defense; Bonnie Petite, naturalist and President, Conference House Park–Raritan Bay Conservancy; Larry Plotnick, Queens County Bird Club; Don Riepe, Park Ranger, Gateway National Recreation Area, and Chapter Director, American Littoral Society; Richard Rosenblum; Herb Roth, North Shore Audubon Society; Oscar W. Ruiz, New York City Audubon Society; Don Smith, Hackensack Meadowlands, DeKorte Park; Howard Snyder, Founder and President, Mariners Marsh Conservancy, and former Vice President, New York City Audubon Society; Norman I. Stotz, former President, New York City Audubon Society; Tom Torma, South Shore Audubon; Steve Walter; Marie Winn, author of *Red-tails in Love: A Wildlife Drama in Central Park*; and John and Mary Yrizarry, Sterling Forest League of Naturalists. Not only did they willingly supply extremely accurate and interesting site information, but they reviewed the material with us (sometimes over and over), coordinated it with the maps, and updated it when necessary, always with enthusiasm and encouragement. Their understanding of the significance of the project and the necessity for perseverance has resulted in a unique guidebook.

To those who reviewed and commented on various parts of the guide, we thank Deborah Allen, The Linnaean Society of New York; Marianne Anderson, Van Cortlandt Park; David E. Avrin, Assistant Superintendent, Gateway National Recreation Area; Mary Davis, Director of Conservation, Westchester County Department of Parks, Recreation, and Conservation; Sue Gilmore, Gateway National Recreation Area; Susan Guliani, Superintendent of Operations, Jones Beach State Park; Susan Hinz, Brooklyn Center for the Urban Environment; Rick Lepkowski, Central Park Conservancy; Pete McCarthy, Gateway National Recreation Area; Mark McKeller, Van Cortlandt Park; Tom O'Connell, Gateway National Recreation Area; Jan Orzeck-Byrens, Director of Marketing and Public Information, Prospect Park; Starr Saphir, field trip leader, New York City Audubon Society; and Dave Taft, Gateway National Recreation Area. We greatly appreciate their thoughtful input. Thanks also to

Ronald V. Bourque, Peter Joost, David S. Künstler, Peter Rhoades Mott, Don Riepe, Norman I. Stotz, and Steve Walter, who reviewed and fine-tuned the checklist of the birds of New York City.

We thank Betty Hagedorn and the late Rita Holz, who methodically checked various fine points, specifically in the borough chapters. Thanks also go to Caryl Baron for her technical assistance on document formatting and to Jane Kashlak for indexing. So many people answered our pleas for specific information and advice. We are particularly appreciative of help from Heather Amster, Real Property Supervisor, New York State Department of Environmental Conservation; Michael Crewdson, author, *Wild New York*; Linda D'Anna, Natural Resources Group, City of New York/Parks and Recreation; Anne Galli, Hackensack Meadowlands; Carl Howard, Esq., U.S. Environmental Protection Agency; Jeff Mason, Assistant Director of Operations, Jones Beach State Park; Wendy Paulson, The Nature Conservancy, and Advisory Council, New York City Audubon Society; Dorothy Poole, former member of the Board of Directors, New York City Audubon Society; Shawn Spencer, City of New York/Parks and Recreation, Staten Island; and Michael Sperling, South Shore Audubon. They always led us in the right direction and to the right person.

We thank especially those who edited our rough drafts: Mary T. Adelstein, editor; Peter P. Blanchard III, the Trust for Public Land and Advisory Council, New York City Audubon Society; Peter Joost, Board of Directors and Chair, Wildife/Endangered Species Committee, New York City Audubon Society; and Lauren Pera, co-editor, *The Urban Audubon*, New York City Audubon Society. Their suggested changes and reassurance moved the project forward with style and ease. And we greatly appreciate the care and thoroughness of the final draft readers, Emanuel Levine and Norman I. Stotz.

After a wide search, we found the illustrator Louise Zemaitis just down the coast, on Cape May. We thank her for the lovely drawings.

The maps are an integral part of this guidebook. Fortunately, we teamed up with Mark Stein, whose special (and spatial) creative talents are conveyed in each site map. We thank him for assiduously changing park boundaries, trails, and stream locations when new information was supplied and, of course, for his clear, handsome maps.

We are grateful to Furthermore, the publication program of The J. M. Kaplan Fund, for providing funding for these illustrations and maps.

New York City Audubon's President Lynn Rollins and Executive Director Sean Andrews (1999–2000) nourished the project during the incubation period. We are very appreciative of their support.

Thanks again to each of you for your patience and stick-to-itiveness. The guidebook's completeness and liveliness are due to you.

The New York City Audubon Society
Guide to Finding Birds
in the
Metropolitan Area

Red-tailed Hawk

Introduction

Few people associate New York City with wildlife or birdwatching. Instead, images of the theater, museums, financial institutions, skyscrapers, restaurants, ethnic diversity, population density, and even crime and dirt are more likely to come to mind. Considering these urban attributes, it may come as a surprise that New York City offers marvelous birding opportunities.

In New York City's parks and green spaces and along portions of its 578-mile waterfront are some of the best places in the world to watch birds. In fact, New Yorkers need only take a bus, subway, or ferry to Central Park, Jamaica Bay Wildlife Refuge, Pelham Bay Park, Prospect Park, or Staten Island to see hundreds of species of birds. The diversity is vast and changes constantly throughout the year.

Whether the viewer is a novice or an expert, there are places to watch common and rare birds, birds in winter, birds in migration, birds in courtship, and nesting birds. This guidebook introduces metropolitan New Yorkers, nearby suburbanites, and visitors from afar to the wealth of birding opportunities in and around the city.

How This Guidebook Was Assembled

No individual possesses all the information needed for a comprehensive guide to New York City birding sites. We relied on the expertise and insight of numerous naturalists. These resource people possess not only a unique understanding of their sites and a love of birds, but also a willingness to share their enthusiasm. To provide clear, accurate information, they devoted many hours compiling information and reviewing drafts and site maps. Also consulted were organizations that serve birders, protect birds, and conserve habitat. Among these organizations is a champion of urban birding and the guidebook's sponsor, the New York City Audubon Society.

Why the New York City Area Is a Marvelous Birding Place

Extraordinary birding in New York City is the result of a combination of geography, topography, and habitat diversity. New York City is located at a geographic nexus of migration and nesting distribution for numbers of species. For tens of thousands of years, since the end of the last ice age and long, long before the city and suburbs were built, birds migrated to and through the area. Large numbers of arctic, boreal, northern temperate, and southern temperate species follow this migration route. New York City is situated north enough and south enough to be included in both the nesting and migratory range of many species. Add the resident species, which nest locally, and vagrants, which are off course, and the total species count exceeds 300. On an annual basis, more than 200 different species frequent the New York City metropolitan area.

Topographically, New York City is situated at the eastern edge of North America at a point where the coastline takes a turn in an east–west direction. Both New York State's Westchester County (on Long Island Sound) and Long Island (on the Atlantic Ocean) extend in this direction. Birds flying due south from eastern Canada and northeastern United States encounter Long Island Sound or the Atlantic Ocean. Reluctant to make long-distance water crossings, many species do not venture offshore. They follow along the east–west New York State (also Connecticut) coastline, forming a concentrated stream of migrants at the New York Bight (the mouth of New York Harbor). In the reverse direction, many birds from South America or southern United States on the way to New England or eastern Canada go through the New York metropolitan area, avoiding an Atlantic Ocean crossing.

After a night or day in flight, birds migrating over the city alight somewhere in the metropolitan area for rest and food. Because of the numbers of migrants and the fragmented nature of open space suitable for landing, unusually dense concentrations of birds occur during migration.

Specific habitat requirements for most North American bird species can be found in the New York City area. These include ocean, harbor, river, back bay, tidal marsh, freshwater marsh, swamp and riparian forest, pond, reservoir, lake, upland forest, grassland, brushland, beach, dune forest and grassland, city streets, and suburban neighborhoods.

The location of New York City and the surrounding metropolitan area is at a historic and essential junction for hundreds of millions of birds that migrate through each year. The area is also a haven for nesting and wintering species.

How to Use This Guidebook

This guide can be used in several ways. The first five chapters cover birding sites in the boroughs followed by chapters devoted to nearby sites in Nassau County, Westchester County, and New Jersey. Residents and visitors can scan the descriptions to learn what is available within these geopolitical entities and find a birding place that suits them.

Readers can also determine the types of birds they wish to see and the appropriate seasons for field observations. For example, if a birder wishes to see birds migrating in spring, he or she may browse through the sites, examining the "rating" for spring migration. If a site has a three-asterisk rating for spring migration, it should be excellent for viewing spring migrants.

Once readers know when and where they wish to go and what type of birds they wish to see, they can then pick a time of day. Many site descriptions include optimal weather conditions, times of day, and where applicable, optimal tides.

Suggestions about site access, exploration, and enjoyment of birdlife are described in the text. Maps are provided for sites in the five boroughs, Nassau County, Westchester County, and nearby New Jersey that pinpoint trails, ponds, viewing locations, restrooms (!), and transportation nodes. Directions by both public transportation and car are given for each site within the five boroughs. For nearby birding places outside the city limits, directions by car are provided.

Before visiting a site, readers should note the specific safety recommendations, which are located at the end of the each site description.

Information is provided on pelagic birding (observing avian species, primarily seabirds, offshore) and hawkwatching. In addition, special day-trip birding sites (within a two-and-a-half-hour drive from Manhattan), which include two newly established national wildlife refuges, are depicted. Local birding events, Christmas Bird Counts and Winter Waterfowl Counts, and such resources as New York State Important Bird Areas, conservation organizations, web sites, and hot lines are enumerated.

Readings are suggested that include field guides (for both novice and expert birders), natural history reference books, and local periodicals.

The Birding Seasons: A Calendar for Birders

Getting to know the seasons for birding is one of the best ways to maximize your chances of seeing lots of bird species or a particular species. The permanent residents that live and breed here can be found at all seasons of the year. Migratory nesters arrive from late winter through midsummer. After raising families, they return to their "wintering" grounds. Twice each year, many millions of songbirds, waterfowl, raptors, and seabirds pass through the metropolitan area. They follow their own schedule (not necessarily our Gregorian calendar), each species with its own point of origin and its own final destination. When birds fly to their breeding grounds, we refer to the span of time as "spring migration," although some species migrate in winter and some in summer. The term "fall migration," is used when birds return to their wintering grounds. This period can start as early as June for some species and as late as December for others. Although peak dates vary greatly by species, the following calendar acquaints birders with the normal schedules of most birds. (For accounts of migration, see Paul Kerlinger's *How Birds Migrate* [1995], Scott Weidensaul's *Living on the Wind: Across the Hemisphere with Migratory Birds* [1999], and Kenneth P. Able's *Gathering of Angels: Migrating Birds and Their Ecology* [1999], all listed in "Suggested Readings.")

Nesting/Breeding Season

February through July; species-dependent, with larger birds such as egrets, ducks, hawks, shorebirds, and gulls starting before most songbirds.

Last days of April through May and into June; Neotropical songbirds (songbirds that migrate south of the United States, such as vireos, thrushes, warblers, grosbeaks, and others).

March through May; non-Neotropical songbirds.

Autumn Migration (Postbreeding Migration)

Late June through November, peaking in August and early September; shorebirds.

Late July through mid-October, peaking the last week of August through the first few days of October; Neotropical songbirds.

Mid-September through November, peaking the last days of September through October; non-Neotropical songbirds.

Last of August through December, peaking in mid-September through the first week of November; hawks.

Mid-September through December, with large numbers moving through sometime after October 1; waterfowl (sea ducks usually peak after October 20).

Winter

November through March/April; some birds come and go during this time, depending on weather conditions.

Spring Migration

February through June; hawks, gulls, and waterfowl.

Late February through April; non-Neotropical.

Late March through April and into May, peaking in May (usually starting late in the first week and declining in the last week); Neotropical songbirds and shorebirds.

Ranking of Birding Sites

To help readers plan birding excursions to sites where they can find birds at the seasonally appropriate times, we have assigned each site a set of asterisks for each of the four seasons: nesting, spring migration, fall migration, and winter. Lack of an asterisk indicates that birding is not very productive; one asterisk, birding is somewhat productive; two asterisks, birding is productive; and three asterisks, birding is very productive. A given site may be good for a particular season but not productive in other seasons. Readers can also refer to the checklist showing seasonal status and abundance of each species.

Using the Checklist

Included in the guidebook is a checklist of 355 birds that have been documented to occur within the five boroughs of New York City and the adjoining waters. Because the checklist was constructed for birders by birders, it is not meant to be a scientific document but rather a tool to help birders understand what species can be expected in a given season and their relative abundance at that time. For example, if a birder wants to know when to see an American Redstart and how common it is in a given season, he or she can see from the checklist that this species does not occur in the New York City area in winter. It is common in spring, rare in summer, and common in early autumn. The estimate of relative abundance for each species in a particular season is a rough estimate. The checklist also indicates which species are known to nest (or have nested) within the city limits.

The abundance of a species relates to habitat. A bird "common" in a given season is found in its specific, or native, habitat. Use this guide to go out birding and to familiarize yourself with which habitats are suitable to which species.

The species names used in this guidebook are the official designations given by the American Ornithologists Union (AOU) at the time of this writing. AOU is the scientific organization that selects the common and scientific names of North American birds. The decision to change Oldsquaw to Long-tailed Duck was not official, so Oldsquaw it is!

Personal Safety

People who bird in New York City and the metropolitan area must take precautions to ensure their own well-being. The New York area is generally safe, especially if you bird with companions. Should you find yourself in a location where you cannot see other people, do not venture forth alone. Even when birding in small groups, be aware of where you are and what is going on around you. Occasionally the most experienced New York City birders have encountered trouble. A short note pertaining to personal safety is included in each site description. Heed the warnings. If you use common sense, you are unlikely to have problems.

Other people are not the only dangers to birders in the metropolitan area. Automobile traffic, railroad tracks (mostly electrified), tow-away zones for automobiles, and automobile theft and break-ins need to be considered along with poison ivy, mosquitoes, and ticks.

Minute deer ticks (the nymph is the size of a sesame seed; the adult is the size of an apple seed) and dog ticks are active in spring, summer, and fall in a variety of habitat, but principally in woodlands, grasslands, and bushy areas. Deer ticks can transmit Lyme disease. (For information about Lyme disease, contact the American Lyme Disease Foundation at 914-277-6970 or at www.aldf.com.) The oil in poison ivy can cause an uncomfortable rash to those who are susceptible. Learn how to identify this plant and avoid it. If you go into poison ivy areas or tick habitat, minimize skin exposure by wearing a hat, long-sleeved shirt, and long pants tucked into socks. For easy tick spotting, wear light-colored clothing.

Safety and Law of the Birds

Although some birds seen in cities are habituated, there are many that have rarely encountered a human being. Maintain a distance from wild birds. Stay on the trails and paths. By chasing birds through the underbrush or forest, you disturb them and crush the vegetation. You may deprive migrants, which are on a tight energy budget, of valuable time to find food, fatten up, and continue on their journey. Disturbances can cause nesting birds to abandon the nest. Give birds space.

Native birds are protected under the Migratory Bird Treaty Act, which prohibits the taking of nests, eggs, and feathers, except for scientific purposes. It also prohibits killing (except those species for which there are designated hunting seasons), harrassing, or "adopting." Taking in a young bird that appears to be abandoned is illegal. It is best to leave the youngster alone because the parents may be close by and will continue to care for it. Or call your local birding organization to obtain the name of a certified rehabilitator, who is licensed to care for injured and abandoned birds.

Birding in New York City is an adventure. Frequently, birding is better in this urban area than in the wilderness. The concentration, diversity, and numbers of birds are astounding. Where else in North America or the world can you see 75 or 100 species of birds in one day? With binoculars around your neck and perhaps a scope over your shoulder, you wend you way through busy streets or maneuver for a seat on a crowded subway. You reach your birding destination. While you observe a Snowy Egret spearing a crustacean, an Osprey carrying a fish to its nesting platform, a Red-bellied Woodpecker probing a decayed tree for insects, or a Long-eared Owl eyeing you from its cedar tree perch, out of the corner of your eye you may see the Arthur Kill oil refineries, a 747 jet on its way to Paris, or the Manhattan skyline. This guide provides you with the kind of information that will lead to many memorable birding experiences. Go forth with a friend and enjoy.

Chapter One

Saltmarsh Sharp-tailed Sparrow

The Bronx

The Bronx is northernmost of New York City's five boroughs and the only one physically attached to the mainland; Manhattan and Staten Island are islands by themselves, and Queens and Brooklyn are part of Long Island. Two of the city's largest public parks, Pelham Bay Park and Van Cortlandt Park, are in the Bronx, as is the venerable New York Botanical Garden. These urban parks, plus a string of parklands along the Hudson River—Spuyten Duyvil Shorefront Park, Riverdale Park, and Wave Hill—provide diverse habitats that are especially scenic and wonderful for birding.

Pelham Bay Park

Nesting**   Spring Migration**   Fall Migration***   Winter***
Middletown Road and Watt Avenue to Westchester County, Bruckner Expressway and Hutchinson River to Long Island Sound

Pelham Bay Park, located on Long Island Sound in the northeast corner of Bronx County, contains woodlands, scrublands, meadows, salt-marshes, freshwater ponds, sandy beaches, rocky shores (a continuation of New England's rock-bound coast), and a re-vegetated landfill along with golf courses, ball fields, tennis courts, and a riding stable. Comprising 2,764 acres with 13 miles of shoreline, it is the largest park managed by the City of New York/Parks and Recreation. Pelham Bay Park is one of four city parklands that are designated Important Bird Areas in New York State by the National Audubon Society.

Although Pelham Bay Park is best known for owls in winter, including Barn, Great Horned, Long-eared, Northern Saw-whet, and on rare occasions, Eastern Screech-Owl, Snowy, Barred, and Short-eared owls, it provides very good birding opportunities in all seasons. Approximately 250 bird species have been recorded in the park since the mid-1980s. Breeding bird species tally to 80 and include Yellow-crowned Night-Heron, Red-tailed Hawk, Great Black-backed Gull, Great Horned Owl, Red-eyed Vireo, Cedar Waxwing, American Redstart, Saltmarsh Sharp-tailed Sparrow, Rose-breasted Grosbeak, and Orchard Oriole.

Pelham Bay Park is divided by Eastchester Bay into two distinct areas. The southern portion, southwest of the bay, has a nature center (with restrooms), a track-and-field facility, tennis courts, playgrounds, ball fields, and the Bronx Victory Column and Memorial Grove, a World War I memorial, as well as a meadow, part of the Thomas Pell Wildlife Sanctuary, and re-vegetated landfill (off limits). This zone is accessible by subway and bus lines. The northern portion, north of Eastchester Bay and east of the Hutchinson River, includes a nature center (summers only), Orchard Beach (restrooms at the pavilion), Hunter Island, Twin Islands, Woodlands, the Meadow, Rodman's Neck, Turtle Cove, Wedgewood/Pelham Wood, Bartow-Pell Mansion Museum, the northern portion of the Thomas Pell Wildlife Sanctuary, golf courses, and riding stables. The northern section is the better birding area (mostly by virtue of its size and habitat diversity), but it is less accessible by public transportation, except in the summer when buses run directly to Orchard Beach.

Going to Pelham Bay Park by car will enable you to move from habitat to habitat easily, covering the major birding areas in a single day.

Hunter Island

For winter birding, start in the northern section at the northeast corner of the Orchard Beach parking lot. (Parking at this lot is free from October to April; a small fee is charged in summer.) Follow the Kazimiroff Nature Trail (paved at the start), named in memory of a Bronx historian, north to the high point (90 feet above sea level) of the park. From late November to early March, Great Horned Owl may be found in the mature pines and Northern Saw-whet Owl in the younger ones. Although you have crossed no body of water, you are actually on Hunter Island, one of three islands annexed (with landfill) in the 1940s as part of Robert Moses' design. Continue north until you reach an intersection. In the vicinity of this intersection, look right (northeast) to a large northern red oak with a cavity at the top of its trunk. Here, from the end of January to April, is an active Great Horned Owl nest. Follow the nature trail by continuing left or straight at the nest and then bearing right, looking along the shore for wintering waterbirds. When you reach the southeast part of Hunter Island, search the spruces for Barn Owl and other Great Horned Owl.

Long-eared Owl are irruptive migrants that may not be seen for years and then make an appearance in the park for one winter. Roosts established in the past have been in deciduous trees in less disturbed areas of Hunter Island as well as in conifers elsewhere.

Wintering hawks can be seen from the Hunter Island trails. Red-tailed Hawk are common; Cooper's Hawk and Sharp-shinned Hawk are rare.

In spring and fall, Hunter Island, with its wildflowers, trees, and shrubs, abounds with migrants, and in summer, nesters. On mornings after northwest winds, look in the mature oaks, hickories, and tulip trees for migratory warblers. But before starting out on the nature trails, investigate the brushy edge of Hunter Island north of the Orchard Beach parking lot for thrushes, warblers, and sparrows.

Twin Islands (Little or West Twin Island and Big or East Twin Island)

In all seasons, good birding is found from the shores of Twin Islands (like Hunter Island, Twin Islands were annexed to the mainland to construct Orchard Beach). Starting at the north end of the Orchard Beach promenade, where you reach the southeastern shore of Twin Islands, search the waters of Long Island Sound for loons, grebes, cormorants, waterfowl, and gulls. Wintering Bufflehead could be close in shore, Common Goldeneye and large rafts of Lesser Scaup off shore, and Great Cormorant (winter only) on the distant rocks. For a good view, use a spotting scope. In late winter, locate Middle Reef far out in the Sound, where as many as 15 harbor seals have been seen at low tide. On occasion, harp seals haul out here also. You can continue from the end of the promenade north along Big (East) Twin Island to a small rise at the north end for an even better view of Long Island Sound. From here you are also likely to see Brant and American Wigeon.

The Meadow and Adjacent Woodland

Roughly between mid-March and late April, male American Woodcock perform courtship flights at dusk in the Meadow, which is behind (west of) the southern part of Orchard Beach. The Meadow is experiencing a natural succession of trees and shrubs steadily encroaching on open grassland, but a large stand of rare northern gamma grass, with a very dense network of rhizomes, is resisting the invading woody vegetation.

Willow Flycatcher nest here mid-June through July. Other probable nesters are shrubland birds, such as Gray Catbird, Northern Mockingbird, Yellow Warbler, and Eastern Towhee. Red-tailed Hawk hunt here throughout the year as well as in other parts of the park. During migration, Northern Harrier may patrol the large, open expanses.

In the midst of winter, the woodlands northwest of the Meadow, near the bus depot road, are home to woodpeckers, Black-capped Chickadee, Tufted Titmouse, and White-breasted Nuthatch. Also, Fish Crow can be heard and seen in this location as well as in the general Orchard Beach area. Great Horned Owl have nested in the non-native white poplar woodlands to the south of the Meadow. To locate owl roosts and nests, check trees for "whitewash" and look on the ground for pellets.

Rodman's Neck

South of the Meadow is a 54-acre peninsula, Rodman's Neck. The southern portion, which is off limits to the public, is the New York City Police Department's firing range and occasionally an emergency disposal area for explosives.

Eastchester Bay and Turtle Cove

After you have driven or walked north across the Pelham Bridge at the head of Eastchester Bay, turn right onto City Island Road. Follow this road to the first turnoff of the traffic circle and park; this is Rodman's Neck. From the parking area, walk north and west, passing a pine grove (check here in winter for Northern Saw-whet Owl), to the edge of Eastchester Bay and Turtle Cove. At low tide in May, search the bay's waterfront for Greater and Lesser yellowlegs. In fall and winter, look for waterbirds, such as Red-throated and Common loons, Great Cormorant, Canvasback, scaup (search for Horned Grebe among the scaup), and Red-breasted Merganser. At Turtle Cove, Hooded Merganser are regular visitors in winter. Now, with increased tidal flushing through a culvert, wading birds such as Great Egret, Snowy Egret, and Glossy Ibis frequent the site. The egrets are particularly evident in September as they intently follow aquatic prey in the shallows.

Canada Goose and Mallard remain in Eastchester Bay and Turtle Cove during the spring and summer. At the edge of the saltmarsh, Great Blue Heron, Great Egret, Snowy Egret, Green Heron, and Black-crowned Night-Heron stalk the shallows.

Bridle Path

In migration and nesting season, the bridle path, which encircles Pelham and Split Rock golf courses, is a good place to look for landbirds. Start on the path as it goes under the railroad bridge near the golf course parking lot. (It is a good idea to ask permission to park here, because the lot is part of the golf concession.) Eastern Phoebe have nested under the small bridge that spans the stream from the Split Rock Golf Course. Beautiful oak woodlands line the fenced-in golf courses. Follow the bridle path for approximately 2 miles until it crosses Shore Road. (Allow horse-back riders plenty of room by stepping off the path as they approach.) Shortly thereafter, it meets up with the Siwanoy Trail. You can stay on the bridle path to return to the parking lot or you can follow the trail through the Bartow-Pell Mansion grounds and go on to the Lagoon.

Wedgewood/Pelham Wood

North of the Pelham Golf Course is a healthy, wet oak and sweetgum forest, rare in New York City, called Wedgewood/Pelham Wood. It is an ideal place to search for songbirds in migration and sparrows, such as Fox Sparrow, and Pine Siskin in winter. Park to the right off Shore Road, just south of the Westchester County border.

The Lagoon

In the fall, Osprey fish and roost at the Lagoon. From August 15 to October 5, they put on a great aerial show if menhaden (of the herring family) are present. In all seasons except summer, this is a good place to see waterbirds. Investigate the foot of the Lagoon for loon, Pied-billed Grebe, American Black Duck, and Bufflehead. In August, an immature Bald Eagle has been seen at the shoreline. On the east side of the Lagoon (near the northwest corner of the Orchard Beach parking lot), canoes and kayaks can be launched to explore the otherwise inaccessible inlets and marshes.

Bartow-Pell Mansion Museum

The International Garden Club manages the Bartow-Pell Mansion, which was completed in 1842 and now has landmark status. The house and grounds are open to the public on Wednesdays, Saturdays, and Sundays, from noon to 4:00 PM. Contact the museum to double-check the schedule. In winter, Northern Saw-whet Owl are most often found in the lower branches of conifers and holly trees behind the north end of the mansion, but they will roost in any evergreen shrub or tree in the vicinity if it is not heavily pruned. Look for the telltale whitewash. If undisturbed, they will often remain in the same roost for weeks. A Barred Owl has been found near the mansion, and there could be a Great Horned Owl nest in the Nor-way Spruce. In May and again in August, look for shorebirds in the vernal pond beyond a small cemetery behind the mansion. (Turn right at the cemetery and then left.)

Wild Turkey—and occasionally deer—can be seen at dawn at the Bartow-Pell Mansion traffic circle, south of the gated area.

Thomas Pell Wildlife Sanctuary and Goose Creek Marsh

The largest saltmarsh in the Bronx is Goose Creek Marsh, part of the Thomas Pell Wildlife Sanctuary, located east of the Hutchinson River Parkway and west of Split Rock Golf Course. In spring and summer, look for Green Heron, Clapper Rail, Marsh Wren, Saltmarsh Sharp-tailed Sparrow, and Swamp Sparrow. At dusk in late autumn, Short-eared Owl course the saltmarsh. Red-eyed Vireo can be found in the surrrounding forest. You can reach the marsh by following the Siwanoy Trail, a meandering 6-mile walk, starting at either the golf course parking lot or the south end of Orchard Beach.

Goose Island

Goose Island can be viewed from outside the park at Co-op City's Einstein Loop on the south side of the Hutchinson River. Great Egret, Snowy Egret, as many as 50 pair of Black-crowned Night-Heron, and Yellow-crowned Night-Heron nest in the trees and shrubs on Goose Island. In spring and early summer, do not land a boat on this island. These sensitive species should be observed from a distance of at least 100 yards to avoid disturbing parents or young. If disturbed early in the nesting phase, parents are likely to abandon their nests. After the eggs have hatched, the chicks jump out of the nests if agitated. Because the parents do not feed their young on the ground, the chicks will starve to death.

Landfill

In the southern section, the landfill, an 88-acre garbage mound, has been capped and recently re-vegetated, increasing the quantity and quality of habitat for grassland birds.

Peregrine Falcon, a species formerly on the federal endangered species list (and still endangered in New York State), frequently winter at the landfill. (See chap. 3, "Manhattan/Riverside Park," for additional information on Peregrine Falcon.) Look for them along the fence posts. American Pipit and Snow Bunting also winter here, and up to six Rough-legged Hawk have been seen hunting (at the same time) in the area. Occasionally in winter, before the landfill was capped, Short-eared Owl were seen here. At any time of year, Barn Owl may be present. During the 1999 breeding season, the first spring after re-vegetation, a pair of Great Black-backed Gull nested on top of the landfill and a pair of American Kestrel were present, most probably nesting in the area.

Southern Meadow and Vicinity

The meadow in the southern section is being managed for grassland birds, all of which, from Upland Sandpiper to Grasshopper Sparrow, have been sighted here at least once over the years. In May and June and again in August, migrating Bobolink are likely to be seen. It is hoped that the management efforts will attract migrating Eastern Meadowlark. Tree Swallow nest in the boxes provided. Eastern Bluebird are in the area and may use the nest boxes in the future. A pond near the landfill entrance attracts shorebirds such as Solitary Sandpiper.

Fall Hawkwatch

For two years, 1988 and 1989, a formal hawkwatch was conducted in the Orchard Beach parking lot. Every diurnal raptor species of the region was sighted. In a single year, in mid-September, up to 15,000 Broad-winged Hawk were seen, and on September 21, 1988, 230 Osprey were counted as they passed through the area on their way south. In early October with the first cold front, 20 Peregrine Falcon were observed. In mid-October, 400 Sharp-shinned Hawk and 25 Merlin were counted. By December, a total of 19 Bald Eagle were recorded. The counting and fascination with the mass movements of birds of prey continue. Ask the Urban Park Rangers about their hawkwatch tours.

From mid-August through early December on days with northwest winds, migrating hawks can be seen flying over the Orchard Beach parking lot and also over the Lagoon. Wind speeds of 20 mph will usually produce dramatic, often low-altitude, flights. Migration continues until early December. Pick a fall day with brisk northwest winds to go hawkwatching at Pelham Bay Park. If the wind velocity is less than 20 mph, Central Park's Belvedere Castle is usually a better location.

Nature Centers

Various nature tours start from the Pelham Bay Nature Center in the southern section and the Orchard Beach Nature Center (summer only) at the north end of Orchard Beach. Contact the Urban Park Rangers for a list of activities. Visitor guides and maps of Pelham Bay Park are available from the office of the Pelham Bay Park Administrator.

When to Go

If you are looking for waterbirds and shorebirds, it is generally best to go at low tide at any time of year. Tide schedules are published in the *Eldridge Tide and Pilot Book*, which can be found at any bait and tackle shop on City Island. Also, you can call the Urban Park Rangers or access a web page of the National Oceanic and Atmospheric Administration (NOAA) (www.opsd.nos.noaa.gov/tides/nyneWP.html). When you make your inquiry, refer specifically to tide schedules for City Island and Willets Point.

During May through July, early mornings are usually best for spotting nesting and spring migrants, although nesting Great Horned Owl can be seen at the end of January through April. From March through April, as dusk approaches, American Woodcock perform courtship dances in the clearings. At any time of year, Wild Turkey can be found. Hawk migration starts in late August and continues until early December. Wintering waterfowl are seen from late November to mid-March.

Optimal Weather Conditions

A northwest wind is favorable for fall hawk migration, especially after bad weather. When a warm front moves up from the southwest after a period of unfavorable northerly and easterly winds, spring migrants are most plentiful. In winter, heavy snow forces hawks, owls, and some winter finches (such as Purple Finch, Common Redpoll, and Pine Siskin) toward the coastal regions of Pelham Bay. Very cold winters tend to drive waterfowl into the open waters of Long Island Sound and Eastchester Bay. A cloudy day, when the air temperature is close to the water temperature, allows the best viewing of distant rafts of waterfowl.

Personal Safety

Many of the birding areas are isolated and deserted. It is best, and safer, to bird with a friend or two at Pelham Bay Park. In late spring and summer, mosquitoes can be a problem. Dog ticks and deer ticks are rare.

Getting There

The Metropolitan Transit Authority (MTA) puts out a free New York City subway map indicating major subway/bus connections, which can be obtained at subway station ticket booths. Detailed bus schedules can be picked up on board Bronx buses. Or you can contact NYC Transit at 718-330-1234 or www.mta.nyc.ny.us for subway and bus information.

SUBWAY: From Manhattan, take the Bronx-bound 6 subway to Pelham Bay Park, the last stop. Walk directly over the footbridge into the southern section of Pelham Bay Park.

SUBWAY to BUS: From Manhattan, take the Bronx-bound 6 subway to Pelham Bay Park, the last stop. To reach the northern section in summer, from the bus stop on the left of the footbridge, take the Bx5 (on summer weekdays, its route is extended) or the Bx12 (a shuttle that operates in summer), both of which go directly to Orchard Beach. To reach the

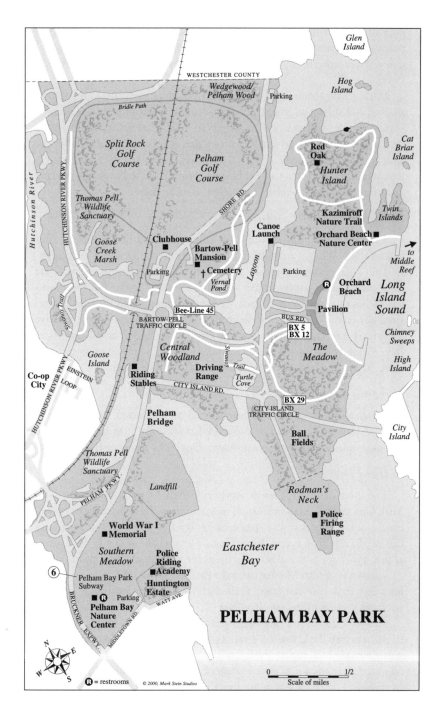

Glen
Island

WESTCHESTER COUNTY

Wedgewood/
Pelham Wood   Parking

Bridle Path

Hog
Island

*Split Rock
Golf
Course*

*Pelham
Golf
Course*

Red
Oak

*Hunter
Island*

Cat
Briar
Island

*Thomas Pell
Wildlife
Sanctuary*

Kazimiroff
Nature Trail

Twin
Islands

■ **Clubhouse**

SHORE RD.

**Canoe
Launch**

Orchard Beach ■
Nature Center

*Goose
Creek
Marsh*

**Bartow-Pell
Mansion** ■

† **Cemetery**

*Vernal
Pond*

Lagoon

Parking

**Orchard
Beach**

*Long
Island
Sound*

to
Middle
Reef

Parking

Pavilion

BARTOW-PELL
TRAFFIC CIRCLE

Bee-Line 45

BUS RD.

**BX 5
BX 12**

*Chimney
Sweeps*

*Goose
Island*

*Central
Woodland*

**Riding
Stables** ■

**Driving
Range**

Siwanoy Trail

*Turtle
Cove*

*The
Meadow*

*High
Island*

**Co-op
City**

EINSTEIN
LOOP

HUTCHINSON RIVER PKWY.

CITY ISLAND RD.

BX 29

CITY ISLAND
TRAFFIC CIRCLE

*City
Island*

**Pelham
Bridge**

**Ball
Fields** ■

*Thomas Pell
Wildlife
Sanctuary*

Landfill

PELHAM PKWY.

*Rodman's
Neck*

■ **Police
Firing
Range**

**World War I
■ Memorial**

*Southern
Meadow*

**Police
Riding
■ Academy**

*Eastchester
Bay*

⑥ — Pelham Bay Park
Subway

**Huntington
Estate**

WATT AVE.

PELHAM BAY PARK

Ⓡ ■ Parking

**Pelham Bay
Nature
Center**

BRUCKNER EXPWY.

MIDDLETOWN RD.

N
W E
S

Ⓡ = restrooms   © 2000, Mark Stein Studios

0   1/2
Scale of miles

Hutchinson River

HUTCHINSON RIVER PKWY.

Siwanoy Trail

northern section after Labor Day through the spring, take the Bx29. Pick up the bus at the bus stop downstairs from the subway train platform and across the street. Ask the bus driver to let you off at the City Island traffic circle. From the circle, it is about a mile to Hunter Island.

BUS: From Queens, take the QBx1 across the Whitestone Bridge to the Pelham Bay subway station and then follow the bus instructions above.

BUS: From Westchester, take the Bee-line 45 to the Bartow-Pell Mansion Museum. Ask the driver to let you off at the Bartow traffic circle. Call 914-682-2020 for complete information.

CAR: Drive north on the Bruckner Expressway, I-95. To go to the southern section, get off at Exit 7C (Country Club Road/Pelham Bay Park) and drive along the service road to the second traffic light. Turn right on Middletown Road and go to the parking lot on the left.

To go to the northern section, take Exit 8B (Orchard Beach/City Island). This road takes you across the Pelham Bridge to a traffic light. Take the right turn to the City Island traffic circle and then take the third turnoff to Orchard Beach. Or go straight from Pelham Bridge to the Bartow traffic circle, from which you can also go to Orchard Beach (first turnoff) or to Shore Road to Pelham/Split Rock golf courses and Bartow-Pell Mansion (second turnoff).

For Additional Information on Pelham Bay Park

Bartow-Pell Mansion Museum, 718-885-1461
Bronx Urban Park Rangers (lead tours), 718-430-1832
City of New York/Parks and Recreation, www.nycparks.org
New York City Audubon Society (leads tours), 212-691-7483 and
    www.nycaudubon.org
Orchard Beach Nature Center (leads tours, in summer only),
    718-885-3466
Pelham Bay Nature Center (leads tours), 718-885-3467
Van Cortlandt and Pelham Bay Parks Administrator's Office,
    718-430-1890
Resource persons: Ronald V. Bourque, Board of Directors, and former President, New York City Audubon Society; Robert DeCandido, Urban Park Ranger; and David S. Künstler, Wildlife Manager, Van Cortlandt and Pelham Bay Parks, City of New York/Parks and Recreation

Van Cortlandt Park

Nesting**   Spring Migration**   Fall Migration**   Winter*
Van Cortlandt Park South (West 240th Street) to Westchester County,
Broadway to Jerome Avenue and Van Cortlandt Park East

Van Cortlandt Park, covering 1,146 hilly acres in the northwest Bronx, is the third largest city park. More than half the park's acreage contains deciduous forests, scrubland, meadows, ridges, wetlands, brooks, and a man-made lake, which provide vital avian habitat. In 1998, the National Audubon Society designated the park an Important Bird Area in New York State. Foresters and botanists, answering *Wild New York's* survey on the health of forest ecosystems in New York City, awarded second prize to the Northwest Forest portion of Van Cortlandt Park.

City of New York/Parks and Recreation manages the park with assistance from the Friends of Van Cortlandt Park, a nonprofit organization founded in 1992 by a group of Bronx residents concerned with environmental education and preservation of their neighborhood park.

New York City took title to this vast acreage more than one hundred years ago. During the early and mid-1900s, the Major Deegan Expressway and Henry Hudson and Mosholu Parkways were built, splitting the parkland into five segments: the Northwest Forest, Croton Woods, the Northeast Forest, the southwest zone, and the southeast zone.

A total of 177 different bird species has been recorded in Van Cortlandt Park since 1970. And at least 50 species breed here, including Great Horned Owl, Eastern Wood-Pewee, Great Crested Flycatcher, Northern Rough-winged Swallow, and Rose-breasted Grosbeak. In the southeastern zone, where two municipal golf courses are located, birding is limited. However, just north of the Mosholu Golf Course in the mature oak and sweetgum forest surrounding the Allen Shandler Recreation Area, 10 species of warbler may be seen on a spring morning in mid-May. The rest of the park offers wonderful birding opportunities. Each section is accessible by mass transit. With a car, all birding areas can be visited in one day.

Northeast Forest

Enter the Northeast Forest (not far from a bus stop) at Van Cortlandt Park East and Katonah Avenue, a wide road that leads to the Nursery and the trailhead for the new John Muir Trail. This 1½-mile trail starts near the Nursery gate and meanders east–west through prime birding habitat in the Northeast Forest, Croton Woods, and the Northwest Forest, where it passes through a rare, mature oak and sweetgum forest. During spring migration, look for woodpeckers, flycatchers, vireos, wrens, thrushes, warblers, tanagers, and grosbeaks. Pileated Woodpecker have been seen on occasion in April and early May. Continue until you spy on the left a *Phragmites* (or common reed) marsh off in the distance. Walk through a tunnel under the Major Deegan Expressway to Croton Woods. (Refer to Croton Woods for the continuation of the John Muir Trail.)

You can also start at Van Cortlandt Park East and East 235th Street (near where you can park your car). Enter the park at a small stand of red cedar that encircles the Stockbridge Indian Monument commemorating a Native American battle. If you are there in mid-May, check the oaks lining the street for a variety of warbler species. Continue west on the path until you come to an intersection. Explore the area to your left (south). Then take the right, pass the *Phragmites* marsh, and come to Nursery Road. Make a left (west) and continue under the Major Deegan Expressway into Croton Woods.

In winter and fall, you will likely flush Common Snipe and American Woodcock from the perimeter of the marsh.

Croton Woods

Croton Woods is an uncommon oak and tulip tree forest, with sugar maple, covering 158 acres. At least 108 bird species have been sighted in these woods, 32 of them nesting species. Nesting birds include Great Horned Owl and Indigo Bunting. During spring migration, these moist woods provide prime habitat for upland birds. The Old Croton Aqueduct Trail runs north–south through these lush woods. You may wish to explore this mile-long trail or continue on the John Muir Trail, which eventually takes you to the Northwest Forest.

To continue on the John Muir Trail, go west away from I-87 (Major Deegan Expressway) and bear right (north) at an intersection. Head north for a short period and look for a well-worn, edged trail on the left. Take this trail until you come to a wide flat trail, the Old Croton Aqueduct Trail, which runs north–south. In this area, Great Horned Owl are found in winter, and Pileated Woodpecker have been seen in late March to early April. Make a left (south) on the Old Croton Aqueduct Trail, passing an old gatehouse. During spring migration, check the gatehouse area for Prothonotary Warbler.

Just south of a stream, turn right (west), taking the steps downhill (the stream should be on your right) until you reach a trail at the bottom bordering the Van Cortlandt Golf Course fence. In spring, Black-billed and Yellow-billed cuckoos have been found along this portion of the trail. Turn left (south), with the fence on your right, hugging it as the trail turns and bears west along the Mosholu Parkway Extension and then south to another tunnel, this one under the Mosholu Parkway Extension. Pass through and continue up the hill on your left; the parkway is now on your right. Heading west, stay on the trail that is closest to the parkway and eventually you will reach an intersection with a bridge on your right. At this point, if you turn left (south) uphill, you are on Vault Hill. If you continue west, you will enter the Parade Ground. To continue on the

John Muir Trail to the Northwest Forest, turn right (north) and cross the bridge spanning the Henry Hudson Parkway. (Refer to the Northwest Forest section to continue on the final stretch of the John Muir Trail.)

Northwest Forest

The Northwest Forest is a dramatic 188-acre woodland atop a north–south ridge with rocky outcroppings. It can be entered directly from Broadway (western edge) and Mosholu Avenue (near both a parking lot and a bus stop at the riding stables). Or you can reach the forest by continuing on the John Muir Trail from Croton Woods. When you cross a bridge over the Henry Hudson Parkway, you are in the Northwest Forest. Follow the trail to the brick building on your left. At this point you are near the end of the John Muir Trail. You may choose to stay on the road, passing the stables, to reach the intersection of Broadway and Mosholu Avenue, where you can pick up public transportation.

Or you may choose to explore the Northwest Forest. The Cass Gallagher Nature Trail, named in memory of a Bronx resident devoted to protecting the park, passes through this century-old oak and tulip tree forest with an understory of sassafras, wild grape, spicebush, and mapleleaf viburnum. Other trails include the Bridle Path and Putnam Trail, an old railroad bed. Many of the same migrants and breeding species seen in the Northeast Forest and Croton Woods can be found here. If you arrive as the setting sun filters through the trees, this forest can be most impressive.

Southwest Zone

From the Van Cortlandt Golf Course (near a municipal parking lot, where there is paid and free parking year round), there is a good view of Van Cortlandt Lake. The Golf House (with restrooms) is open during the warm months. Here you can buy a snack and eat it on a deck overlooking the lake while you watch Northern Rough-winged and other swallows (mostly Tree and Barn) hawking for insects. Double-crested Cormorant can be seen drying their outstretched wings. Also in warm weather, you can view basking eastern painted turtles and red-eared sliders. In winter, Gadwall, Northern Shoveler, Hooded Merganser, and Ruddy Duck are regularly seen on the lake.

Walk up the west side of the lake, following the John Kieran Nature Trail (named in honor of the author of *A Natural History of New York City*, listed in "Suggested Readings") as it goes through the lake area and freshwater wetlands and loops around to the eastern edge of the Parade Ground. (You can pick up a trail map from the Urban Park Rangers at the Urban Forest Ecology Center, which is on the southern end of the Parade

Ground.) When you reach the bridge over Tibbetts Brook at the north end of Van Cortlandt Lake, look for foraging Great Blue Heron and Great Egret along the shore of the northern portion of the lake. Follow the Kieran Trail north to the concrete bridge. In April and again in August, look to the right in the swamp's vegetation for migrating Virginia Rail and Sora. Virginia Rail have over-wintered here, as have large numbers of Rusty Blackbird. In early May, look for Prothonotary Warbler foraging for insects in the Buttonbush. During nesting season, Eastern Kingbird and Baltimore Oriole may be seen as they feed young.

Go north along the wetlands and take the first path on the left. The footbridge is the best vantage for Wood Duck and Warbling Vireo. In September and October, look for American Bittern, and in winter look for Green-winged Teal and Wild Turkey. In any season, Tibbetts Brook and its associated wetlands are prime areas for birdwatching.

Continue on the trail to the Parade Ground (where Teddy Roosevelt reviewed his troops), now a large stretch of playing fields and cricket pitches. Migrating Vesper and Savannah sparrows have been seen here in mid-March and mid-October. To reach the subway or bus from here, cross the Parade Ground to Broadway. In mid-April, make a detour to the wetland behind the pool, a prime habitat for Solitary Sandpiper or, in September, Ruby-throated Hummingbird and Bobolink.

If you wish to continue birding to the north, trails begin on the east side of the Parade Ground. One starts at the base of Vault Hill (former burial plot of the Van Cortlandts; also in 1776, a hiding place for city records) and goes north along the base (next to the golf course). Another takes a sharp left uphill and then right following the ridge. (Both eventually cross over the Henry Hudson Parkway to the Northwest Forest.) Vault Hill rises 169 feet above sea level and offers a lovely view of the Parade Ground and, on a clear day, the Manhattan skyline. Watch Chimney Swift, which nest nearby, flying overhead. Several fertile acres of meadow with little bluestem, switchgrass, and wildflowers such as bird's-foot trefoil and round-headed bush clover form prime butterfly habitat from May to July. Among the Lepidopteran fauna, look for American Lady and skippers such as the hoary edge.

Hawkwatch

The Parade Ground and Vault Hill are good places to look for migrating hawks, particularly inland migrants such as Sharp-shinned, Cooper's, Broad-winged, and Red-tailed hawks, American Kestrel, and Bald Eagle.

In any wooded section of the park in any season, if you come across a flock of noisy, nervous American Crow, chances are they have encountered a hawk and are in the process of mobbing it. If the din is deafening, follow the crows, and you may be rewarded by seeing a Great Horned Owl.

Urban Forest Ecology Center

The Urban Forest Ecology Center (with restrooms), run by the Urban Park Rangers and located to the east of Broadway at West 246th Street on the south end of the Parade Ground, is the only city nature center addressing the protection and preservation of urban forests. It also houses the Junior Bird and Nature Club for children eight years and over. You can pick up a trail map from the center.

Van Cortlandt House Museum

The Van Cortlandt House, built in 1748 by Frederick Van Cortlandt, is a national landmark and an exceptional example of Georgian architecture. Tours are run every day except Monday.

Special Notes

Roger Tory Peterson, while a member of the Bronx County Bird Club (now defunct), often walked the same trails you will explore.

Woodlawn Cemetery is just south of the Northeast Forest and offers good birding in winter. There are many evergreens that serve as roosts for owls. Merlin, Red-breasted Nuthatch, and Hermit Thrush can also be found. A pond in the northeast corner is good for ducks. The cemetery, which opens at 9:00 AM, is best investigated by car. Ask for a map at the entrance gate (where Bainbridge Avenue meets Jerome Avenue).

New York City Audubon Society Speaks Out

The New York City Planning Commission has approved a plan to locate a federally required water filtration plant under the Mosholu Golf Course in Van Cortlandt Park. New York City Audubon is concerned with long-term protection of both city parks and city drinking water. Audubon has taken a strong position against decreasing and degrading city parkland and has led various seminars and workshops on the protection of upstate watershed areas from which the city's water supply originates.

When to Go

Spring songbird migration includes the period March 15 to May 31, with peak warbler migration around May 5 to 21. The best birding is often between dawn and 11:00 AM, but in the Northeast and Northwest forests, the hours between 2:00 and 5:00 PM can also be good.

During the spring–summer breeding season (May to mid-July), the best time of day is one-half hour after dawn (the peak) to 10:30 AM. Nesting Wood Duck and young can be seen from May 15 to June 15.

Autumn hawk migration runs from September through mid-November, with the peak for Broad-winged Hawk from September 12 to 22. Hawk-watching is best started at 10:00 AM and can continue until 4:00 PM. There are good birding opportunities in winter. On rare occasions, Long-eared Owl can been seen from mid-November to early January, usually on Vault Hill. Great Horned Owl may be seen from late January to mid-March in any crow or squirrel nest in the wooded sections. Wild Turkey is present year round, evoking earlier and wilder woodlands of the Northeast.

Optimal Weather Conditions

During mid-May, when large numbers of warblers and songbird arrive, "fallouts" or groundings can be impressive, especially on the first clear day following a few days of inclement weather. The cause can be weather conditions, habitat, or topographical situations (e.g., coastline) or a combination of these things. In general, warm and sunny days are good throughout spring migration and on into the breeding season. During fall hawk and songbird migration, look for a day with northwesterly winds between 5 and 15 mph. To see hawks distinctly, wait for a day with cumulus and cirrus clouds to act as a backdrop, although hawks can also be seen against clear blue skies. In winter, reliable days for birding are sunny and windless. If the swamp and lake are not frozen over, they are good places to investigate for waterfowl and other waterbirds.

Personal Safety

Birding with a friend or two is best not only for your safety but also for those extra sets of eyes and ears. Be mindful of the joggers and bicyclists using the trails (bikers are permitted on paved paths and the Putnam Trail only). Watch out for poison ivy. Dog and deer ticks are rare.

Getting There

The Metropolitan Transit Authority (MTA) puts out a free New York City subway map indicating major subway/bus connections, which can be obtained at subway station ticket booths. Detailed bus schedules can be picked up on board Bronx buses. Or you can contact NYC Transit at 718-330-1234 or www.mta.nyc.ny.us for subway and bus information.

BUS: From Manhattan to the southwest zone, take the Manhattan Express bus BxM3 to 244th Street and Broadway, adjacent to the park. From Manhattan to the Northwest Forest, take the Manhattan Express

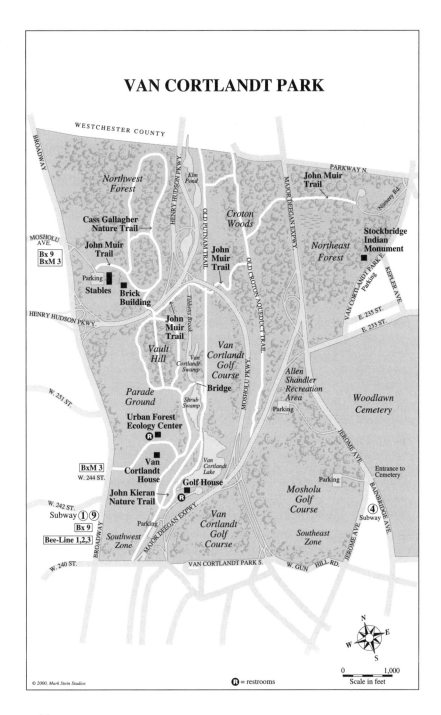

VAN CORTLANDT PARK

WESTCHESTER COUNTY

BROADWAY

Northwest Forest

Cass Gallagher Nature Trail →

PARKWAY N.

John Muir Trail

Nursery Rd.

MAJOR DEEGAN EXPWY

MOSHOLU AVE.

Bx 9
BxM 3

John Muir Trail

Parking

Stables

Brick Building

Elm Pond

HENRY HUDSON PKWY.

OLD PUTNAM TRAIL

Croton Woods

John Muir Trail

Northeast Forest

■

Stockbridge Indian Monument

VAN CORTLANDT PARK E.

Parking

KEPLER AVE.

E. 235 ST.

E. 233 ST.

HENRY HUDSON PKWY.

John Muir Trail

Vault Hill

Tibbetts Brook

OLD CROTON AQUEDUCT TRAIL

Van Cortlandt Golf Course

Van Cortlandt Swamp

Bridge

Allen Shandler Recreation Area

Parking

Woodlawn Cemetery

W. 251 ST.

Parade Ground

Urban Forest Ecology Center
Ⓡ ■

Shrub Swamp

MOSHOLU PKWY.

JEROME AVE.

BxM 3
W. 244 ST.

■
Van Cortlandt House

John Kieran Nature Trail →
Ⓡ

Van Cortlandt Lake

Golf House
■

Mosholu Golf Course

Parking

Entrance to Cemetery

BAINBRIDGE AVE.

W. 242 ST.
Subway ①⑨

Bx 9

Bee-Line 1,2,3

W. 240 ST.

BROADWAY

Southwest Zone

Parking

MAJOR DEEGAN EXPWY

Van Cortlandt Golf Course

VAN CORTLANDT PARK S.

Southeast Zone

W. GUN HILL RD.

JEROME AVE.

④
Subway

AVE.

N
W E
S

© 2000, Mark Stein Studios

Ⓡ = restrooms

0   1,000
Scale in feet

bus BxM3 to Mosholu Avenue (it stops near the stable) and walk two blocks east. The Manhattan Express buses pick up on Madison Avenue and drop off on Fifth Avenue. Call Liberty Lines at 718-652-8400 for exact locations and schedules.

From Westchester to the western edge of Van Cortlandt Park, take the Bee-line 1, 2, or 3 to stops along Broadway. Call 914-682-2020 for complete information.

SUBWAY to BUS: From Manhattan to the Northeast Forest, take the Bronx-bound 4 subway to Woodlawn, the last stop. Then take the Bx34 bus from Bainbridge Avenue to its end at Katonah Avenue and East 242th Street. You can walk from the bus turnaround south to Nursery Road to connect with the John Muir Trail.

From Manhattan to the Northwest Forest, take the Bronx-bound 1 or 9 subway to Van Cortlandt Park/242nd Street, the last stop. Take the Bx9 bus from Van Cortlandt Park/242nd Street to Mosholu Avenue (riding stables), where there is an entrance to the Northwest Forest.

SUBWAY: From Manhattan to the southwest zone, take the Bronx-bound 1 or 9 subway to Van Cortlandt Park/242nd Street, the last stop. The entrance to the Parade Ground is just north of this subway stop.

CAR: You can reach all four birding areas in Van Cortlandt Park by car in one day following the suggested route below.

To start at the Northeast Forest, exit I-87 North (Major Deegan Expressway) at East 233rd Street. Proceed through the intersection of 233rd Street and Jerome Avenue. Turn left (north) at the next traffic light onto Van Cortlandt Park East. Continue north until East 235th Street or East 237th Street. Park along Van Cortlandt Park East (not on the park side) after East 246th Street to access Nursery School Road.

To go on to the southwest zone from your parking spot on Van Cortlandt Park East, return to 233rd Street and take a right, staying in the right lane. Proceed to the next intersection (Jerome Avenue and 233rd Street) and bear a half-right, where you will immediately access I-87 South. Go onto the highway and proceed ¾ of a mile to Van Cortlandt Park South exit. After exiting, take the left at the light and left again at the next light. Bear left *under* I-87 toward Van Corltandt Park Golf Course. (Do not get on I-87 North.) Continue on and park in one of the two secure parking lots used by golfers ($2.00 fee), or park in the free lot located on the left before the ticket booth. The latter is not secure.

To continue on to the Northwest Forest, exit the golf course parking lot and continue on to the traffic light at Van Cortlandt Park South. Turn right (west) and bear right (north) on Broadway just before the light at the elevated subway. Continue for 1½ miles to the light at Mosholu Avenue. Van Cortlandt Park will be on your right the entire distance. Turn right on Mosholu Avenue and park in the free lot on your right. Walk past the orange gate and access any of the paved trails on your left. All trails in this section are circular and lead back to Mosholu Avenue.

For Additional Information on Van Cortlandt Park

Bronx Urban Park Rangers (lead tours), 718-430-1832
City of New York/Parks and Recreation, www.nycparks.org
Friends of Van Cortlandt Park, 718-601-1460
New York City Audubon Society (leads tours), 212-691-7483 and www.nycaudubon.org
Urban Forest Ecology Center, 718-548-0912
Van Cortlandt and Pelham Bay Parks Administrator's Office, 718-430-1890
Van Cortlandt House Museum, 718-543-3344
Resource persons: Carl Jaslowitz; and David S. Künstler, Wildlife Manager, Van Cortlandt and Pelham Bay Parks, City of New York/Parks and Recreation

New York Botanical Garden

Nesting* Spring Migration** Fall Migration** Winter*
Fordham Road to Gun Hill Road, Southern Boulevard and Dr.Theodore Kazimiroff Boulevard to Bronx River Parkway

Incorporated by New York State legislature more than 100 years ago, the New York Botanical Garden is a major horticultural institution. Covering 250 acres in central Bronx, it comprises gardens, a gorge, ponds, wetland area, and a 40-acre virgin forest. The Enid A. Haupt Conservatory (with restrooms), a Victorian greenhouse with landmark status, and Main Building are devoted to education and research.

The forested area, ponds, marsh, and waterfall overlook provide good birding, especially when migrating vireos, kinglets, thrushes, and warblers are the objects of the search. Although the park is lovely at all times of year, in springtime both the birds and gardens—with their daffodils, tulips, blazing azalea bushes, and blossoming ornamental trees (including cherries and magnolias)—are magnificent. Spring, summer, and fall are good for egrets, herons, and waterfowl in the wetland areas. In winter, Northern Goshawk have been sighted in the forest.

Enter at either the Mosholu Gate (pedestrians only) or the Conservatory Gate (main entrance). A wide trail (Mill Road) runs north–south through the forest, which can be accessed from several points. A suggested entry point is at the north side of the Rock Garden. When you reach the trail, walk south through the forest, birding as you go, and pause at the waterfall overlook, which provides vistas of the gorge and river below. From the high points, scan the trees above the river for vireos and warblers. Continue south and cross the Bronx River via Hester Bridge, which spans the gorge, and access the river trail. The river trail will lead to an impressive waterfall.

Additional areas that should be investigated are the two ponds (Twin Lakes) located at the north end of the property and a small wetland at the southwestern portion near the Everett Children's Adventure Garden. If Twin Lakes is not frozen, various ducks with striking plumage, such as Wood Duck, Northern Shoveler, and Green-winged Teal, may be present.

Trams shuttle visitors around the grounds. Once the $1.00 fare is paid, you can get off and on (there are four stops) at no additional charge. Maps are available at the information booths. Gifts, including a great array of botanical and horticultural books, can be bought at the Plant Shop (with restrooms) and lunches at the seasonal cafés, Garden Café and Terrace Room (with restrooms), and the Snuff Mill (with restrooms).

Special Notes

The New York Botanical Garden offers free guided birdwalks year round on Saturdays and Sundays at 12:30 PM. Call the garden to obtain current information.

The famous Bronx Zoo (founded in 1895 as the New York Zoological Society, now the Wildlife Conservation Society) is located just to the south, across Fordham Road. The zoo and the botanical garden together make up what is known as Bronx Park.

When to Go

For migrating songbirds, spring is the best time of year, with the peak being May 1 to 25. Start at 10:00 AM when the park opens. Migration in autumn is protracted, with peak songbird and hawk movement from September 15 to October 15. Peak Broad-winged Hawk migration is September 12 to 22, and Bald Eagle may pass through at any time. Mid-December through mid-March is the best time to search the forest for hawks, owls, and wintering songbirds.

The New York Botanical Garden opens at 10:00 AM, Tuesday to Sunday, throughout the year. It is not open on Monday except when a holiday falls on Monday. Closing hours vary according to season. There is a general grounds admission charge, except on Wednesday and Saturday, as well as a parking fee.

Optimal Weather Conditions

Bright, sunny, warm days are best for spring birding. Hawkwatching is good to excellent on partly sunny autumn days with northwesterly winds. In winter, go out on clear, windless days.

Personal Safety

If you wish, you can bird alone because the New York Botanical Garden has a large and efficient security staff, and a security fence encloses the entire property.

Dog ticks are found in the forest. Watch out for the few areas of poison ivy.

Getting There

The Metropolitan Transit Authority (MTA) puts out a free New York City subway map indicating major subway/bus connections, which can be obtained at subway station ticket booths. Detailed bus schedules can be picked up on board Bronx buses. Or you can contact NYC Transit at 718-330-1234 or www.mta.nyc.ny.us for subway, bus, and train information.

SUBWAY to BUS: From Manhattan, take the Bronx-bound D subway to the Bedford Park Boulevard station. From the southeast corner of the Grand Concourse and Bedford Park Boulevard, take the eastbound Bx26 bus to the botanical garden.

Or take the Bronx-bound 4 subway to Bedford Park Boulevard. Upon exiting this elevated station, turn right and cross Jerome Avenue. From the southeast corner of Jerome Avenue and Bedford Park Boulevard, take the eastbound Bx26 to the botanical garden.

Or take the Bronx-bound 2 subway to Allerton Avenue. From the northeast corner of Allerton Avenue and White Plains Road, take the Bx26 to the botanical garden.

CAR: From Manhattan, take the Triborough Bridge to Bruckner Expressway East and then to Bronx River Parkway North. Exit the parkway at 7W/Fordham Road and continue on Kazimiroff (Southern) Boulevard to the Conservatory Gate entrance. There is a parking charge.

From Westchester County, take the Cross County Parkway to Bronx River Parkway South. Exit the parkway at 7W/Fordham Road and continue on Kazimiroff (Southern) Boulevard to the Conservatory Gate entrance.

MANHATTAN SHUTTLE BUS: The New York Botanical Garden operates a shuttle bus to and from Manhattan (from the Metropolitan Museum of Art and the American Museum of Natural History) on week-

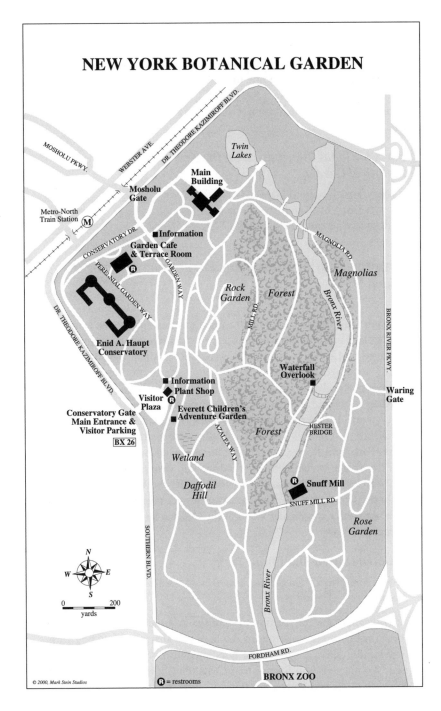

NEW YORK BOTANICAL GARDEN

MOSHOLU PKWY.

WEBSTER AVE.

DR. THEODORE KAZIMIROFF BLVD.

Twin Lakes

Main Building

Mosholu Gate

Metro-North Train Station Ⓜ

CONSERVATORY DR.

■ **Information**

Garden Cafe & Terrace Room
Ⓡ

PERENNIAL GARDEN WAY

GARDEN WAY

MAGNOLIA RD.

Rock Garden

Forest

Magnolias

Bronx River

MILL RD.

DR. THEODORE KAZIMIROFF BLVD.

Enid A. Haupt Conservatory

BRONX RIVER PKWY.

Waterfall Overlook ■

■ **Information**
Plant Shop
◆
Visitor Plaza Ⓡ
■ **Everett Children's Adventure Garden**

Waring Gate

Conservatory Gate Main Entrance & Visitor Parking
`BX 26`

AZALEA WAY

Forest

HESTER BRIDGE

Wetland

Daffodil Hill

Ⓡ **Snuff Mill**

SNUFF MILL RD.

SOUTHERN BLVD.

Rose Garden

N
W   E
S

0   200
yards

Bronx River

FORDHAM RD.

© 2000, Mark Stein Studios

Ⓡ = restrooms

BRONX ZOO

ends, April through October. Reservations are required, and tickets cost $7.00. Call the botanical garden for information.

METRO-NORTH TRAIN: From Grand Central Station in Manhattan, take Metro-North/Harlem line to the New York Botanical Garden stop. The Mosholu Gate is across Kazimiroff (Southern) Boulevard, just a few hundred feet east of the station. Call 212-532-4900 for schedule information.

For Additional Information on the New York Botanical Garden

New York Botanical Garden (leads tours),
718-817-8700 and www.nybg.org
Resource person: Carl Jaslowitz

Spuyten Duyvil Shorefront Park/Riverdale Park/ Wave Hill

Nesting*   Spring Migration**   Fall Migration**   Winter*

Spuyten Duyvil is an early Dutch name for the steeply sloped area where the Harlem and Hudson Rivers meet. Spuyten Duyvil Shorefront Park, managed by City of New York/Parks and Recreation, is a small hillside (0.187 acre) overlooking the two rivers on the southwestern tip of the Bronx. The park is a natural stopover for songbirds migrating near the Hudson River and offers open views of ducks on the rivers. Just a few blocks north is Riverdale Park, a narrow strip of land (97 acres) running parallel to the Hudson River for 1¼ miles, also managed by City of New York/Parks and Recreation. Its deciduous woodlands, brushy clearings, and freshwater wetland attract woodpeckers, vireos, swallows, thrushes, and warblers. Inland from Riverdale Park sits the Wave Hill estate and grounds. The formal gardens and lawns attract migrating songbirds. All three sites offer spectacular views of the Hudson River and New Jersey's Palisades.

Spuyten Duyvil Shorefront Park

Spuyten Duyvil Creek and Metro-North Railroad Line to Palisade Avenue.

Starting from the intersection of Johnson Avenue and Kappock Street (near the bus stop), walk toward the high-rise apartment building with a blue façade. Make a right at the building and proceed downhill on Palisade Avenue to Edsall Avenue to the beginning of a woodchip path. Take this path to the end (only a few hundred feet), where there is a good view of the river, and across to Manhattan's Inwood Hill Park. Scan the trees along the path and the river for migrants. Walk west on Edsall Avenue and check the pond under the Henry Hudson Bridge for ducks.

You can also start from the Spuyten Duyvil Metro-North Railroad Station and walk along Edsall Avenue, birding the same areas as above.

Return to Johnson Avenue (which soon becomes Palisade Avenue), turn left (west), and walk past private residences to the tiny gated overlook on the left. Check for birds in the trees lining the street and in the bushes on the hillside below. Stop to take in the wonderful view of the river below.

Go back to Palisade Avenue and continue north until you reach West 232nd Street, birding in the trees and bushes on the right-hand (east) side of the avenue.

Riverdale Park

232nd Street to 254th Street, Hudson River to Palisade Avenue

Look for the entrance to the southern section of Riverdale Park at the northwest corner of 232nd Street and Palisade Avenue. Enter the southern section of the park through an opening in the fence, take the trail closest to the river, and walk north, checking the treetops as you go. In a quarter of a mile, take the trail on your right and exit this section. Walk north on Palisade Avenue. In a short distance, after passing a group of private residences, you can re-enter the park. This northern section of Riverdale Park has oak woods, clearings, and a freshwater wetland. Explore any of the trails and check the trees and brushy areas for migrants. The park ends at West 254th Street, half a mile from the start of the northern section.

A breeding bird census conducted in 1988 identified 34 breeders, including Eastern Wood-Pewee, Great Crested Flycatcher, and Red-eyed Vireo. Additional interesting forest edge breeders were Yellow-billed Cuckoo, Eastern Screech-Owl, Red-bellied Woodpecker, Rose-breasted Grosbeak, and eight pair of Orchard Oriole.

The Urban Park Rangers conduct nature walks in Riverdale Park.

Wave Hill

Roughman's Bush to 254th Street, Riverdale Park to Sycamore Avenue and Independence Avenue

At this point, you can either walk one block north to 255th Street and the Hudson River to Metro-North's Riverdale Station and return to Manhattan or continue on to Wave Hill's lovely gardens, wooded trails, and scenic views overlooking the Hudson River.

To reach Wave Hill, take a right on West 254th Street and then take another right on Sycamore Avenue. Check in the large pines on the right and the orchard on the left for birds. Continue to the intersection of 252nd Street and Independence Avenue and turn right on Independence. In a short distance, Wave Hill's main entrance (249th Street) appears on the right. Wave Hill is a city-owned cultural and environmental institution operated by a private, nonprofit board of directors. The 28-acre park and Wave Hill House (with restrooms) are open regularly from 9:00 AM, to 5:30 PM every day except Monday. There is an entrance fee. Investigate the garden in front of the greenhouse to the right of the entrance as well as the stately oaks and beeches in the lawn area. The lawn offers an unrestricted view overlooking the Hudson River and in the fall is an opportune place to hawkwatch.

When to Go

Spring is the time to visit these sites for migrating songbirds; the peak is May 10 to 25. Go to Spuyten Duyvil Shorefront Park and Riverdale Park between 8:00 and 11:30 AM and to Wave Hill starting at 9:00 AM, when it opens. At Wave Hill, fall hawk migration is best from September 15 to October 15. The peak of the Broad-winged Hawk migration is September 12 to 22; for Red-tailed Hawk, October 25 to November 10. The best hours are 10:00 AM to 3:00 PM. When there are strong west and northwest winds, some hawks fly at eye level using the updrafts along the steep westward facing hills overlooking the Hudson River. Mid-November to mid-March, at midmorning to midafternoon, is good for watching wintering ducks, including Canvasback and Common Merganser, at Spuyten Duyvil Shorefront Park. The abundance and variety of ducks depend on freezing conditions farther north; in short, the colder the winter up north, the better the chance for variety and numbers of ducks on open water in the New York City area.

Optimal Weather Conditions

Bright, sunny, warm days are best for spring birding. Hawkwatching is good on partly sunny autumn days with northwesterly winds. In winter, go out on clear, windless days.

Personal Safety

Our suggested tour runs through relatively safe but remote residential areas. All the same, it is best to bird in small groups of two to four. Spuyten Duyvil and Riverdale Parks have dog ticks, poison ivy, and greenbrier. Watch for joggers and unleashed dogs along Palisade Avenue and in Riverdale Park.

Getting There

The Metropolitan Transit Authority (MTA) puts out a free New York City subway map indicating major subway/bus connections, which can be obtained at subway station ticket booths. Detailed bus schedules can be picked up on board Bronx buses. Or you can contact NYC Transit at 718-330-1234 or www.mta.nyc.ny.us for train, subway, and bus information.

METRO-NORTH TRAIN: From Grand Central Station in Manhattan, take the Hudson line to the Spuyten Duyvil station and start the suggested route above. You can return to Manhattan on the Hudson line from the Riverdale station.

BUS: From Manhattan, take the express bus BxM1 or BxM2 to Kappock Avenue and Johnson Avenue and follow the suggested route above. The Manhattan Express picks up on Madison Avenue and drops off on Fifth Avenue. Call Liberty Lines at 718-652-8400 for complete schedules.

SUBWAY to BUS: From Manhattan, take the Bronx-bound 1 or 9 subway to the 231st Street station and pick up the Bx10 bus going west. Take it to the Kappock Street and Johnson Avenue stop. Then follow the suggested route above. Or take the Bronx-bound 4 subway to Bedford Park Boulevard station. Turn left, upon exiting this elevated station, and walk west over the train yard to the Bx10 westbound bus. Take it to the Kappock Street and Johnson Avenue stop and then follow the suggested route above. (For your return, the Bx10 and Bx7 can take you back to the 231st Street subway station. Only the Bx10 will take you back to the Bedford Park Boulevard subway station for the 4.)

CAR: Take the Major Deegan Expressway (I-87) north to the Henry Hudson Parkway south and continue on to West 227th Street, the exit just before the Henry Hudson Bridge. Proceed along the service road that parallels the Henry Hudson Parkway to the stop sign at Independence Avenue. Make a U-turn and go under the parkway to the stop sign at the intersection of Johnson Avenue and Kappock Street. Make a sharp right and a right again and proceed onto Johnson Avenue to Edsall Avenue near the Spuyten Duyvil Shorefront Park.

Or take the Henry Hudson Parkway (Westside Highway) north, paying the toll at the Henry Hudson Bridge, to the exit at West 232nd Street. Make a left at the traffic light and proceed over the parkway. Take a left again onto the westbound service road and continue the stop sign at Independence Avenue. Make a U-turn and go under the parkway to the stop sign at the intersection of Johnson Avenue and Kappock Street. Make a sharp right and a right again and proceed onto Johnson Avenue to Edsall Avenue near the Spuyten Duyvil Shorefront Park.

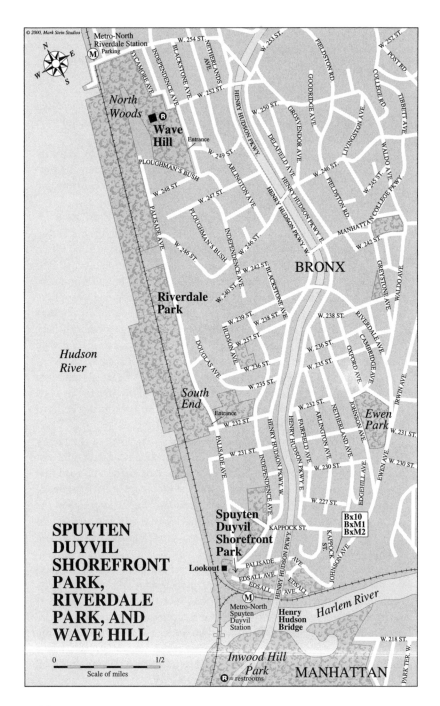

© 2000, Mark Stein Studios

Metro-North
Riverdale Station
Ⓜ Parking

W. 254 ST.
W. 253 ST.
W. 252 ST.
FIELDSTON RD.
POST RD.

North
Woods

Ⓡ
Wave
Hill
Entrance

PLOUGHMAN'S BUSH

W. 250 ST.
W. 252 ST.
W. 249 ST.
W. 248 ST.
W. 247 ST.
W. 246 ST.
W. 245 ST.

SYCAMORE AVE.
INDEPENDENCE AVE.
BLACKSTONE AVE.
NETHERLANDS AVE.
HENRY HUDSON PKWY.
DELAFIELD AVE.
GROSVENDOR AVE.
GOODRIDGE AVE.
FIELDSTON RD.
LIVINGSTON AVE.
WALDO AVE.
COLLEGE RD.
TIBBETT AVE.

PLOUGHMAN'S BUSH

PALISADE AVE.
ARLINGTON AVE.
INDEPENDENCE AVE.
HENRY HUDSON PKWY. W.
HENRY HUDSON PKWY. E.
MANHATTAN COLLEGE PKWY.
W. 242 ST.

BRONX

Riverdale
Park

W. 246 ST.
W. 246 ST.
W. 242 ST.
W. 240 ST.
W. 239 ST.
W. 238 ST.
W. 237 ST.
W. 236 ST.
W. 235 ST.

BLACKSTONE AVE.
HUDSON AVE.
DOUGLAS AVE.

W. 238 ST.
W. 236 ST.
W. 235 ST.

GREYSTONE AVE.
WALDO AVE.
RIVERDALE AVE.
CAMBRIDGE AVE.
OXFORD AVE.
IRWIN AVE.

Hudson
River

South
End
Entrance

W. 232 ST.
W. 231 ST.
W. 227 ST.

PALISADE AVE.
INDEPENDENCE AVE.
HENRY HUDSON PKWY. W.
HENRY HUDSON PKWY. E.
FAIRFIELD AVE.
ARLINGTON AVE.
NETHERLAND AVE.
JOHNSON AVE.
EDGEHILL AVE.
EWEN AVE.

W. 230 ST.

Ewen
Park
W. 231 ST.
W. 230 ST.

SPUYTEN
DUYVIL
SHOREFRONT
PARK,
RIVERDALE
PARK, AND
WAVE HILL

Spuyten
Duyvil
Shorefront
Park
KAPPOCK ST.

Bx10
BxM1
BxM2

Lookout ■

PALISADE
EDSALL AVE.
EDSALL AVE.
EDSALL AVE.

Ⓜ
Metro-North
Spuyten
Duyvil
Station

Henry
Hudson
Bridge

KAPPOCK ST.
JOHNSON AVE.
HENRY HUDSON PKWY.

Harlem River

W. 218 ST.
PARK TER. W.

Inwood Hill
Park
Ⓡ = restrooms

MANHATTAN

0   1/2
Scale of miles

34

There is ample parking at the Spuyten Duyvil station, or you can drive to a higher vantage point on Palisade Avenue. There is a parking lot for ten cars on the left, where Palisade Avenue makes a sharp right. This is the best location from which to bird both sections of Riverdale Park. There is a four-car lot at West 254th Street from which to bird the north section of the park. Refrain from leaving anything in your car in plain sight. Parking at Wave Hill is limited but free and secure.

For Additional Information on Spuyten Duyvil Shorefront Park, Riverdale Park, and Wave Hill

Bronx Urban Park Rangers (lead tours), 718-430-1832
City of New York/Parks and Recreation, www.nycparks.org
Wave Hill, 718-549-3200 and www.wavehill.org
Resource persons: Michael J. Feller, Natural Resources Group, City of New York/Parks and Recreation; Carl Jaslowitz

Chapter Two

Barn Swallow with Tree swallows

Brooklyn

Brooklyn (Kings County), the most populous of the five boroughs with well over 2.3 million residents, is the second largest borough in area (81.8 square miles) after Queens. It occupies the southwestern end of Long Island, fronting on New York Bay and the Narrows, Harlem River, and Jamaica Bay. In the heart of the borough are three landscaped parklands, Prospect Park, Brooklyn Botanic Garden, and Green-Wood Cemetery, each of which offers very good birding. Other unusual Brooklyn birding opportunities are found at Floyd Bennett Field and Dead Horse Bay, part of the Jamaica Bay district of the Gateway National Recreation Area.

Prospect Park

Nesting**   Spring Migration***   Fall Migration***   Winter**
Parkside Avenue to Grand Army Plaza, Prospect Park South and Prospect Park West to Flatbush Avenue and Ocean Avenue

In 1865, several years after landscape architects Frederick Law Olmsted and Calvert Vaux completed Central Park in Manhattan, they were commissioned to design Prospect Park. They created a 526-acre public park, considered to be one of their finest works, with rolling meadows, rugged woodlands, and an artificial system of waterways. In 1980, the New York City Landmarks Preservation Commission granted Prospect Park scenic landmark status, and in 1998 the National Audubon Society designated it an Important Bird Area in New York State.

The City of New York/Parks and Recreation manages Prospect Park in partnership with the Prospect Park Alliance, a nonprofit advocacy and preservation organization. They have launched a long-term reforestation project to revitalize and stabilize the extensive woodlands which, combined with Prospect Lake, cover half of the park. Starting with the ravine area, they have added thousands of cubic yards of new topsoil and planted thousands of native species of herbs, shrubs, and trees. The Alliance is also restoring the Boathouse, a landmarked terra cotta-clad pavilion, where the National Audubon Society of New York State and the Alliance will operate an environmental education center, opening in April 2001.

Prospect Park is a migration hot spot. During spring migration, 100 bird species can be seen on a peak day, including 5 species of vireo, Eastern Bluebird, numerous warblers, Vesper Sparrow, Lincoln's Sparrow, White-crowned Sparrow, Rose-breasted Grosbeak, Indigo Bunting, Bobolink, Orchard Oriole, and Baltimore Oriole. Earlier in migration, Yellow-bellied Sapsucker may be seen, and later in migration, Black-billed and Yellow-billed cuckoos.

The park also offers good birding during winter and nesting seasons. The Christmas Bird Count, conducted by the Brooklyn Bird Club, has recorded more than 60 species in Prospect Park, almost half of the species counted in the entire borough. The Christmas Bird Count is a longtime tradition in New York City. It has been held in Brooklyn since 1903, in the Bronx since 1902, and in Manhattan since 1900.

Nesting species in Prospect Park include Green Heron, Wood Duck, Red-tailed Hawk, White-eyed Vireo, Red-eyed Vireo, Warbling Vireo, Carolina Wren, House Wren, Wood Thrush, Brown Thrasher, Yellow Warbler, Orchard Oriole, and Baltimore Oriole. The Brooklyn Bird Club collects nesting data during the month of June.

Some of the park's best birding locations are found in the woodland areas, the Vale of Cashmere, the Midwood, the Ravine, and Lookout Hill. Other prime birding sites include the Peninsula, which overlooks Prospect Lake, the Lullwater, and Long Meadow. These habitats attract a wide diversity of birds. A total of 275 species has been recorded in Prospect Park since 1905.

People visit Prospect Park for recreation and cultural events as well as for birding. There are tennis courts, ball fields, bridle paths, a wildlife center and zoo (entrance fee), ice skating rink (winter only), bandshell (with restrooms), carousel, and parade grounds (with restrooms). Aside from the Boathouse, notable buildings in Prospect Park include the Grecian Shelter, Tennis House (location of Brooklyn Center for the Urban Environment), Picnic House (with restrooms), Litchfield Villa (location of the Prospect Park Alliance and meeting place for the Brooklyn Bird Club), and Lefferts Homestead.

Vale of Cashmere, the Midwood, Long Meadow, and Lookout Hill

Your birding adventure starts at the park's main entrance (at its northernmost tip), at Grand Army Plaza, opposite the Memorial Arch. (There is a farmers' market here every Saturday morning, even in winter.) Follow the footpath on the left toward the park's eastern side and go south past the Rose Garden to the Vale of Cashmere. Dense ornamental shrubbery in this area provides excellent bird habitat. Continue south across Nellie's Lawn, checking for ground-feeding birds as you go, to the East Drive. Walk south and down the hill alongside East Drive through Battle Pass, where, in 1776, the American colonists tried in vain to hold off the advancing British troops in the Battle of Long Island. At the bottom of the hill, you will arrive at the rear of the wildlife center and zoo. Turn right (west), cross East Drive, and enter the Midwood. This is a particularly rich area for thrushes and warblers in the spring. First work the trail at the bottom of the ridge (part of the Harbor Hill terminal moraine that stretches along northern Long Island), and then work back toward the north. Climb the ridge, cross over Boulder Bridge, walk into the Ravine, and turn right. Follow the footpath westward to Long Meadow. Turn left and walk past Swan Boat Lake, checking it for Great Egret, Yellowed-crowned Night-Heron, and an occasional Wood Duck. Continue southwest, checking the ball fields for ground-feeding birds such as Killdeer, Northern Flicker, American Robin, and sparrows, and scanning the sky for raptors. Go past the rear of the Friends (Quaker) Cemetery and walk southeast along the bridle path to Center Drive.

Cross Center Drive and ascend Lookout Hill, the highest point in the park. Its prominence serves as a beacon for spring and fall migrants. On a good spring "wave day," (i.e., when migrants appear in large numbers), 25 species of warbler have been seen here. Covering Lookout Hill takes time. It is best to start from the top, then circle the hill along the lower paths several times, and return to the top. This can take a whole morning if there is a fallout of migrants. An alternative approach leads to the base of Lookout Hill from the park entrance at 16th Street and Prospect Park Southwest.

The Peninsula and the Lullwater

Proceed down the south side of Lookout Hill, investigating its wooded slope, particularly the dense thickets above the Well House, for Carolina Wren and various warblers, including infrequent Orange-crowned Warbler. Also check the forest immediately to the south of the Maryland Monument (commemorating the Maryland Four Hundred who faced the

British army, thereby protecting George Washington's retreat). Then proceed down the hill and cross the road and meadow onto the Peninsula. Bird this area thoroughly and proceed to the Thumb. From the rustic, log-braced shelter, check the water and Duck Island, directly across from the shelter, for roosting herons or raptors and interesting ducks, such as American Wigeon and Bufflehead. (The other islands, the Three Sisters and West Island, are also important roosting and nesting areas.) Work back along the north edge of the peninsula, past the *Phragmites* thickets, to a footpath that leads under the Terrace Bridge. Black-crowned Night-heron often roost in this area.

Proceed along the footpath under the bridge and along the Lullwater, a stretch of the stream where it widens. Green Heron nest in this area, and a variety of waterfowl, such as Wood Duck, Common Moorhen, and American Coot, may be found here. In winter, there are feeding stations along the trails on both sides of the Lullwater that attract Yellow-bellied Sapsucker, Downy and Hairy woodpeckers, Black-capped Chickadee, Tufted Titmouse, Dark-eyed Junco, Fox Sparrow, White-throated Sparrow, House Finch, and American Goldfinch. Proceed along the Lullwater trail to the Lullwater Bridge at the Boathouse. Cross the bridge, checking the surrounding trees as well as the water. Baltimore Oriole have nested in the trees above the bridge, Barn Swallow in crevices under the bridge, and Green Heron in trees within sight of the bridge. From here, walk behind the Boathouse and bear right to return to East Drive. Walk past the zoo and retrace your steps to Grand Army Plaza. Or cross Flatbush Avenue and walk up Eastern Parkway past the public library (with restrooms) to the main entrance of the Brooklyn Botanic Garden. (To enter the Botanic Garden at Empire Boulevard and Flatbush Avenue, exit the park just past Lefferts Homestead and the carousel and cross Flatbush Avenue.)

An alternate route, particularly in the fall, starts at the south end of Prospect Park at the Wollman Memorial Rink parking lot. Facing Prospect Lake, bear left around the south side of the lake, keeping it on your right. When you reach the northeast side, go to the peninsula, and then work the water course northward along the Lullwater. Instead of crossing the Lullwater Bridge, follow the edge of the Lullwater to Pagoda Pond, actually a wooded swamp, and on to Center Drive at the Nethermead Arches. Bear right along Center Drive to a footpath that takes you into the Midwood. Follow this trail north, through the Midwood, back to Park Drive East at the zoo. Walk the drive south back to the parking lot at the skating rink.

In fall, check Long Meadow from the west side of the ridge, particularly for migrating hawks. For large fallouts of flickers and robins, check

Long Meadow, the ball fields, and Nethermead (smaller meadow) in early morning. Killdeer, Common Snipe, and Eastern Meadowlark have also been seen in these areas very early in the morning, before the influx of dog walkers and their exuberant pets.

Special Notes

The reforestation project has caused some areas along the glacial ridge to be fenced off, limiting one's ability to cross the park and the ridge. A walkway, known as Rocky Pass, allows access through the restoration area. It starts at the beginning of the ravine and ends at the Nethermead Arches. The fencing will be in place past the year 2000 to allow native plantings to mature, but it does not obstruct birders from reaching the important sites.

The Prospect Park Alliance provides *A Guide to Nature in Prospect Park* and a map of the park and the Brooklyn Botanic Garden that can be purchased at Litchfield Villa (in the park at 5th Street; 95 Prospect Park West, Brooklyn, N.Y. 11215), Lefferts Homestead, or Wollman Memorial Rink.

The Brooklyn Bird Club, a private nonprofit membership organization founded in 1909, publishes a checklist and *Map for Birdwatchers* for Prospect Park, as well as a number of other resources for birders, including a quarterly newsletter, *The Clapper Rail*. It offers field trips and field studies such as an annual Breeding Bird Census.

The Brooklyn Center for the Urban Environment (BCUE), located at Tennis House, was founded in 1978 as a nonprofit, educational organization. BCUE provides numerous public programs, runs tours in Prospect Park in conjunction with the Brooklyn Bird Club, offers school groups a special introductory course in bird biology that covers migration, bird behavior, ecology, and the use of field guides, and publishes, a newsletter, *CityGreen*.

When to Go

In spring, April 15 to May 31 is good for songbirds, the peak for warblers being May 5 to 20. Sunrise until 10:00 A.M. and then again from 3:00 P.M. until sunset are the best times of day.

In summer, breeding and nonbreeding species can be seen from July 1 to August 15. Dragonflies (more than 15 species) and butterflies (more than 25 species, especially prevalent at the buddleia bushes in Butterfly Meadow atop Lookout Hill) can be seen from July 1 to August 31. In addition to the birds and insects, mammals take to the air as well. At the lake, Nethermead, Swan Boat Lake, Lookout Hill, and Long Meadow, there are 6–8 species of bats, including little brown, big brown, red, hoary, and silver-haired, that are present and can sometimes be seen at dusk from July 1 to September 30.

In fall, warblers can be seen from August 15 to September 30, peaking around August 31 to September 10; other songbirds, September 1 to 30, peaking around September 15; sparrows, September 15 to October 30, peaking October 7 to 15; and raptors, October 1 to November 30. Any time of day is fine for fall birding.

In winter, waterfowl can be expected between September 1 and April 30, and raptors (Sharp-shinned, Cooper's, and Red-shouldered hawks, American Kestrel, and Merlin) from November 1 to March 31, at any time of day.

Optimal Weather Conditions

Large fallouts of spring migrants occur on a clear day when the mornings with west or southwest winds are cool (high 50s to low 60s) and midday temperatures rise to 65–75,° after a period of rain. In fall, birding is best on a day with northwest winds, especially at the beginning of a cold snap.

Personal Safety

It is advisable to bird in Prospect Park with at least one companion, particularly in secluded wooded areas.

Getting There

The Metropolitan Transit Authority (MTA) puts out a free New York City subway map indicating major subway/bus connections, which can be obtained at subway station ticket booths. Detailed bus schedules can be picked up on board Brooklyn buses. Or you can contact NYC Transit at 718-330-1234 or www.mta.nyc.ny.us for subway and bus information.

SUBWAY: From Manhattan, take the Brooklyn-bound 2 or 3 subway train to the Grand Army Plaza stop. When you come out from the subway stop, walk 300 yards to the park's main entrance and follow the suggested route above. Or take the Brooklyn-bound F subway train to the 15th Street/Prospect Park stop. Go into the park and follow Center Drive to Lookout Hill. Or take the Brooklyn-bound D or Q subway train to the Seventh Avenue stop (near Grand Army Plaza) or the Prospect Park stop (near the zoo) or the Parkside Avenue stop (near the lake).

Or take the C subway train to the Franklin Avenue stop, transfer to the Shuttle (S), and then take it to the end at Prospect Park.

BUS: In Brooklyn, take the B41 that runs along Flatbush Avenue in both directions, making stops at the north end (Grand Army Plaza) in

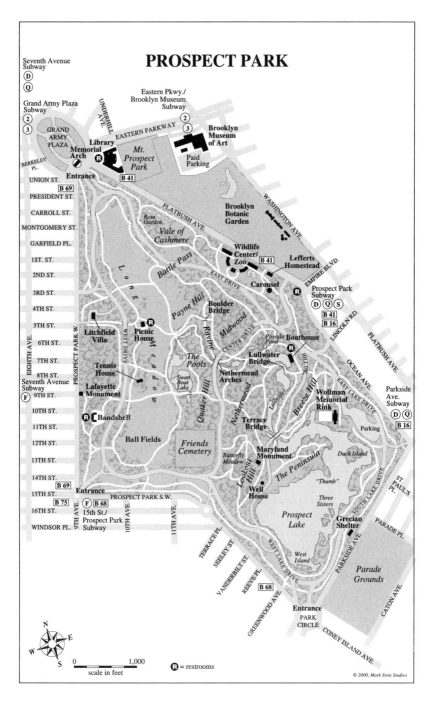

PROSPECT PARK

front of the public library (restrooms), in front of the zoo, and at the south end at Empire Boulevard (D, Q, and S subway stop). Or take the B68 that runs along Prospect Park Southwest in both directions, the B69 that runs south along Prospect Park West (and north along Eighth Avenue), the B75 that turns from Ninth Street into Prospect Park West, or the B16 that runs in both directions along Ocean Avenue and Caton Avenue, all of which make stops near park entrances.

CAR: From Manhattan, cross the Manhattan Bridge and take Flatbush Avenue to Grand Army Plaza. Go part way around the circle to Prospect Park West. At Prospect Park West and 5th Street, look on your left for free (limited) public parking at Litchfield Villa, which is near the southwestern end of Long Meadow. Or you can continue to Prospect Park Southwest and to Parkside Avenue. Take Parkside Avenue and follow it to the point at which it meets Ocean Avenue. Turn into the park entrance on the left, which leads to a parking lot (free) near Wollman Memorial Rink.

From the Belt Parkway (Shore Parkway), take the Flatbush exit north (11N) and follow Flatbush Avenue to Parkside Avenue. Go left for two blocks. Look for the entrance on the right, at the corner of Parkside Avenue and Ocean Avenue, that leads to the skating rink parking lot (free).

For Additional Information on Prospect Park

Brooklyn Urban Park Rangers (leads tours), 718–438–0100
Prospect Park Alliance (leads tours), 718–965–8951 and
    www.prospect park.org; events hotline, 718–965–8999
Brooklyn Center for the Urban Environment (leads tours),
    718–788–8500 and www.bcue.org
Brooklyn Bird Club (leads tours), www.brooklynbirdclub.org
National Audubon Society of New York State, 518–869–9731
New York City Audubon Society (leads tours), 212–691–7483 and
    www.nycaudubon.org
Resource persons: Robert Gochfeld, editor of Brooklyn Bird Club's
The Clapper Rail; Paul Keim, President, Brooklyn Bird Club; and John
C. and Mary Yrizarry, Sterling Forest League of Naturalists

Brooklyn Botanic Garden
Nesting   Spring Migration**   Fall Migration**   Winter
Empire Boulevard to Eastern Parkway, Flatbush Avenue to Washington Avenue

Located to the east of Prospect Park, across Flatbush Avenue, and to the south of the Brooklyn Museum lies the Brooklyn Botanic Garden. Founded in 1910 as the research arm of the Brooklyn Institute of Arts and Sciences, it was built, like Prospect Park, on a portion of the Harbor Hill moraine that extends from Montauk Point in eastern Long Island to New York City. The Brooklyn Botanic Garden covers 52 acres featuring speciality gardens: the Japanese Hill-and-Pond, Herb, Osborne, and Cranford Rose gardens as well as the renowned Cherry Esplanade. The Brooklyn Botanic Garden conducts the New York Metropolitan Flora Project, an ongoing inventory of all the plants in the New York metropolitan area. As a semi-public institution, it has specific hours and suggests an entrance donation for adults, seniors, and students (free for children under 16). Picnics, radios, bicycles, and ball playing are not allowed.

The Eastern Parkway Gate entrance is near the 2 and 3 subway stop. If coming from Prospect Park or the D/Q subway, there is a convenient entrance on Flatbush Avenue where it meets Empire Boulevard. Maps can be picked up at any entrance. The Steinhardt Conservatory (with restrooms) serves food year round.

The Brooklyn Botanic Garden is a natural retreat for birds because they are attracted by the concentration and diversity of its berry-producing trees and shrubs as well as by its several ponds. During spring and fall migration, thousands of birds drop down into the botanic garden for shelter, food, and water.

The Japanese Hill-and-Pond Garden has the strongest draw for waterbirds. A good number, including Pied-billed Grebe, Wood Duck, American Wigeon, and Northern Shoveler, are also found around Terminal Pond at the southeast end of the Plant Family Collection and at the Lily Pool. Birding along the stream in the north section can also be productive.

Hummingbirds have been seen in the Herb Garden during migration. Fruit-bearing trees such as the crab apples northeast of Cherry Esplanade, the prickly ash along the path opposite the Japanese Hill-and-Pond Garden, and the paper mulberry northwest of the Osborne Garden attract many resident birds and fall migrants such as Red-eyed Vireo, White-breasted Nuthatch, and Cedar Waxwing. Resident species include Downy Woodpecker, Black-capped Chickadee, and Tufted Titmouse.

Chimney Swift and Tree and Barn swallows fly overhead or occasionally perch in the tops of tall trees.

Ground feeders, such as the Northern Flicker, Hermit Thrush, Eastern Towhee, Chipping Sparrow, White-throated Sparrow, and Dark-eyed Junco, are found throughout the botanic garden. The lawns and shrubby edges of the Systematic Collection, Osborne Garden, and Cherry Esplanade are prime locations for sighting these species.

When to Go

The best time for spring migrants is from May 1 to 15; for fall migrants, from September 15 to November 25.

Optimal Weather Conditions

Large fallouts of spring migrants occur on a clear day when the mornings are cool (low 50s) and midday temperatures rise to 60–70°, after rainy periods with west or southwest winds. In fall, birding is best on a day with or after winds west to north.

Personal Safety

The botanic garden is an enclosed, limited-access park. In addition, guards regularly patrol the grounds. It is safe to bird alone.

Getting There

The Metropolitan Transit Authority (MTA) puts out a free New York City subway map indicating major subway/bus connections, which can be obtained at subway station ticket booths. Detailed bus schedules can be picked up on board Brooklyn buses. Or you can contact NYC Transit at 718-330-1234 or www.mta.nyc.ny.us for subway and bus information.

SUBWAY: Take the Brooklyn-bound 2 or 3 subway train to the Eastern Parkway/Brooklyn Museum stop, which will bring you right to a Brooklyn Botanic Garden entrance. Or take the Brooklyn-bound D or Q subway train to the Prospect Park stop. Exit at the Empire Boulevard end of the subway station. Across Flatbush Avenue you will see an entrance to the botanic garden.

Or take the C subway train to the Franklin Avenue stop, transfer to the Shuttle (S), and take it to the end at Prospect Park.

BUS: Take the B41 that runs north or south along Flatbush Avenue to the Empire Boulevard stop (at Wendy's on the corner). From the bus stop you will see an entrance to the garden.

CAR: From Manhattan, cross the Manhattan Bridge and take Flatbush Avenue to Grand Army Plaza. Go around the circle to Eastern Parkway. Take a right on Washington Avenue. You can use the parking lot (there is a parking fee) for the Brooklyn Museum, which is on your right. You can enter the Brooklyn Botanic Garden from the parking lot or you can walk along Washington Avenue to the Steinhardt Conservatory entrance.

From the Belt Parkway (Shore Parkway) take the Flatbush exit north (11N), then follow Flatbush Avenue to Washington Avenue. You can use the parking lot for the Brooklyn Museum, which is on your left.

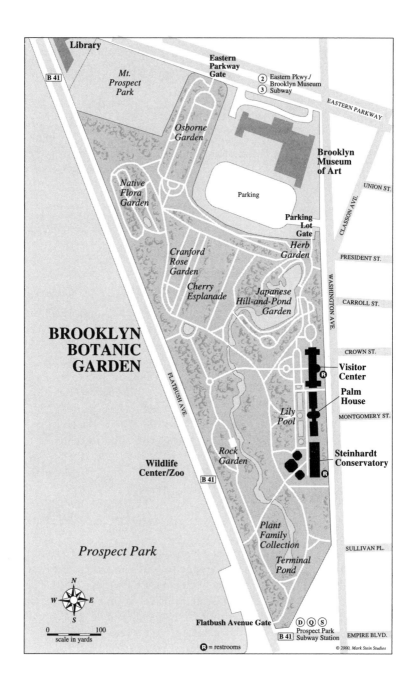

Library

B 41

Mt.
Prospect
Park

Eastern
Parkway
Gate

② Eastern Pkwy./
Brooklyn Museum
③ Subway

EASTERN PARKWAY

Osborne
Garden

Brooklyn
Museum
of Art

UNION ST.

Native
Flora
Garden

Parking

Parking
Lot
Gate

CLASSON AVE.

PRESIDENT ST.

Cranford
Rose
Garden

Herb
Garden

Cherry
Esplanade

Japanese
Hill-and-Pond
Garden

WASHINGTON AVE.

CARROLL ST.

BROOKLYN
BOTANIC
GARDEN

CROWN ST.

Ⓡ Visitor
Center

Palm
House

FLATBUSH AVE.

Lily
Pool

MONTGOMERY ST.

Wildlife
Center/Zoo

B 41

Rock
Garden

Steinhardt
Conservatory

Ⓡ

Plant
Family
Collection

SULLIVAN PL.

Prospect Park

Terminal
Pond

N
W   E
S

0   100
scale in yards

Flatbush Avenue Gate

Ⓓ Ⓠ Ⓢ
Prospect Park
B 41   Subway Station

EMPIRE BLVD.

Ⓡ = restrooms

© 2000, Mark Stein Studios

For Additional Information on the Brooklyn Botanic Garden

Brooklyn Botanic Garden, 718-623-7200 and www.bbg.org
Brooklyn Bird Club (leads tours), www.Brooklynbirdclub.org
New York City Audubon Society (leads tours), 212-691-7483 and
www.nycaudubon.org
Resource persons: John C. and Mary Yrizarry, Sterling Forest
League of Naturalists

Green-Wood Cemetery

Nesting*   Spring Migration**   Fall Migration**   Winter*
Fort Hamilton Parkway to Fifth Avenue and 24th Street, 36th Street and
37th Street to McDonald Avenue

In 1840, long before Prospect Park was conceived, Green-Wood Cemetery opened as a nonsectarian burial ground. More than half a million people are memorialized here with extraordinary Victorian mausoleums and monuments; those memorialized include De Witt Clinton, Horace Greeley, Reverend Henry Ward Beecher, Samuel F.B. Morse, Peter Cooper, Duncan Phyfe, Boss Tweed, and even Whistler's father. Green-Wood Cemetery, 478 acres of rolling hills and ponds landscaped with exotic trees, shrubs, and marine vegetation, lies on the highest point in Brooklyn. It is not surprising that it has become a haven for botanists, historians, art lovers, and of course, birders, particularly during migration.

Four ponds, Sylvan Lake, and Valley, Crescent, and Dell waters, thrive. (A fifth pond, Dale Water, has been filled in.) These ponds attract herons, egrets, geese, ducks, (a male Eurasian Wigeon arrives at Sylvan Lake every fall), Solitary Sandpiper, and Spotted Sandpiper. An American Bittern is often found among Valley Water's water lilies in the fall. And there is always the chance of spotting an unusual migrant such as Pied-billed Grebe, Green-winged Teal, Hooded Merganser, or American Coot.

The cemetery's avenues are lined with old oaks, and with European linden, maple, and tulip trees, which attract warblers, tanagers, grosbeaks, and orioles. Fruit trees and berry bushes are magnets for fall migrants.

Tombstones and monuments act as perches for late fall bluebirds. The old burial grounds, low and grassy, attract resident Red-tailed Hawk and Eastern Meadowlark. Cemetery workers keep track of the Red-tailed Hawk and can point out their whereabouts.

A colony of Monk Parakeet nest in the landmarked gatehouse's gothic spires. These blue-green parrots, native to the mountainous regions of Argentina, are classified as released exotics. Legend has it that the now-wild birds escaped in the 1960s when a crate of caged Monk Parakeet broke open at JFK airport. Our winters are similar to those in the Andes, so they have thrived, nesting on the lighting fixtures at the Brooklyn College athletic field as well as on the highest spire of the main entrance gatehouse here. The parrot's catchy name comes from the patch of gray on its head resembling a monk's cap.

Start your birdwalk as you enter through Green-Wood Cemetery's main gate. (You can't miss the parrots.) Follow along Central Avenue, a recognized birding hot spot. Two blocks ahead you will find Pierrepont Hill (the vast acreage was originally the Pierrepont family farm) to your right. Continue on Central Avenue to the Four Corners, where big oaks, fruit trees, black birch, and magnolia trees hold birds in every season. Stay on Central Avenue to the giant weeping birches. Look underneath them and around them for a variety of thrushes and warblers. Continue for another block, which brings you to Peter Cooper Circle. Bird the trees around the circle and then climb up Ocean Hill, the highest point in Brooklyn, which can be a good site in fall for hawkwatching. (A signer of the Declaration of Independence is buried here. Can you find him?)

In spring, go on to Cypress Avenue, lined for half a mile with very old oaks. When the catkins are ripe, the avenue is warbler heaven.

Then go on to Crescent and Dell waters, but do not miss Dale Water, which is now a dump for leaves and mulch. Solitary Sandpiper, Spotted Sandpiper, and flocks of sparrows (Chipping, Field, and White-throated) are attracted to this area.

Other people prefer to bird Green-Wood Cemetery by starting at Valley Water, then on to Sylvan Lake, Dale, Dell and Crescent waters, Cypress Avenue, and return via Ocean Hill and Central Avenue. Either way you are bound to have an exciting birding experience.

Special Note

You will need to obtain permission to enter Green-Wood Cemetery, which is open from 8:00 A.M. to 4:00 P.M. You can either get a pass as you enter the main gate or call the main office ahead of time, mentioning which birding group you represent, and ask for permission to bird on a specific day. The administrators and gatekeepers are very receptive to birders.

Cameras are not allowed in the cemetery.

Personal Safety

It is safe to bird Green-Wood Cemetery on your own. It is also a wonderful place to explore with other birders.

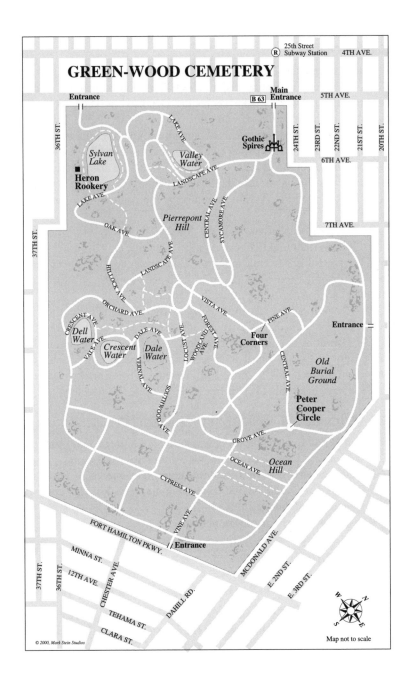

GREEN-WOOD CEMETERY

25th Street
Ⓡ Subway Station   4TH AVE.

Entrance

Main
B 63   Entrance   5TH AVE.

36TH ST.

Gothic
Spires

24TH ST.
23RD ST.
22ND ST.
21ST ST.
20TH ST.

Sylvan
Lake

Valley
Water

6TH AVE.

Heron
Rookery

LAKE AVE.

LANDSCAPE AVE.

37TH ST.

LAKE AVE.

OAK AVE.

Pierrepont
Hill

CENTRAL AVE.

SYCAMORE AVE.

7TH AVE.

LANDSCAPE AVE.

HILLOCK AVE.

ORCHARD AVE.

VISTA AVE.

PINE AVE.

Entrance

CRESCENT AVE.

Dell
Water

VALE AVE.

DALE AVE.

FOREST AVE.

Four
Corners

Crescent
Water

Dale
Water

LOCUST AVE.

WOODLAND AVE.

CENTRAL AVE.

Old
Burial
Ground

VERNAL AVE.

SOUTHWOOD AVE.

Peter
Cooper
Circle

GROVE AVE.

OCEAN AVE.

Ocean
Hill

CYPRESS AVE.

VINE AVE.

FORT HAMILTON PKWY.   Entrance

MCDONALD AVE.

MINNA ST.

E. 2ND ST.

E. 3RD ST.

37TH ST.
36TH ST.
12TH AVE.

CHESTER AVE.

DAHILL RD.

TEHAMA ST.

CLARA ST.

© 2000, Mark Stein Studios

Map not to scale

Getting There

The Metropolitan Transit Authority (MTA) puts out a free New York City subway map indicating major subway/bus connections, which can be obtained at subway station ticket booths. Detailed bus schedules can be picked up on board Brooklyn buses. Or you can contact NYC Transit at 718-330-1234 or www.mta.nyc.ny.us for subway and bus information.

SUBWAY: From Manhattan, take the Brooklyn-bound R subway train to Brooklyn's 25th Street station, one block west of the main entrance.

BUS: From Brooklyn, take the B63 at Atlantic Avenue. The bus runs along Brooklyn's Fifth Avenue, stopping at the main entrance on 25th Street.

CAR: From Manhattan, take the Manhattan Bridge over the East River. It leads right into Flatbush Avenue. Continue on Flatbush Avenue until you reach Fifth Avenue (2 miles). Take a right on Fifth Avenue and continue on until you reach the main entrance opposite 25th Street (2 miles). There is free parking inside the cemetery.

Or from Manhattan, take the Brooklyn Battery Tunnel under the East River and exit immediately after the toll plaza onto Hamilton Avenue. Follow Hamilton Avenue until it becomes Third Avenue. Continue for about eight blocks on Third Avenue to 25th Street. Turn left on 25th Street and proceed two blocks to Fifth Avenue. The cemetery main entrance is straight ahead. There is free parking inside the cemetery.

For Additional Information on Green-Wood Cemetery

Green-Wood Cemetery, 718-768-7300 and www.green-wood.com
Brooklyn Bird Club (leads tours), www.brooklynbirdclub.org
Linnaean Society of New York (leads tours), 212-252-2668
New York City Audubon Society (leads tours), 212-691-7483 and
    www.nycaudubon.org
Resource person: Richard Rosenblum

Floyd Bennett Field

Nesting**   Spring Migration**   Fall Migration**   Winter**
Rockaway Inlet to Shore Parkway, Flatbush Avenue to Jamaica Bay

In 1931, New York City built its first municipal airport, Floyd Bennett Field, on a group of marshy islands at the mouth of Jamaica Bay that were landfilled with garbage, rubble, and dredge spoil. The maintained grassland areas between runways inadvertently provided habitat for grassland birds. When Floyd Bennett Field was decommissioned 40 years later, the management practice of suppressing woody vegetation ceased, and natural succession started to occur. In 1985, the U.S. Department of Interior's National Park Service and the New York City Audubon Society initiated a grassland restoration and management project (GRAMP) for 140 acres (out of 1,500) of Floyd Bennett Field. Trees and shrubs were removed, and mowing was resumed. The managed grasslands are particularly lovely in spring, when the wildflowers and grasses display hues of green, red, blue, and yellow.

Very good birding is found at the North Forty and along Floyd Bennett Field's shorefront as well as in the grassland areas. Observers have recorded up to 30 species nesting in these areas.

Floyd Bennett Field is part of the Gateway National Recreation Area, a five-district park with sections in Brooklyn, Queens, Staten Island, and New Jersey, which was established in 1972 along with a San Francisco's Golden Gate Park. These parks were the first national recreation areas of the national park system that were in an urban setting. The airport administration building and flight tower are landmark buildings, as are the runways, which are now used on occasion for bicycle races and in line skating. Floyd Bennett Field's other recreational areas include ball fields, a cricket field, two public campgrounds, a model airplane field, and community gardens.

Floyd Bennett Field Grasslands

During spring migration, Floyd Bennett Field is the place to look for Upland Sandpiper, Savannah Sparrow, Grasshopper Sparrow, Bobolink, and Eastern Meadowlark. Northern Harrier, occasional nesters, can be seen throughout the year hunting the fields and open shrubland. The Savannah Sparrow is the only grassland species still nesting there regularly, reflecting a wider decline of these species throughout the region as a result of habitat loss. Other nesters are Ring-necked Pheasant, American Woodcock, Northern Flicker, White-eyed Vireo, Tree Swallow (in man-made nest boxes), Gray Catbird, Brown Thrasher, and Common Yellowthroat.

In early October, migrating Tree Swallow flock in swarms of more than 1,000 birds, feeding on the bayberry shrubs around the field. And in the fall, as many as 14 American Kestrel have been sighted at one time sitting along the fence that encloses the New York City Police Department's runway (formerly used by the U.S. Coast Guard).

Sharp-shinned Hawk, Cooper's Hawk, Red-tailed Hawk, American Kestrel, and Merlin are winter residents, as on occasion are Rough-legged Hawk and Snowy and Short-eared owls. Hawks are seen in the small stands of tall cottonwoods trees between runways. Scattered about the field are Japanese black pines of various sizes and densities, many of which are dying. The National Park Service is replacing them with native pines. In Ecology Village, an educational environmental center, the existing pine grove provides nighttime winter roosts for Sharp-shinned and Cooper's hawks and, from time to time, day roosts for Barn Owl. Because the pines are neither tall nor dense, owls do not feel secure among them. These birds of prey are easily flushed from their roosts, often before birders get a good look.

The many runways and roads that crisscross Floyd Bennett Field make walking easy, but the distances are long. In winter, the wind is cold, and in summer, there is little shade. We recommend exploring by car. Besides providing mobility and shelter, the car can act as a blind that allows you to get close to birds. When the car is not in motion, harriers, kestrels, and owls may fly within 20 feet of you. But if you get out of your car, a Cooper's Hawk as far as 100 yards away will be frightened off its perch. Try using a scope on a window mount.

North Forty

Aside from the grassland area, there is a remote section at the north end, west of the model airplane area, called the North Forty. It is accessible by a trail that winds through shrubland and *Phragmites* to a man-made, two-acre pond named the Return-a-Gift Pond. If you checked "Return a Gift to Wildlife" on your New York State tax return, you helped pay for the trail and pond. During spring, summer, and fall, look for American Robin, Gray Catbird, Brown Thrasher, Common Yellowthroat, Eastern Towhee, and Northern Cardinal in the shrubbery at the beginning of the trail. Some of these birds nest nearby. When you reach the pond, you may see Pied-billed Grebe, Great Blue Heron, Great Egret, Snowy Egret, Black-crowned Night-Heron, Glossy Ibis, Wood Duck, Gadwall, American Black Duck, Mallard, Northern Shoveler, Green-winged Teal, Hooded Merganser, and Solitary, Spotted, and Least sandpipers.

The Jamaica Bay shoreline on the eastern edge of Floyd Bennett Field offers good birding opportunities. At low tide, exposed rocks, jetty, and concrete pilings make wonderful perches for cormorants, shorebirds, gulls, and terns. The birding is best in winter, when there is no fishing activity to disturb the birds. This area can be reached by going from Gateway National Recreation Area's entrance on Flatbush Avenue straight down Floyd Bennett Drive to a sharp left turn. Following the turn, proceed north, and make the first left on a road that leads directly to a parking area on the immediate right. From this parking area, walk 100 yards east to Jamaica Bay.

Good birding (best in spring) is also found at the northeastern end of the north runway (Raptor Point). When you reach this point, walk around to the right and look south to the beach and marsh for waterfowl and American Oystercatcher. Although you are permitted to walk this beach, it is recommended that you do not. View the birds from the bulkhead area so you do not disturb them. Across the bay are two large uninhabited islands (which are off limits), Canarsie Pol and Ruffle Bar, that host gulls, Barn Owl (in nest boxes put up by the National Park Service), and colonial nesters such as Great Egret, Snowy Egret, Black-crowned Night-Heron, Yellow-crowned Night-Heron, Glossy Ibis, and a few Little Blue and Tricolored herons (mainly at Canarsie Pol). In spring and summer, you may see these egrets, herons, and ibis flying over the bay's waters, in transit to and from their nests.

Special Note

At certain times of the year, parking areas may be restricted to fishermen with special permits or to participants in special events. For advice, check at the information desk at the Ryan Visitor Center (with restrooms and a display area on the history of aviation) on Hangar Row along Flatbush Avenue.

New York City Audubon Society Speaks Out

In the past, the National Park Service has pressed for expansion of the baseball fields into the grasslands. New York City Audubon opposes any plans that will encroach on this sensitive grassland area.

In 1992, New York City Audubon and the Trust for Public Land published a protection plan, *Buffer the Bay Revisited*, emphasizing the importance of safeguarding Jamaica Bay's fragile coastal area and estuarine ecosystem. North of Floyd Bennett Field lies Vandalia Dunes, a 227-acre former landfill slated for protection under this plan. In the mid-1990s, real estate developer Gateway Estates proposed a broad-footprint complex that would cover most of the open land with parking lots, a shopping center, residential units, schools, playgrounds, offices, recreation facilities, and new entrance ramps for the Belt Parkway. New York City Audubon opposed this project, voicing three main concerns: degradation of the bay's waters as the result of construction, increased traffic, and large-scale commercial use; placement of new housing and schools on what could be highly toxic soil; and loss of critical open land that absorbs and filters storm surges and provides wildlife habitat. As of the publication of this guidebook, developers have broken ground for the shopping complex.

When to Go

During the first through third weeks in April, Upland Sandpiper, Savannah Sparrow, and Eastern Meadowlark migrate through. During May, the Grasshopper Sparrow and Bobolink move through. From early April through May, migrating Osprey, Northern Harrier, and American

Kestrel can be seen. From mid-April through May, nesting birds arrive. From the second week in September to the end of October, when there is a cold front with strong northwesterly winds, raptors such as Northern Harrier, Sharp-shinned Hawk, American Kestrel, and Merlin move through. By the middle of November, most resident winter hawks have arrived, and waterfowl are arriving in increasing numbers. By the end of February, winter birding is slowing down.

Personal Safety

It is always best to bird with at least one other person, even at Floyd Bennett Field.

When you are on the North Forty Trail or on trails through and around the Ecology Village campgrounds, be on the lookout for poison ivy. After leaving the trail, check yourself and your clothing for dog ticks.

Obey the speed limit and stop signs when driving the roads and runways. Exercise caution when driving on the runways during bicycle races. Exercise extra caution when approaching runway intersections at which there are no stop signs.

Getting There

The Metropolitan Transit Authority (MTA) puts out a free New York City subway map indicating major subway/bus connections, which can be obtained at subway station ticket booths. Detailed bus schedules can be picked up on board Brooklyn buses. Or you can contact NYC Transit at 718-330-1234 or www.mta.nyc.ny.us for subway and bus information.

SUBWAY to BUS: From Manhattan, take the Brooklyn-bound 2 subway to Brooklyn College/Flatbush Avenue, the last stop. Then take the Q35 Green bus line from the bus stop on Nostrand Avenue in front of the famous Lord's Bakery. Allow time for a snack before heading south on Flatbush Avenue. Ask the bus driver to let you off at the main entrance (at the traffic light) to Gateway National Recreation Area and Floyd Bennett Field. Cross Flatbush Avenue at the controlled traffic light (take care—this is a six-lane divided thoroughfare) and walk into the well-marked entrance. Walk past the entrance booth to a long fenced road on the left. Take it and the next left to the Ryan Visitor Center (the building with the airport control tower). You can pick up an updated map of the area there.

CAR: From Manhattan, take the Brooklyn Bridge over the East River and follow signs to Brooklyn/Queens Expressway (Route 278) toward the Verrazano-Narrows Bridge. The Brooklyn/Queens Expressway becomes the Gowanus Expressway. The Gowanus Expressway (Route 278) will split off to the right to go over the Verrazano Bridge. Stay left (you do not

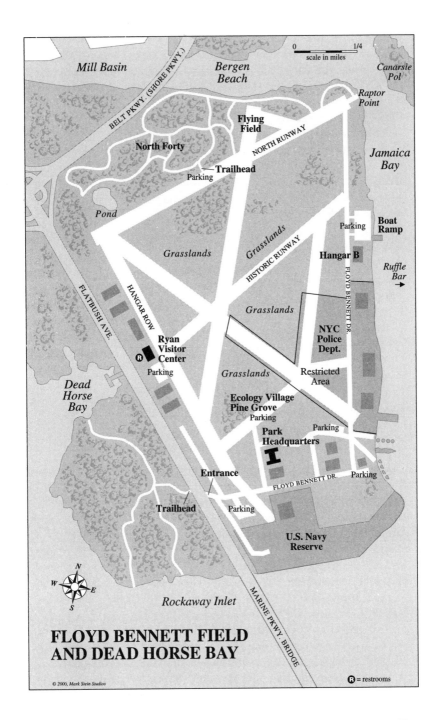

Mill Basin

Bergen
Beach

Canarsie
Pol

BELT PKWY. (SHORE PKWY.)

Raptor
Point

Flying
Field

NORTH RUNWAY

Jamaica
Bay

North Forty

Trailhead
Parking

Pond

Parking

Boat
Ramp

Grasslands

Grasslands

HISTORIC RUNWAY

Hangar B

Ruffle
Bar
→

FLATBUSH AVE.

HANGAR ROW

Grasslands

Grasslands

FLOYD BENNETT DR.

Ryan
Visitor
Center

Parking

NYC
Police
Dept.

Dead
Horse
Bay

Grasslands

Restricted
Area

Ecology Village
Pine Grove
Parking

Parking

Park
Headquarters

Entrance

Parking

Parking

FLOYD BENNETT DR.

Trailhead

Parking

U.S. Navy
Reserve

N
W   E
S

Rockaway Inlet

MARINE PKWY. BRIDGE

FLOYD BENNETT FIELD
AND DEAD HORSE BAY

© 2000, Mark Stein Studios

Ⓡ = restrooms

0   1/4
scale in miles

55

want to go over the Verrazano-Narrows Bridge to Staten Island) on Shore Parkway (the Belt Parkway). Continue on the parkway until Exit 11S, which brings you onto Flatbush Avenue. Go south on Flatbush Avenue about 1 mile to a traffic light (100 yards before the toll booths), where, on the left, there is an entrance to Gateway National Recreation Area and Floyd Bennett Field. As you drive in, a parking lot is on your right at which groups often park and then tour the field on foot.

If you wish to pick up a map of the area, follow the instructions above for walkers to the Ryan Visitor Center. Drive on and turn left on a limited access road that goes toward the Ryan Visitor Center. Watch for a second left-hand turn to the center. If driving around Floyd Bennett Field, an updated Park Service map will be helpful.

For Additional Information on Floyd Bennett Field

> Ecology Village (leads tours), 718-338-4306
> Floyd Bennett Field, 718-338-3799
> Gateway National Recreation Area, Brooklyn District, 718-338-3338
>   and www.nps.gov/gate
> New York City Audubon Society (leads tours), 212-691-7483 and
>   www.nycaudubon.org
> Resource person: Ronald V. Bourque, Board of Directors and former
> President, New York City Audubon Society

Dead Horse Bay

Nesting   Spring Migration**   Fall Migration**   Winter**
Rockaway Inlet to Shore Parkway, Lower Bay to Flatbush Avenue

The small bay and uplands (138.8 acres) directly across Flatbush Avenue from the entrance to Gateway National Recreation Area and Floyd Bennett Field is Dead Horse Bay, part of Gateway's Jamaica Bay district. The bay has the reputation of attracting disoriented birds, such as Red-necked Grebe and Surf and White-winged scoters, from late autumn through winter. By scanning the bay with a scope, you may sight an out-of-place bird, an accidental. Throughout the winter, waterfowl, including loons and grebes, are scattered across the bay. The regulars are Brant, American Wigeon, scaup, Bufflehead, and Red-breasted Merganser. In summer, look for Least Tern and Boat-tailed Grackle.

The southern section of Dead Horse Bay is easily accessible through a series of well-maintained trails. From the trailhead on the west side of Flatbush Avenue, take the far right-hand trail to the shore of the bay. As you emerge from the trail onto the sandy beach, inch forward quietly until the shore is in sight. This slow approach is unlikely to disturb the shorebirds. Sometimes horse bones are found in the sand, evidence of the bay's past as a manufacturing center for fertilizer made from horse carcasses.

Walk left when you reach the beach and follow around the tip of a peninsula to the base of the Marine Parkway (Gil Hodges) Bridge that spans Rockaway Inlet. For this walk, the tide is an important consideration. The full moon/new moon high tides may swamp the beach. At low tide you will see exposed mud and sand flats and a sand spit at the mouth of the bay. Here waterfowl, gulls, and shorebirds gather, including American Oystercatcher and Greater Yellowleg in spring and fall and Common and Least terns in summer. To consult the tide schedule, call the Jamaica Bay Wildlife Refuge at 718-318-4340. In the winter, look out into the inlet for Oldsquaw, black and white riders of the chop, far from their summer haunts in Greenland and northern Canada.

While on the beach at Rockaway Inlet, scan the towers of the Marine Parkway Bridge for the resident Peregrine Falcon. (See chap. 3, "Manhattan/Riverside Park," for more information on New York City Peregrine Falcon.)

To return to Flatbush Avenue, you can continue to the bridge and turn left onto the bicycle/pedestrian path to the traffic light, or you can take inland trails back to the trailhead at Flatbush Avenue. The inland trails are generally less productive, except in winter, when raptors patrol the uplands.

Special Note

From the peninsula that separates Dead Horse Bay from the Rockaway Inlet, you will notice at low tide large quantities of broken glass in the sand and mud flats. Erosion is exposing this underlying garbage dump. The proposed Jamaica Bay Ecosystem Restoration Project (JABERP) plans to bolster these areas against further erosion. The National Park Service, U.S. Army Corp of Engineers, and New York State Department of Environmental Conservation will sponsor JABERP. When visiting sites around Jamaica Bay, you may encounter this restoration work.

When to Go

You can go birding at Dead Horse Bay at any time of year without restrictions. The best time for waterfowl is from November to March, and for woodcock courtship behavior, early April at dusk.

During the last week of May to the first week in June, horseshoe crabs breed and lay their eggs, which attract hundreds of Ruddy Turnstone, Laughing Gull, occasionally Sanderling, and other shorebirds. Horseshoe crab eggs are a specific food source for these species.

Personal Safety

It is recommended that you go birding at Dead Horse Bay with at least one other person. If you walk the bicycle/pedestrian path, be on the lookout for speeding cyclists.

Getting There

Follow the directions above to Floyd Bennett Field.

For Additional Information on Dead Horse Bay

Gateway National Recreation Area, Brooklyn District, 718-338-3338 and www.nps.gov/gate

New York City Audubon Society (leads tours), 212-691-7483 and www.nycaudubon.org

Resource person: Ronald V. Bourque, Board of Directors and former President, New York City Audubon Society

Chapter Three

Wood Thrush

Manhattan

The borough of Manhattan fuels New York City. Residents, business people, diplomats, and tourists flock to its financial institutions, corporate headquarters, cultural institutions, and the United Nations. Incongruous as it may seem, birding enthusiasts from all over the world visit Manhattan to go birding. In the midst of skyscrapers, concrete, and asphalt lie three large islands of green—Central Park, Inwood Hill Park, and Riverside Park—that attract migrant, over-wintering, and, of course, resident birds.

Central Park

Nesting*   Spring Migration***   Fall Migration***   Winter*
Central Park South (59th Street) to 110th Street, Fifth Avenue to Central Park West

Central Park, an 843-acre rectangle that stretches 2½ miles north–south and ½ mile east–west, was designed in 1858 by Frederick Law Olmsted and Calvert Vaux. In 1965 it was designated a National Historic Landmark, and in 1974 it became New York City's first Scenic Landmark. The Central Park Conservancy, a nonprofit organization, manages the park under contract with the City of New York/Parks and Recreation. The Conservancy provides 85% of the park's annual operating budget, funds major capital improvements, supports horticultural care and management, and offers programs for volunteers and visitors.

Central Park is one of the best birding spots in the United States, attracting birdwatchers from all over the world. Birds migrating, spring and fall, along the East Coast find Central Park a welcoming place to rest and stoke up energy for the next leg of their journey. On a single wave or fall-out day, as many as 30 warbler species may be seen, establishing the park as one of the most famous warbler traps on this coastal migration path. For some spring migrants, Central Park is their breeding destination. And in fall, hawks migrating along the flyway soar directly above this city park.

Since the creation of Central Park, 275 bird species have been recorded; 192 are regular visitors or year-round residents, and 83 are in-frequent or rare visitors. A free Central Park checklist can be obtained at the Dairy (mid-park at 65th Street; restrooms nearby) and at Belvedere Castle (mid-park at 82nd Street; restrooms nearby).

Central Park also attracts a goodly number of birders. On a warm Sun-day in May, more than 500 birders have been counted birdwatching in the Ramble. Birding enthusiasts include visiting bird groups from other parts of New York State and neighboring states as well as visitors from distant states and abroad. On a spring weekday morning, you will see the business-suited folk catching a little birding on their way to work. During fall migration, hawkwatchers, eyes trained aloft, congregate at Belvedere Castle.

Birders team up on their own or join bird walks sponsored by the New York City Audubon Society, Central Park Conservancy, the Linnaean Society of New York, The Nature Conservancy, and the Urban Park Rangers. They also join walks led by independent naturalists. Any of these walks, which are scheduled year round but occur most frequently during migration, provide top-notch birding experiences for novices and experts alike.

In 1998, the National Audubon Society designated Central Park an Important Bird Area in New York State, recognizing the significance of its man-made avian habitats, which include meadows, grassy hillocks, rocky crags, woodlands, ravines, streams, ponds, lakes, and a reservoir. The best and most popular birding areas are the Ramble, Belvedere Cas-tle, Locust Grove and Pinetum, the Jacqueline Kennedy Onassis Reser-voir, and the North Woods and surroundings.

The Ramble

This 37-acre jumble of hills (Olmsted's "wilderness") in the center of the park runs from 72nd Street to 79th Street. You can approach this world-famous birding area at 72th Street, just west of Bethesda Fountain. Walking along the rising sidewalk past pine trees, you come to a gathering of beech trees at the edge of Cherry Hill. The beeches produce a banquet of insects just in time for arriving spring warblers. Birders stand on an an-cient rocky outcrop and name Chestnut-sided, Magnolia, Black-throated

Blue, and Black-throated Green warblers, American Redstart, and Canada Warbler, among others.

The grassy crown of Cherry Hill is adorned with two rows of pin oaks planted at right angles that attract flocks of birds when insects hatch in spring. Nearby, leaning like the Tower of Pisa, is a tulip tree. In its mighty branches you may see Swainson's Thrush, Scarlet Tanager, Baltimore Oriole, and even Summer Tanager. The orioles find mates, disperse to nearby elms, and begin building nests. Red-eyed Vireo look the trees over and sometimes nest here.

Downslope toward Bow Bridge stands a young swamp white oak, a singing perch for generations of Song Sparrow. Beneath it, barberry bushes defend summer nests of Gray Catbird and Brown Thrasher.

From the curve of Bow Bridge you look out on Rowboat Lake and may see Double-crested Cormorant, egrets, Green Heron, Black-crowned Night-Heron, Canada Geese, Mute Swan (which nest here), ducks, gulls, and Belted Kingfisher. Cross the bridge and you are in the heart of the Ramble. An intricate system of trails leads to the Summer House, the Gill, Willow Rock, the Oven, the Point, and the feeding station at Azalea Pond. Black Tupelo, Evodia, and Maintenance Meadows surround the Azalea Pond, where spring and fall birds rest and feed. On the meadows are found Yellow-rumped and Palm warblers, Chipping, Field, and White-throated sparrows, Dark-eyed Junco, and Indigo Bunting, all gobbling seeds and chasing bugs. In fall, fruiting trees are crowded with feeding Yellow-bellied Sapsucker, Northern Flicker, thrushes, Cedar Waxwing, and Rose-breasted Grosbeak. If they are joined by a Sharp-shinned or Copper's hawk, escaping birds explode in all directions.

To leave the Ramble, walk to the maintenance building (with restrooms), turn right (east), and walk to the edge of East Drive. Continue north and up the winding sidewalk to a rise, where you will see Turtle Pond. Take the left path along the shady side of the pond and scan the dabbling Mallard for possible Wood, American Black, or Northern Pintail ducks. Depending on the season, the trees lining the sidewalk and shore attract passing Belted Kingfisher, kingbirds, Tufted Titmouse, kinglets, warblers, and orioles. As you walk forward, you will see Belvedere Castle above you.

Belvedere Castle and the Fall Hawkwatch

From the vantage of Belvedere Castle's viewing deck, you can watch treetop songbirds without incurring "warbler neck," a muscle strain caused by repeatedly looking upward into the treetops. And it provides the perfect spot for watching the fall migration of hawks. Ten thousand hawks (of 15 species) have been counted migrating over Central Park in a single autumn season. On a good September day, observers have tallied thousands of Broad-winged Hawk and as many as 125 American Kestrel, 75 Osprey, and 10 Bald Eagle. In early October, Peregrine Falcon come through along with the accipiters. The migration of accipiters begins in mid-September and continues into early November. In a single day, it is possible to see more than 100 Sharp-shinned Hawk, dozens of Cooper's Hawk, and on rare occasions, Northern Goshawk. Turkey Vulture become numerous by mid-October. In late October, Red-shouldered and Red-tailed hawks pass over. In November and early December, the last of the migrating Bald Eagle, Northern Harrier, and buteos are seen. Also in October, flocks of songbirds such as Blue Jay, Eastern Bluebird, and Cedar Waxwing are seen as well as waterbirds, including Common Loon, Double-crested Cormorant, Canvasback, and Greater Scaup. It is not uncommon to count several thousand Snow and Canada geese winging their way over this urban parkland.

The Urban Park Rangers of the City of New York/Parks and Recreation sponsor the Hawkwatch with support from the New York City Audubon Society and the Linnaean Society of New York. A ranger or other hawkwatcher is on hand to help birders spot and identify hawks.

The Belvedere Castle observation deck also provides a good view of Turtle Pond, home to five species of turtle. In spring and fall, you will see red-eared sliders, the park's most common turtle. They crowd each other for space on the rocks to bask in the sun. The Conservancy has provided an unobtrusive nature blind, on the shore near the Delacorte Theatre, from which turtles and, of course, birds can be viewed.

In summer, scan the pickerel weed and sedge on the far shore of the pond for dragonflies. During their fall migration, watch hundreds of green darner dragonflies and monarch butterflies pass through this region.

Locust Grove and Pinetum

On the west side of the Great Lawn, just north of Delacorte Theatre, is the Locust Grove. Locust wood is popular with woodpeckers for digging winter roosts because it is relatively soft. Here you may see Red-bellied, Downy, and in recent years, Red-headed woodpeckers. If we can produce a starling-proof bird house, all of these woodpeckers might stay and nest.

North of the Locust Grove you enter the Pinetum. It is a good place to see Northern Saw-whet Owl, Red-breasted and White-breasted nuthatches, Golden-crowned and Ruby-crowned kinglets, and Yellow-rumped and Pine warblers in spring and fall. When you exit the Pinetum at the West Drive, you pass a mighty sycamore. Cross over the 86th Street Transverse and arrive at the reservoir.

Jacqueline Kennedy Onassis Reservoir

The 106-acre Jacqueline Kennedy Onassis Reservoir stretches from 85th Street to 94th Street, slightly closer to the East Side (Fifth Avenue) than to the West Side (Central Park West). In late March and April, migrating loons, grebes, cormorants, ducks, and coots stop here. Later in the spring and in summer, egrets forage along the water's edge for choice morsels to take back to their young waiting in nests, most likely on the East River's Brother Islands. (North and South Brother Islands are designated New York State Important Bird Areas.) In winter, look for cormorants, ducks, and gulls. Rarities such as Tufted Duck and Iceland Gull have appeared here.

North Woods and Surroundings

At the park's northern end, a 90-acre woodland area includes the Loch (where you may see wandering warblers in mid-August), the Pool, and the Wildflower Meadow (where flocks of Ruby-crowned Kinglet and American Goldfinch feed on fall grasses). In the 1990s, the Central Park Conservancy restored a portion of this forest area by enriching the soil and replacing exotic invasive plants with native species.

In August 1998, six Eastern Screech-Owls, raised at the Raptor Trust in New Jersey, were released in the park's North Woods. As of March 2000, at least three were seen here. Another was returned to the Raptor Trust after an injury. It is now believed that the owls are nesting in Central Park. The records from Ludlow Griscom, Geoffrey Carleton, and others show that screech owls nested in the park in the 1920s and 1960s.

The Charles A. Dana Discovery Center (with restrooms), which runs nature programs for all ages, is located to the east of the North Woods at 110th Street and Fifth Avenue. During spring and fall migration, New York City Audubon leads family birdwalks from the center on weekends. Contact the chapter for the schedule.

South of the Discovery Center at Fifth Avenue and 105th Street is the entrance to the Conservatory Garden, which delights flower lovers most of the year. The walks are lined with crab apple trees. In late fall, the trees are filled with American Robin, Gray Catbird, and huge flocks of Cedar Waxwing devouring the fruit.

Nature Notes at the Loeb Boathouse

A notebook of Central Park bird sightings was begun in 1975 and is kept in the Loeb Boathouse (with restrooms) on the eastern shore of Rowboat Lake. Birdwatchers come to the Boathouse to have a snack and study the notebook before they enter the Ramble. They check pages with recent dates and learn what birds are around and where they may be seen. Other birders record their discoveries before they leave the park. Although birders are delighted to tell you about special sightings, reading the register gives you a sequential picture of Central Park's natural phenomena.

Wintering Owls

As many as five species of owl winter in the park. Of these, Long-eared and Northern Saw-whet owls are the most commonly sighted. Great Horned Owl are seen on occasion. Barn and Barred owls are very rare. Owl perching locations are reported in Nature Notes at the Loeb Boathouse. Now that the Eastern Screech-Owl is a resident of the park, they too can be seen (heard) in winter.

Christmas Bird Count

In the 1900 Christmas Bird Count, the lone counter in New York City was 12-year-old Charles H. Rogers (who later became the well-known Princeton University ornithologist). On Christmas Day, he went to Central Park and reported 12 Herring Gull, 1 Downy Woodpecker, 4 European Starling, "abundant" White-throated Sparrow, 2 Song Sparrow, and 1 American Robin. On December 19, 1999, Central Park celebrated the 100th Christmas Count. More than 100 people counted 6,462 birds representing 62 species—the most people, the most birds, and the most species in the history of the Central Park count. The New York City Audubon Society is responsible for the Lower Hudson Count, which includes all of Manhattan (and parts of New Jersey). Contact the chapter if you would like to take part (see Appendix 1, "Metropolitan Birding Resources").

Winter Waterfowl Count

In mid-January, the Federation of New York State Bird Clubs conducts a statewide waterfowl count. In Central Park, much of the water freezes over or is drained, but waterfowl are counted in the open water on the Meer, the Pool, the Resevoir, the west side of Rowboat Lake, and the northeastern corner of the 59th Street Pond. Many places in and around New York City are not yet counted. If you wish to participate, get in touch with the federation (see Appendix 1, "Metropolitan Birding Resources").

Central Park Breeding Bird Census

In 1998, the New York City Audubon Society, with help from the Linnaean Society of New York and the City of New York/Parks and Recreation, conducted a breeding bird census of the entire park, following the protocol of the Cornell Laboratory of Ornithology. Thirty-one species were confirmed as nesters. American Robin were the most numerous and widespread, with more than 200 nesting territories. Next (but very far behind) were Common Grackle with 19 territories, Baltimore Oriole with 17, Northern Cardinal with 13, Blue Jay with 13, Northern Flicker with 10, and Red-bellied Woodpecker with 9. Among the species with few territories were Great Crested Flycatcher, Eastern Kingbird, Northern Rough-winged Swallow, Wood Thrush, and Brown Thrasher. These nesters were distributed from the Hallett Sanctuary (closed to the public) in the southeast to the Blockhouse in the northwest. Nonnative species such as pigeons (Rock Dove), House Sparrow, and European Starling were not included in the study. For a copy of the census, contact New York City Audubon, 71 West 23rd Street, New York, N.Y. 10010.

Nesting Red-tailed Hawk

Since 1994, a pair of Red-tailed Hawk has nested on an ornamental window pediment of a Fifth Avenue apartment at 74th Street. The best vantage for observing nesting and fledging activities is from the west side of Central Park's model boat pond (Conservatory Water). During April, May, and June, a scope trained on the nest is likely to be at this location. Don't hesitate to ask if you can take a look. Central Park birders are pleased to share the antics of the red-tails. For the full saga, read Marie Winn's *Red-Tails in Love: A Wildlife Drama in Central Park* (see "Suggested Readings").

New York City Audubon Speaks Out

From 1997 to 1999, at least eight "Manhattan" Red-tailed Hawk died from ingesting a poison, suspected to be Avitrol 4-aminopyridine, an avicide that the Environmental Protection Agency lists as "acutely hazardous." In New York City, Avitrol was used to "control" pigeons. It threatens all seed-eating birds and birds of prey, such as Red-tailed Hawk and Peregrine Falcon, that feast on pigeons. In August 2000, Governor George E. Pataki signed into law a bill banning the use of Avitrol in New York City. The New York City Audubon Society strongly supported this legislation. The use of Avitrol is still legal in the rest of New York State.

New York City Audubon Society Advocates for Central Park's Habitat and Wildlife

Members of New York City Audubon sit on the Central Park Conservancy's Woodlands Advisory Board, which addresses management and restoration needs. Recent problems that affect wildlife include damage to plantings from off-path trampling and bike riding, breakdown in the storm water drainage system, the use of lead sinkers on fishing lines, dogs off leash, and invasive vegetation.

When to Go

Spring migration extends from late February through the first week of June, peaking in May. The last days of April can also be good for viewing the earlier migrants (sparrows and other songbirds that winter in the United States and pass through before those from the Tropics). Often the early birder finds the best sighting, so set out at sunrise.

Autumn migration stretches from mid-August to early December. The arrival of migrating songbirds peaks in September and October. For raptors, join the hawkwatch at Belvedere Castle. The best hours are between 10:00 AM and 4:00 PM.

In winter, any time of day is good for birding. For information about owl roosts, refer to the Nature Notes at the Loeb Boathouse.

Optimal Weather Conditions

Some of the most spectacular waves of migrating birds have occurred on sunny spring mornings after nights of southerly to southwesterly winds. Fog in the morning, particularly in May, also produces good birding days.

In autumn, clear blue skies following passage of a cool or cold front make for the best birding days. Fallouts can also occur the morning after a nighttime rainstorm. The hawkwatch is best on days when the winds are from west to north and when there is ample cloud cover. Hawkwatching also can often be good on clear days with west-to-north winds after the passing of a cold front.

Personal Safety

Central Park is a popular place for joggers, bikers, and strollers, particularly on weekends if the weather is nice. In springtime, it also teems with birders. Nevertheless, you should take caution in the secluded spots, especially in the North Woods and the Ramble, not only for your safety but also for your sense of decorum. Public displays of intimate behavior may be encountered. We recommend that you bird with others.

Getting There

The Metropolitan Transit Authority (MTA) puts out a free New York City subway map indicating major subway/bus connections, which can be obtained at subway station ticket booths. Detailed bus schedules can be picked up on board Manhattan buses. Or you can contact NYC Transit at 718-330-1234 or www.mta.nyc.ny.us for subway and bus information.

BUS: There are buses that stop along or near Central Park either on Fifth Avenue (only southbound) and Madison Avenue (only north-

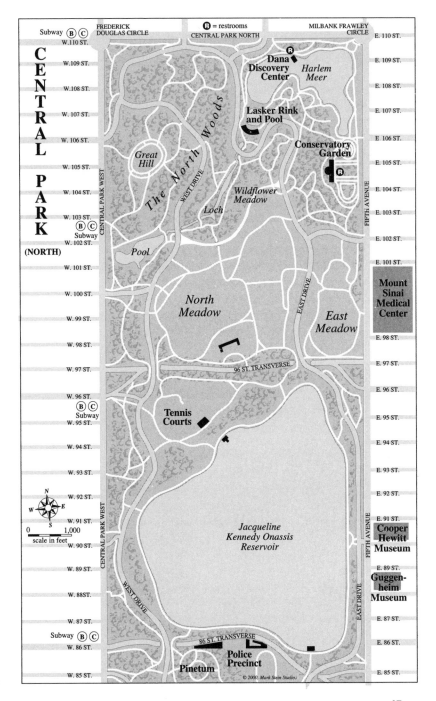

Subway Ⓑ Ⓒ
W.110 ST.

FREDERICK
DOUGLAS CIRCLE

Ⓡ = restrooms
CENTRAL PARK NORTH

MILBANK FRAWLEY
CIRCLE

E. 110 ST.

W.109 ST.
Ⓡ
Dana
Discovery
Center

Harlem
Meer

E. 109 ST.

C E N T R A L   P A R K
(NORTH)

W.108 ST.

E. 108 ST.

W. 107 ST.

**Lasker Rink
and Pool**

E. 107 ST.

W. 106 ST.

E 106 ST.

Great
Hill

**Conservatory
Garden**

E. 105 ST.

W. 105 ST.

Wildflower
Meadow

The North Woods

WEST DRIVE

Ⓡ

E. 104 ST.

W. 104 ST.

FIFTH AVENUE

CENTRAL PARK WEST

W. 103 ST.
Ⓑ Ⓒ
Subway
W. 102 ST.

Loch

E. 103 ST.

E. 102 ST.

Pool

E. 101 ST.

W. 101 ST.

W. 100 ST.

North
Meadow

East
Meadow

EAST DRIVE

**Mount
Sinai
Medical
Center**

W. 99 ST.

W. 98 ST.

E. 98 ST.

W. 97 ST.

96 ST. TRANSVERSE

E. 97 ST.

E. 96 ST.

W. 96 ST.
Ⓑ Ⓒ
Subway
W. 95 ST.

**Tennis
Courts**

E. 95 ST.

W. 94 ST.

E. 94 ST.

W. 93 ST.

E. 93 ST.

N
W   E
S

W. 92 ST.

E. 92 ST.

W. 91 ST.

**Cooper
Hewitt
Museum**

0   1,000
scale in feet

Jacqueline
Kennedy Onassis
Reservoir

E. 91 ST.

W. 90 ST.

FIFTH AVENUE

W. 89 ST.

E. 89 ST.

**Guggen-
heim
Museum**

CENTRAL PARK WEST

WEST DRIVE

E. 88 ST.
W. 88ST.

EAST DRIVE

W. 87 ST.

E. 87 ST.

Subway Ⓑ Ⓒ
W. 86 ST.

86 ST. TRANSVERSE

E. 86 ST.

W. 85 ST.

Pinetum

**Police
Precinct**

© 2000, Mark Stein Studios

E. 85 ST.

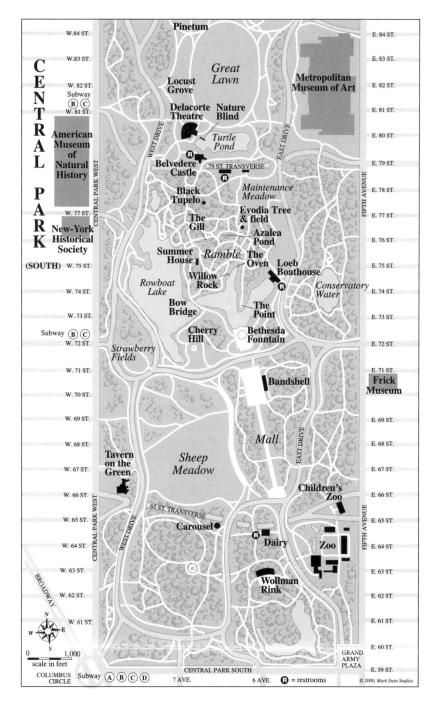

Pinetum

W.84 ST.   E. 84 ST.

W.83 ST.   E. 83 ST.

C   W. 82 ST.   *Great*   **Metropolitan**   E. 82 ST.
             Subway   *Lawn*   **Museum of Art**
E   Ⓑ Ⓒ   **Locust**   E. 81 ST.
             W. 81 ST.   **Grove**
N   E. 80 ST.
                          Delacorte Nature
T   **Theatre   Blind**
             American   *Turtle*   E. 79 ST.
R   **Museum**   *Pond*
             of   Ⓡ
A   **Natural**   **Belvedere** 79 ST. TRANSVERSE   E. 78 ST.
             History **Castle** Ⓡ
L   *Maintenance*
                          Black   *Meadow*   E. 77 ST.
             W. 77 ST.   **Tupelo** **Evodia Tree**
P   **The**   **& field**
                          Gill   **Azalea**   E. 76 ST.
A   **New-York**   **Pond**
             Historical
R   **Society**   **Summer** *Ramble* **The** E. 75 ST.
             House   **Oven** **Loeb**
K   (SOUTH) W. 75 ST.   **Willow** **Boathouse**
                          Rock   Ⓡ
             W. 74 ST.   *Rowboat*   *Conservatory* E. 74 ST.
                          Lake   *Water*
                          Bow   **The**
             W. 73 ST.   **Bridge** **Point**   E. 73 ST.
                          Cherry **Bethesda**
             Subway Ⓑ Ⓒ   **Hill**   **Fountain**   E. 72 ST.
             W. 72 ST.
                          Strawberry
                          Fields   E. 71 ST.
             W. 71 ST.   **Frick**
             W. 70 ST.   **Bandshell**   **Museum** E. 70 ST.

             W. 69 ST.   E. 69 ST.

             W. 68 ST.   *Mall*   E. 68 ST.

             Tavern   *Sheep*
             on the   *Meadow*   E. 67 ST.
             Green   **Children's**
             W. 66 ST.   **Zoo**   E. 66 ST.

             W. 65 ST.   65 ST. TRANSVERSE   E. 65 ST.
                          Carousel Ⓡ
             W. 64 ST.   **Dairy** **Zoo**   E. 64 ST.

             W. 63 ST.   E. 63 ST.
                          Wollman
             W. 62 ST.   **Rink**   E. 62 ST.

             W. 61 ST.   E. 61 ST.

             N
         W ✦ *E*
             S   **GRAND**   E. 60 ST.
             0   1,000   **ARMY**
                                                  PLAZA E. 59 ST.
             scale in feet
             COLUMBUS   Subway Ⓐ Ⓑ Ⓒ Ⓓ   © 2000, Mark Stein Studios
             CIRCLE   7 AVE.   6 AVE.   Ⓡ = restrooms

68

bound)—M1, M2, M3, and M4—or Central Park West (north and southbound)—M10.

SUBWAY: The B and C subway trains run along Central Park West, stopping at 72nd, 81st, 86th, 96th, 103rd, and 110th Streets. The best West Side entrance for reaching the Ramble and Belvedere Castle is at 81st Street, and the North Woods is at 103rd Street.

The 6 subway train runs along Lexington Avenue (three crosstown blocks east of Fifth Avenue) on the East Side, making local stops at 59th, 68th, 77th, 86th, 96th, 103rd, and 110th Streets. The best East Side entrance for reaching the Ramble and the Conservatory Water is at 72nd Street and Fifth Avenue; the entrance for the Reservoir and the popular 1.6-mile jogging track is at 90th Street; and the entrance for the Dana Discovery Center is at 110th Street.

CAR: Some parking is available along Central Park West and along Fifth Avenue as well as on the cross streets. You cannot count on finding an empty space except early on Sunday mornings, when the parking rules are relaxed. There is no parking within the park. We recommend public transportation.

For Additional Information on Central Park

Central Park, www.centralparknyc.org
Belvedere Castle, 212-772-0210
Central Park Conservancy (lead tours), 212-310-6600
Charles A. Dana Center, 212-860-1370
The Dairy, 212-794-6564
Federation of New York State Bird Clubs (conducts the Winter
    Waterfowl Count), P.O. Box 440, Loch Sheldrake, N.Y. 12759
Linnaean Society of New York (leads tours), 212-252-2668 and
    www.linnaeansociety.org
Manhattan Urban Park Rangers (lead tours), 212-304-2365, 212-625,
    and 212-427-4040
The Nature Conservancy (leads tours), 212-997-1880
New York City Audubon Society (leads tours; runs the Lower
    Hudson Christmas Bird Count), 212-691-7483 and
    www.nycaudubon.org
Resource persons: Robert De Candido, Urban Park Ranger, City of New York/Parks and Recreation; Sarah M. Elliott, teacher of nature classes in Central Park and Battery Park and publisher of *The Elliott Newsletter*; Tom Fiore; Roger F. Pasquier, Environmental Defense; and Marie Winn, author, *Red-Tails in Love: A Wildlife Drama in Central Park*.

Inwood Hill Park

Nesting*   Spring Migration**   Fall Migration**   Winter*
Dyckman Street to Spuyten Duyvil Creek, Payson Avenue, Seaman Avenue,
Indian Road to the Hudson River

Inwood Hill Park, managed by the City of New York/Parks and Recreation, is perched on the northernmost tip of Manhattan. The central portion of the park rises steeply into a rocky ridge, Inwood Hill, approximately 230 feet above sea level. The western border at the Hudson River offers magnificent views of the Palisades in New Jersey. Many of its 196 acres are lush woodlands that include a magnificent understory of witch hazel, spice bush, and dogwood. The canopy is red oak and tulip trees. Some of the tallest trees in Manhattan are found in the Clove, a small, forested valley that extends along the eastern base of the ridge. Inwood Hill Park ranked third in the *Wild New York* survey of the healthiest forest ecosystems in New York City.

In a single year, 150 bird species have been spotted in Inwood Hill Park. Hairy Woodpecker, Black-capped Chickadee, and White-breasted Nuthatch nest in the wooded uplands. Eastern Kingbird and Brown Thrasher, which also nest in the park, are seen in the clearings.

At the northeast corner of Inwood Hill Park, where it meets Spuyten Duyvil Creek, two small bays indicate the saltmarsh system that once surrounded Manhattan Island. The Urban Park Rangers conduct nature walks from the Urban Ecology Center (with restrooms) at the Boat Basin, the larger of the two bays. Contact the center for schedule information.

You can start your birdwalk at Inwood Hill Park by entering at 218th Street and Indian Road. During spring migration, check along the bays and shoreline, particularly the mudflats at low tide, for waders (Solitary and Least sandpipers) and gulls. In spring and early summer, Belted Kingfisher and Northern Rough-winged Swallow are regular visitors. In the summer, Great Egret are found, and from time to time, Black-crowned Night-Heron roost in the trees along Baker Bay, the smaller bay. Canvasback are seen in winter, late November through late February, on the Boat Basin.

To explore the ridge, follow the paved paths that go into the woods from the southwest corner of the soccer field. The northern (on the right) path winds its way around and onto the north side of the ridge (under the Henry Hudson Bridge, take the switchback upward). The southern route (on the left) goes into the Clove before climbing the ridge. Either way is good.

At the top of the Clove path there is an intersection; bear hard right on a paved path that goes northward along the east side of the ridge, listening for Indigo Bunting (nesting) that are often on the west side of this path. Eastern Screech-Owl also nest in the vicinity, as do—perhaps—Wild Turkey. Approximately 400 yards after the intersection, a side road comes in on the left (west). Stay on the main road, beyond the point where the side road splits off, to a junction with a small side trail leading to a lookout over a stone wall. Here you are level with the tops of tall trees growing in the valley, a good vantage to view treetop warblers, particularly in the morning when the east side of the ridge catches the sun. These tiny wonders actively forage for insects in the treetops and rapidly dart from tree to tree looking for places to rest and feed.

Back on the main path going south (retracing your steps), take the road to the west that leads to a small overgrown field. Here you can find woodland edge birds. Eastern Bluebird are regular visitors in March and November. From the west side of the field is a view—not to be missed—of the Hudson River and across to the Palisades. In the fall you can watch hawks and waterfowl migrating south along the river. As you gaze across the river to the Palisades, Turkey Vulture may be seen soaring in the updrafts.

After exploring the ridge, you can return the way you came or take the north path, which goes past the Henry Hudson Bridge toll booths before swinging under the bridge and switching back down to the east side of the ridge. The north path leads to the soccer field where you started.

When you are under the bridge, you may choose to take a path that leads westward to the Hudson River and the ball fields. This path crosses the Amtrak railroad tracks via an overpass. For a more direct route to this portion of the river's edge, start at Dyckman Street, at the southern end of the park, and walk westward. From a pier where Dyckman Street meets the river, savor the view across the Hudson and watch for migrating cormorants, ducks, and gulls. Bring a scope and perhaps a chair and search the river for Green-winged Teal, Canvasback, and scaup, particularly in winter.

Although the path system is not extensive, it is easy to get confused. For the sake of orientation, remember that while you are on the ridge, the Hudson River is always to the west.

Special Features

Inwood Hill Park has a number of very interesting geological and historical features. Inwood Hill's stony promontories contain all three types of New York City bedrock—gneiss, marble, and schist. A large outcropping of marble is visible on the northeast side of the intersection of Seaman Avenue and Isham Street. Glacial potholes are exposed on the west side of the rock wall near the upper end of the Clove path.

Inwood was the site of a Native American village (Shorakapkok) and was at one time believed to be the place where, in 1626, according to legend, Peter Minuit "purchased" Manhattan Island from the Manhattan Indians in exchange for objects then valued at 60 guilders (now believed to be worth $600). A rock tablet at the far end of the soccer field commemorates this transaction. In the 1890s, Native American artifacts were unearthed from caves in the ridge on the west side of the Clove. Some caves, actually rock overhangs, are still visible.

During the Revolutionary War, the north end of the ridge (then called Cock Hill) was the site of an earthen fork, and the surrounding areas were the site of a Hessian encampment.

Dyckman House, a colonial-era farmhouse at Broadway and 204th Street (two blocks from the park), houses a small museum with artifacts from the period.

Inwood Hill Park has many wildflowers not found in the more heavily used city parks, among them Dutchman's-breeches, trillium, May apple, and jack-in-the-pulpit. The overgrown meadow on the ridge is particularly attractive to butterflies.

When to Go

The best time to look for spring migrants is the third week in April. Many migrants persist into mid-May. June is a good time to look for nesters. The morning hours from sunrise to midday are best, although on a wave or flight day, the park is a productive place to look all day long. Because Inwood Hill Park has considerable woodlands, it holds migrants longer than does Central Park or Riverside Park.

September and October are peak times to look for fall migrants. Look for hawk flights along the Hudson River from midmorning to midafternoon. Some of these migrants are the same birds that are seen passing Riverdale Park to the north (see chap. 1, "The Bronx").

Optimal Weather Conditions

During spring migration, the best birding days are those following nights of light southwest and, to a lesser extent, westerly winds. The best fall flights, including hawk migration, follow nights of west-to-north winds.

Personal Safety

Most people in Inwood Hill Park are using the ball fields and playgrounds, so with the exception of a few joggers and dog walkers, the birding areas are a bit desolate. We recommend that birders go out in groups of two or more.

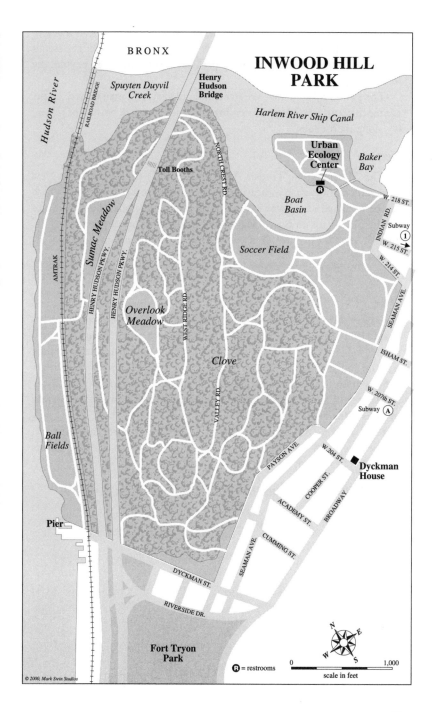

BRONX

INWOOD HILL PARK

Spuyten Duyvil Creek

Henry Hudson Bridge

Hudson River

RAILROAD BRIDGE

NORTH CREST RD.

Harlem River Ship Canal

Urban Ecology Center

Baker Bay

Toll Booths

Ⓡ

Boat Basin

W. 218 ST.

INDIAN RD.

Subway ①

W. 215 ST.

Sumac Meadow

Soccer Field

W. 214 ST.

SEAMAN AVE.

AMTRAK

HENRY HUDSON PKWY.

HENRY HUDSON PKWY.

WEST RIDGE RD.

Overlook Meadow

ISHAM ST.

Clove

VALLEY RD.

W. 207th ST.

Subway Ⓐ

Ball Fields

PAYSON AVE.

W. 204 ST.

■ **Dyckman House**

COOPER ST.

ACADEMY ST.

BROADWAY

Pier

SEAMAN AVE.

CUMMING ST.

DYCKMAN ST.

RIVERSIDE DR.

Fort Tryon Park

N
W   E
S

Ⓡ = restrooms

0   1,000
scale in feet

© 2000, Mark Stein Studios

At the river overlook on the top of the ridge, a hole has been made in the fence, which leads to an open rock ledge. Because the ledges slopes down to a dangerous drop-off to the parkway below, do not go beyond the fence. The paths and stairways are steep and not very well maintained. In the winter they can be slippery. In spring, summer, and fall, beware of poison ivy along their edges.

Getting There

The Metropolitan Transit Authority (MTA) puts out a free New York City subway map indicating major subway/bus connections, which can be obtained at subway station ticket booths. Detailed bus schedules can be picked up on board Manhattan buses. Or you can contact NYC Transit at 718-330-1234 or www.mta.nyc.ny.uc for subway and bus information.

BUS: The M100 goes to Dyckman Street from 124th Street and Third Avenue.

SUBWAY: Take the A subway train to the last stop at 207th Street and Broadway. Walk west two blocks to Seaman Avenue. You can enter Inwood Hill Park at Isham Street (one block north of 207th Street) or, alternately, walk north on Seaman another long block to Indian Road and then west on Indian Road to the north end of the park. Or you can take the 1 subway train to the 215th Street stop. Walk west one block to Broadway and then walk north to 218th Street. Go west on 218th Street four blocks to Indian Road and the park.

CAR: Parking can usually be found on the streets bordering the park, but be sure to check street signs for parking regulations. Parking tickets are given out regularly.

For Additional Information on Inwood Hill Park

Urban Ecology Center, 212-304-2365
Manhattan Urban Park Rangers (lead tours), 212-304-2365,
 212-628-2345, and 212-427-4040
New York City Audubon Society (leads tours), 212-691-7483 and
 www.nycaudubon.org
Resource persons: Joseph DiCostanzo, President, Linnaean Society of New York, and Research Assistant, Great Gull Island Project, American Museum of Natural History; Adele Gotlib; and George Karsch

Riverside Park

Nesting   Spring Migration**   Fall Migration**   Winter*
72nd Street to 155th Street, Riverside Drive to the Hudson River

Riverside Park, only one-eighth of a mile wide, follows the western side of Manhattan along the Hudson River for four miles. In the 1870s, Frederick Law Olmsted prepared the park's conceptual plan, which was implemented over two decades by designer Calvert Vaux and others. In the 1930s, under Robert Moses and landscape architect Gilmore Clarke, the railroad tracks (now used by Amtrak) were covered over south of 124th Street to make a promenade, and landfill was added along the river for recreational facilities. In 1980, the 324-acre park (up to 125th Street) was designated a scenic landmark by the New York City Landmarks Preservation Commission. Riverside Park is managed by the City of New York/Parks and Recreation. The Riverside Park Fund, established in 1986, organizes activities, coordinates volunteers, and raises money toward maintenance and improvements in the park.

Recreational facilities abound in Riverside Park: playgrounds, a skatepark, a waterfront esplanade, a kayak launch, a sailboat marina, soccer and baseball fields, and basketball, handball, volleyball, beach volleyball, and tennis courts. The forested and meadow areas between 116th and 124th Streets have been designated the Riverside Park Bird Sanctuary. This is the place to bird. (An annotated checklist of birds of the sanctuary can be obtained free of charge from the Riverside Park Fund.) Since 1997, the approximately 10 acres of the sanctuary have been undergoing reforestation, which has included the removal of invasive species such as Japanese knotweed, Norway maple, and ailanthus, and the addition of bird-friendly native plants such as serviceberry and several species of dogwood and viburnum. More than 3,000 plants—trees, shrubs, and ground covers—have been added, but there is still much to be done. The forest is primarily a monoculture of black cherry, and its understory is thin except where wild roses have taken over. A wildflower meadow has been started in the sanctuary's fields, but the fields tend to fluctuate between grass lawns and weed jungles, depending on an erratic mowing schedule.

Nevertheless, as many as 144 species of birds have been seen in and around the Bird Sanctuary, most of them migrants. Each year more than 100 species have been recorded, among them Black-billed Cuckoo, Summer Tanager, Lincoln's Sparrow, and small flocks of immature White-crowned Sparrow. Thirty-two species of warbler have been seen here, including Golden-winged, Yellow-throated, Cerulean, Kentucky, and most particularly, Blue-winged, Worm-eating, and Mourning. Cape May Warbler have become very rare, but many of the others are seen here every year, often in remarkable numbers. Riverside Park's position along the Hudson River makes it an ideal stopover for birds during spring and fall migration.

Start at the 116th Street entrance to the Bird Sanctuary (the fenced-in Women's Grove) and walk the wood-chip trail through the grove, looking high in the trees for Great Crested Flycatcher, warblers, Scarlet Tanager, Rose-breasted Grosbeak, and Baltimore Oriole. Next, enter the woods, scanning the ground for thrushes, waterthrushes, Brown Thrasher, and Eastern Towhee. Then take the upper trail to a spot from which you can look down on tree crowns. Here you can catch good views of Blackburnian Warbler (uncommon but a regular visitor) and other treetop warblers. Exit at the upper trail's end and walk north along the fence that marks the eastern edge of the bird sanctuary, checking a hot spot just north of the ruins of a turn-of-the-century viewing pavilion, before you reach the Tomb of the Amiable Child, for flycatchers and warblers. The memorial tomb—the only private gravesite in Manhattan—is dedicated to a five-year-old boy who died near this spot more than 200 years ago; it now also marks the northern end of the bird sanctuary. Return to the upper trail and, some 30 feet south, carefully descend the hill into the fields to look for sparrows: Chipping, Field, Savannah, and Song. Re-enter the woods and take the lower trail (through catbird and cardinal nesting territory in season) back to the Women's Grove.

At some point before, after, or while standing in the fields, look for a Peregrine Falcon nest tray on a ledge on the bell tower of Riverside Church at 120th Street. The ledge is located 300 feet up from the sidewalk on the west face. This site has been an active peregrine nest for 11 consecutive years, producing 28 chicks and fledging 29. In 1993, an additional fledging was brought from the Met Life site to be reared by the Riverside Church pair. Up through the 1999 season, the same adult male has remained at the site. He is a bird hatched from the New York Hospital nest site in 1988. The original female, an unbanded peregrine, was eventually captured and banded at the nest in 1989. Sadly, she was found shot in New Jersey several years later and subsequently died. The next season, a Virginia-raised female (who, at this writing, is still in residence) replaced her. These parents remain on or near the tower year round and can be seen (and heard) attacking intruders violating their airspace, most often Red-tailed Hawk and American Kestrel, but occasionally a Turkey Vulture or Osprey. From time to time, Barn Swallow attack these birds and, amazingly, are able to out maneuver them.

New York City is a particularly successful nesting location for Peregrine Falcon. Water and food—pigeons, Northern Flicker, Blue Jay, and European Starling—are abundant. During migration seasons, their diet reflects the waves of songbirds, shorebirds, woodpeckers, and occasionally waterfowl that fly through the area. There are currently 12 established pairs of Peregrine Falcon in the five boroughs. As of 1999, four nested on high-rise buildings including Met Life and New York Hospital, seven on bridges, and one on a tower. Although over the last few years there have been additional sightings of pairs and single birds, no new nests have been confirmed. New York City Audubon, in conjunction with the Urban Park Rangers, offers trips to some of the nesting sites.

In August 1999, the U.S. Department of the Interior removed (delisted) the Peregrine Falcon from the endangered species list. The peregrine remains on the New York State list because populations have not fully recovered in the state's historic regions (as is also true in the rest of eastern United States). Fifty percent of the New York State population is dependent on man-made nesting platforms, like the one on the Riverside Church tower.

South of the bird sanctuary, pockets of bird habitat can be found all the way down to 90th Street along the path hugging the wall that separates Riverside Park from Riverside Drive. These habitat islands are worth investigating.

Special Note

Manhattan's first known coyote was seen in the Riverside Park Bird Sanctuary. A while later, one was seen and caught in Central Park. Could it have been the same one? The Central Park coyote now resides in the Queens Zoo.

When to Go

If you are looking for quantity, mid-April through late May is the best time for birding in Riverside Park. If you are looking for rarities, visit the park in early September through mid-November. In the fall, Cooper's Hawk, Red-headed Woodpecker, Eastern Bluebird, Eastern Meadowlark, and Rusty Blackbird have been sighted.

There is no need to arrive early. Between 8:00 to 10:30 AM or 3:00 to 5:00 PM are perfect times.

Optimal Weather Conditions

Riverside Park is a good place to bird, even in snow and rain, as long as the wind is no stronger than moderate. Northwest winds in early fall sometimes bring flocks of approximately 150 Broad-winged Hawk flying so low a cowboy could rope them.

Personal Safety

The forested area north of the Women's Grove is little traveled and may be dangerous. Bird with a friend or a group of friends. The rest of the park, especially in nice weather, is filled with people strolling, dog walking, jogging, or going to and from numerous recreational facilities.

In the bird sanctuary, beware of poison ivy trailside.

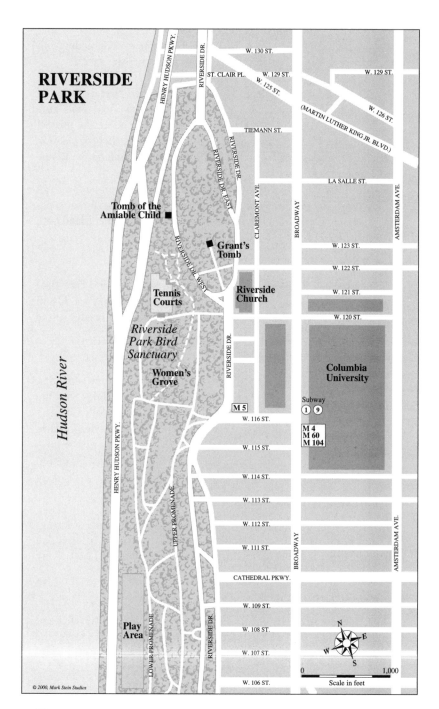

RIVERSIDE PARK

W. 130 ST.

ST. CLAIR PL.

W. 129 ST.

W. 129 ST.

W. 125 ST.

W. 126 ST.

(MARTIN LUTHER KING JR. BLVD.)

HENRY HUDSON PKWY.

RIVERSIDE DR.

RIVERSIDE DR.

RIVERSIDE DR. EAST

TIEMANN ST.

LA SALLE ST.

CLAREMONT AVE.

BROADWAY

AMSTERDAM AVE.

Tomb of the Amiable Child ■

RIVERSIDE DR. WEST

■ **Grant's Tomb**

W. 123 ST.

W. 122 ST.

Tennis Courts

Riverside Church

W. 121 ST.

W. 120 ST.

Riverside Park Bird Sanctuary

RIVERSIDE DR.

Columbia University

Women's Grove

Hudson River

M 5

Subway
① ⑨

W. 116 ST.

M 4
M 60
M 104

W. 115 ST.

HENRY HUDSON PKWY.

W. 114 ST.

W. 113 ST.

UPPER PROMENADE

W. 112 ST.

W. 111 ST.

BROADWAY

AMSTERDAM AVE.

CATHEDRAL PKWY.

W. 109 ST.

Play Area

W. 108 ST.

RIVERSIDE DR.

N

W. 107 ST.

W
E
S

LOWER PROMENADE

© 2000, Mark Stein Studios

W. 106 ST.

0   1,000
Scale in feet

Getting There

The Metropolitan Transit Authority (MTA) puts out a free New York City subway map indicating major subway/bus connections, which can be obtained at subway station ticket booths. Detailed bus schedules can be picked up on board Manhattan buses. Or you can contact NYC Transit at 718-330-1234 or www.mta.nyc.ny.us for subway and bus information.

BUS: Take the M4 or M104 to Broadway and 116th Street. Walk west down the hill to Riverside Drive and the 116th Street entrance to Riverside Park and the bird sanctuary or take the M5 to 116th Street and Riverside Drive.

SUBWAY: Take the 1 or 9 subway train to 116th Street and Broadway. Walk west down the hill to the 116th Street entrance to Riverside Park and the bird sanctuary.

CAR: Although parking is usually available on Riverside Drive north of Grant's Tomb at 123rd Street, driving is not recommended because of possible car break-ins. Public transportation is exceptionally convenient to this part of Manhattan.

For Additional Information on Riverside Park

Riverside Park Fund (lead tours), 212-870-3070
Manhattan Urban Park Rangers (lead tours), 212-304-2365,
    212-628-2345, and 212-427-4040
New York City Audubon Society (leads tours), 212-691-7483 and
    www.nycaudubon.org
Resource persons: Christopher Nadareski, wildlife biologist, New York City Department of Environmental Protection, and New York City Peregrine Project Manager; Geoffrey Nulle, volunteer, Riverside Park Fund, and Park Tender, Riverside Park Bird Sanctuary; and Norman I. Stotz, former President of New York City Audubon Society

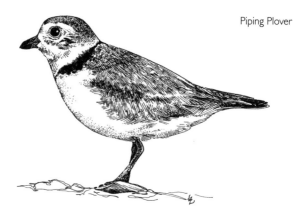

Chapter Four

Piping Plover

Queens

The borough of Queens (named after Catherine of Braganza, Charles II's queen) is almost as large as Manhattan, the Bronx, and Staten Island combined, encompassing 37% of New York City's total area. Its western and northern shorelines follow the East River and Long Island Sound, while its southern shores open on Jamaica Bay and the Atlantic Ocean. Two districts of Gateway National Recreation Area are in Queens: the Jamaica Bay Wildlife Refuge (shared with Brooklyn) and the Breezy Point district. A third, the Jamaica Bay district, is mainly in Brooklyn (see chap. 2, "Brooklyn/Floyd Bennett Field and Dead Horse Bay"); a fourth is on Staten Island (see chap. 5, "Staten Island/Great Kills Park"); and a fifth, the Sandy Hook district, is in New Jersey (see chap. 8, "Nearby Sites in New Jersey"). The wildlife refuge includes saltmarsh, open water, and buffering uplands. The Breezy Point district, on the western end of the Rockaway Peninsula, is a long narrow barrier beach with shoreline on both the Atlantic Ocean and the Rockaway Inlet leading into Jamaica Bay. The district includes Jacob Riis Park, Fort Tilden, and Breezy Point. In 1997, the New York City Audubon Society and the National Audubon Society designated the entire Jamaica Bay complex an Important Bird Area of Global Significance. These federally owned coastal areas, along with city-owned Alley Pond Park and Forest Park, offer extraordinary birding opportunities.

Jamaica Bay Wildlife Refuge
Nesting***   Spring Migration***   Fall Migration***   Winter***
Cross Bay Boulevard and Jamaica Bay

The Jamaica Bay Wildlife Refuge is the U.S. Department of the Interior's only wildlife refuge administered by the National Park Service. All other national refuges fall under the aegis of the U.S. Fish and Wildlife Service. The Jamaica Bay Wildlife Refuge covers 9,000 acres (20 square miles) of open bay, saltmarsh, upland islands, mudflats, two man-made brackish ponds (117-acre East Pond and 45-acre West Pond), several small freshwater ponds, including Big-John's Pond amid East Garden, and North and South gardens. Adjacent uplands in Brooklyn and Queens buffer and protect the refuge and its wildlife.

The Jamaica Bay Wildlife Refuge is internationally recognized as one of the prime birding spots in North America. The total species count to date is 330 (38 are accidental, out of their normal range, and include several New York State records). Birding is excellent year round. It is a rich area for wintering waterfowl, including Snow Goose (at least 700 at one time), Brant, Eurasian Wigeon, and such raptors as Rough-legged Hawk, Snowy Owl, Long-eared Owl, Short-eared Owl, and Northern Saw-whet Owl. In spring, there are numerous shorebirds, such as American Oystercatcher, both yellowlegs, Red Knot, and Dunlin; waterfowl; wading birds; and warblers, which on occasion include Cerulean, Prothonotary, Kentucky, and Connecticut. In the fall, look for Black-bellied Plover, Semipalmated Plover, both yellowlegs, Semipalmated Sandpiper, Dunlin, Stilt Sandpiper, and both dowitchers.

The record of nesting birds is spectacular—approximately 72 species. Among them are Great Egret, Snowy Egret, Little Blue Heron, Tricolored Heron (the best place in New York City to see this species), Cattle Egret, Green Heron, Black-crowned Night-Heron, Yellow-crowned Night-Heron, Glossy, Ibis, Osprey (on man-made platforms), Clapper Rail, American Oystercatcher, Willet, American Woodcock, Laughing Gull, Forster's Tern, Barn Owl (in man-made nest boxes), Willow Flycatcher, American Redstart, Saltmarsh Sharp-tailed Sparrow, Seaside Sparrow, and Boat-tailed Grackle.

In early summer (by July 1), the East Pond water level is lowered to provide an extensive mudflat around the 3-mile perimeter, thereby making it a hot spot for shorebirds.

A checklist, *Birds of the Jamaica Bay Wildlife Refuge*, can be obtained at the Visitor Center (restrooms), which is located at the entrance, or by writing Gateway National Recreation Area, Wildlife Refuge, Floyd Bennett Field, Brooklyn, N.Y. 11234.

West Pond, North Garden, and South Garden

The Jamaica Bay Wildlife Refuge has a well-maintained, easy-to-follow trail system. From the back (west side) of the Visitor Center, take the trail that encircles West Pond, following it in a clockwise direction. At the westernmost end, make a short detour on the Terrapin Trail.

Note that the Terrapin Trail is closed during Diamondback Terrapin nesting season to provide protection for these turtles. From June through July, females leave the waters of the bay to lay their eggs in sandy areas.

Return to the main trail. As it swings right, after you have lost sight of West Pond, you reach the North Garden. The South Garden follows; it is just before you return to the Visitor Center. These garden trails are excellent places to explore in spring and autumn for migrant vireos, gnatcatchers, warblers, and other songbirds. The gardens and fields are also managed to attract butterflies. To date, 70 species have been recorded. Pick up a butterfly checklist at the Visitor Center.

East Pond and Big-John's Pond in East Garden

To reach the East Pond, you must cross over Cross Bay Boulevard at the traffic light opposite the parking lot entrance. The circular trail around East Pond, which is only accessible when the water level is lowered, is located 200 yards to the south. It circles around the southern tip to the east side of the pond and then to its northern end, where a dirt road takes you back to Cross Bay Boulevard. Even when the water level of East Pond is lowered in early summer, it is advisable to wear boots because the trail is muddy and parts of it may be under water. It is best to bird East Pond at approximately one to two hours before high tide in Jamaica Bay. Tide information can be obtained by calling the refuge. At the southern end of the pond, opportunities for nature photography are excellent in early morning. For shorebirds, a spotting scope is very helpful here.

To reach the trail to Big-John's Pond in East Garden and the western access to East Pond, walk left (north) 800 feet after you have crossed Cross Bay Boulevard.

Refuge Regulations

Obtain a permit at the Visitor Center desk if you are a first-time visitor. The following regulations apply: stay on the trails except in garden areas; picnic only at the designated site outside the Visitor Center; no smoking; no radios or other sound-producing equipment; no collecting plants or other wildlife; no feeding wild animals; and no bicycles, motor bikes, or cars on the trails.

New York City Audubon Society Speaks Out

In 1998, the National Park Service proposed a bike path, the Rockaway Gateway Greenway, from North Channel Bridge to the community of Broad Channel. It was designed as a 12-foot-wide paved corridor with 2-

foot-wide shoulders. Meandering for a length of 8,600 feet, it would cut a long, 16-foot-wide swath through the Jamaica Bay Wildlife Refuge. Although New York City Audubon supports bicycle paths, it strongly objected to this initial proposal, particularly to the use of asphalt construction, the disturbance of soils, and the loss of several acres of vegetative habitat in the refuge. New York City Audubon also objected to revocation of the 30-year prohibition of bikes in the refuge. The chapter believes that the proposed plan, along with viable alternatives, should be subject to the Environmental Review process. New York City Audubon supports the alternative of upgrading the existing bike lane that runs along the west side of Cross Bay Boulevard from the bridge to Broad Channel.

Visitor Center

The Jamaica Bay Wildlife Refuge is open from dawn to dusk year round, and the Visitor Center hours are every day from 8:30 A.M. to 5:00 P.M. The main parking lot is open during Visitor Center hours, and parking is free. (Early and late comers can park near the center or ¼ mile south in Broad Channel.) The Visitor Center has a bookstore, natural history exhibit area, and lecture room. National Park Service Rangers offer birdwalks, workshops, and other activities from the center. Before setting out on your walk, check the center's Bird Log for a listing of recent sightings.

When to Go

Birding is good at the Jamaica Bay Wildlife Refuge any time of year. The peak month for spring migration of shorebirds and songbirds is May, earlier for waterfowl and hawks. Walk the trails in the early morning for both spring and fall migrants. Most fall shorebirds are seen at East Pond from mid-July to mid-September. Waterfowl start to arrive in late September, and their numbers build through October and into November.

From mid-March through May, woodcock courtship displays, featuring the aerial exertions and acrobatics of the males, can be seen just before dark in the fields south of the Visitor Center.

Personal Safety

The trails are patrolled by park rangers and are usually safe for solo birding; however, it is still prudent to bird with another person.

From April to September, beware of ticks, mainly dog ticks, along grassy edges of the trails. Also, poison ivy is common trailside.

Getting There

The Metropolitan Transit Authority (MTA) puts out a free New York City subway map indicating major subway/bus connections, which can be obtained at subway station ticket booths. Detailed bus schedules can be picked up on board Queens buses. Or you can contact NYC Transit at 718-330-1234 or www.mta.nyc.nu.us for subway and bus information.

SUBWAY: From Manhattan, take the Queens/Rockaway–bound A subway train to the Broad Channel station. Walk west on Noel Road to Cross Bay Boulevard, then north (right) about ¾ mile to Visitor Center (about 1 mile total).

SUBWAY to BUS: From Manhattan, take the Queens-bound, E, F, or R subway train to Jackson Heights/Roosevelt Avenue. Take the Rockaway-bound Q53 Express bus (Triboro Coach Corp.) and ask to be let off at the Jamaica Bay Wildlife Refuge Visitor Center. These buses run about every half hour. To check on the exact schedule and bus stop location, call 718-335-1000.

CAR: From Manhattan, take the Brooklyn Bridge over the East River and follow signs to the Brooklyn/Queens Expressway (Route 278) toward the Verrazano-Narrows Bridge. The Brooklyn/Queens Expressway becomes the Gowanus Expressway. The Gowanus Expressway (Route 278) splits off to the left to go over the Verrazano Bridge. Stay right (you do not want to go over the Verrazano Bridge to Staten Island) on Shore Parkway (the Belt Parkway). Continue on the parkway until Exit 17S (Cross Bay Boulevard). Then go south through Howard Beach, over the North Channel Bridge. In 1½ miles you reach the entrance to the refuge on the right.

From the Long Island Expressway (Route 495), take Woodhaven Boulevard (it goes south) and follow it to the community of Howard Beach. Follow the instructions above.

For Additional Information on the Jamaica Bay Wildlife Refuge

Jamaica Bay Wildlife Refuge, 718-318-4340 and www.nps.gov/gate
American Littoral Society (leads tours), 718-634-6467 and
    www.alsnyc.org
Brooklyn Bird Club (leads tours), www.brooklynbirdclub.org.
Linnaean Society of New York (leads tours), 212-252-2668 and
    www.linnaeansociety.org
National Park Service Rangers (lead tours), 718-318-4340
New York City Audubon Society (leads tours), 212-691-7483 and
    www.nycaudubon.org

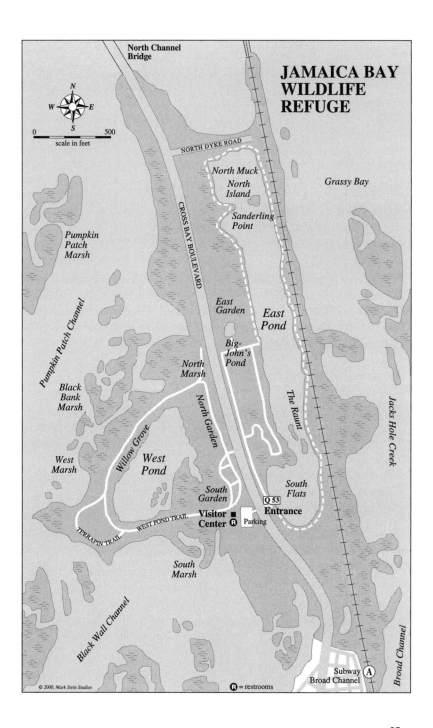

JAMAICA BAY
WILDLIFE
REFUGE

North Channel
Bridge

N
W E
S
0   500
scale in feet

NORTH DYKE ROAD

North Muck

North
Island

Grassy Bay

Sanderling
Point

Pumpkin
Patch
Marsh

CROSS BAY BOULEVARD

East
Garden

East
Pond

Pumpkin Patch Channel

Big-
John's
Pond

North
Marsh

North Garden

The Raunt

Jacks Hole Creek

Black
Bank
Marsh

Willow Grove

West
Marsh

West
Pond

South
Garden

South
Flats

TERRAPIN TRAIL

WEST POND TRAIL

Visitor ■
Center ℞

Q 53
Entrance

Parking

South
Marsh

Black Wall Channel

Broad Channel

Subway Ⓐ
Broad Channel

© 2000, Mark Stein Studios

℞ = restrooms

85

Queens County Bird Club (leads tours), 718-229-4000 (Alley Pond
Environmental Center)
Numerous chapters of National Audubon that are located outside of
the city lead tours in the refuge (see Appendix 1, "Metropolitan
Birding Resources," for a list of chapters).
Resource person: Don Riepe, Park Ranger, Gateway National
Recreation Area area, and Chapter Director, American Littoral
Society

Breezy Point District: Jacob Riis Park/ Fort Tilden/ Breezy Point

Nesting* Spring Migration** Fall Migration*** Winter**
Atlantic Ocean to the Rockaway Inlet into Jamaica Bay, Beach 149th Street
to Rockaway Point

The Breezy Point district of the Gateway National Recreation Area at the
western end of the Rockaway Peninsula covers approximately 5 miles of
uninterrupted Atlantic oceanfront. This barrier beach is included in the
Jamaica Bay complex that was awarded Important Bird Area of Global
Significance status in 1997.

Jacob Riis Park and Fort Tilden

The major attraction at Jacob Riis Park is the fall migration of songbirds.
At Fort Tilden, it is the fall migration of hawks. Under the right conditions,
there are great numbers of low-flying raptors, providing a birding opportu-
nity not found at any other site in the city. In winter during finch irruption
years, this area may be the best place in New York City to find crossbills. Irruptive migrations are not seasonally or geographically predictable. Such
migrations may occur one year and then not again for many years.

Both parks are open from dawn until dusk. The Visitor Center at Fort
Tilden (restrooms), a two-story brick building (Headquarters Building
1), is just inside the Beach 169th Street entrance. Maps of Fort Tilden
and Riis Park are available here.

Jacob Riis Park, created in the early 1900s, is a popular golf and beach
area (27.5 acres with 2 miles of Atlantic Ocean beachfront), graced by a
handsome bathhouse (with restrooms). It includes the requisite 13,000-
car parking lot. Rows of Japanese black pine (now dying, but to be replaced in kind or with native pine species) adjoining the parking lot, the
mall, and golf course attract fall migrants such as woodpeckers, Brown
Creeper, and warblers. When looking for migrating Hermit Thrush and
sparrows, check the ground and low brush in the area.

Much of the 317-acre Fort Tilden, with a mile of oceanfront, is composed of remnant maritime dune vegetation, bayberry and beach plum, that has survived in spite of the area being used, until 1974, as a U.S. Army base. Several bunkers, or gun batteries, reveal its military history.

Follow Range Road, the main road through the center of the parkland, for ¾ mile to a trail on the right that leads to Battery Harris East (World War II bunker), where an observation platform was recently constructed of recycled plastic-wood by the National Park Service. It serves as one of two hawkwatching sites in the park. Aside from hawks, spectacular views of Jamaica Bay, the Atlantic Ocean, and the Brooklyn and Manhattan skylines can be enjoyed from this deck.

Directly across the main road from Battery Harris East is a trail leading through sand dunes, the last remaining natural dune system in the city, to a small freshwater pond where migratory songbirds, especially Yellow-rumped and Palm warblers, congregate during spring and fall migration. On occasion, Snowy Egret and Black-crowned Night-Heron have been seen here.

Go back to the main road and continue to Fisherman's parking lot, where there is a bunker approximately 300 feet to the east, the second hawkwatching site. Great numbers of hawks migrate along the Long Island coastline. They are joined at this end of the Rockaway Peninsula by smaller numbers of hawks flying from Floyd Bennett Field and from other inland points, creating an impressive sight overhead. More Osprey, harriers, and falcons are seen here than at Belvedere Castle in Central Park, but there are fewer Broad-winged and Red-tailed hawks than at the castle. Coastal hawk migration can be very exciting because many of these raptors fly at eye level, making them easy to identify, as they search for prey. Seeing Yellow-rumped Warbler dive for cover as a Sharp-shinned Hawk or Merlin appears from nowhere is one of the thrills of watching hawks at Fort Tilden.

In spring, woodcock can be seen in courtship flights at the western edge of the parking lot. Call the park headquarters to inquire about their late afternoon walks specifically arranged to watch this unusual display.

The east end of Fort Tilden, where you entered, features residences, other buildings, ball fields, and a vegetable garden. The surrounding trees and undercover provide good birding spots. The vegetation along the periphery of the ball fields, especially at the north border of the fort, and the vegetable gardens are good areas in autumn for Horned Lark, Savannah and other sparrows, Eastern Meadowlark, and other grassland birds.

Breezy Point Tip

At the extreme western end of the Rockaway Peninsula, where the dunes reach heights of 10 feet (25 feet above sea level), the National Park

Service manages 1,059 acres that include a beachhead for nesting colonies of endangered and threatened plovers, terns, and skimmers. To protect these birds, recreation is limited to fishing and birding. In spring and summer, the area is subject to closure.

During late spring and summer, Piping Plover, American Oyster-catcher, Common Tern, Least Tern, and Black Skimmer nest on this white sandy barrier beach. The National Park Service fences off the nesting areas in a valiant attempt to ward off dogs, feral cats, and humans. The Common Tern colony has exploded at the expense of the Least Tern colony. In the early 1990s, the skimmers, which have not been here for years, returned. The endangered Piping Plover are holding their own with usually 8 to 10 nesting pairs. In 1999, there were 3 pairs of American Oystercatcher.

For best viewing of the nesting plovers and terns at Breezy Point, a spotting scope is essential. Adults sitting on nests and their young can be seen if you visit in April, May, or June (when entry to the colony is prohibited) and watch from outside the barrier. You will also see adult terns courting and squabbling in the colony.

At the tip of Breezy Point there is a fishing jetty. The beach area around the jetty offers good birding opportunities and beautiful vistas. In the winter, from November to March, the jetty hosts Purple Sandpiper that glean arthropods from the algae growing on the rocks. Also in winter and in fall, Horned Grebe, Bufflehead, Red-breasted Merganser, Snowy Owl, Horned Lark, and Snow Bunting are seen. In the spring, gannet, sandpipers, and cormorants may be encountered here. Use extreme caution when venturing onto the jetty, especially when heavy surf wets the rocks. During subfreezing weather, the rocks can be glazed with ice.

Special Note

Naturalists may also enjoy Fort Tilden's butterflies and dragonfly migration. Monarchs stage a spectacular southern migration during September. From late September through mid-October, keen observers may see migratory question marks, mourning cloaks, and red admirals. Recent studies counted 14 species of dragonfly present on the site from late July through September.

Annual International Coastal Cleanup

If you are out on the Rockaway Peninsula (or any other waterfront anywhere in the United States) on the third Saturday in September, join the beach cleanup. Every year, volunteers take to inland lakes, rivers, streams, and ocean beaches to remove the debris that floats ashore. (Sixty percent of the trash comes from land-based sources!) Cumulatively, more than one million people in over 100 countries have participated since the cleanup became an international event in 1989. The Center for Marine Conservation in Washington, D.C., oversees this monumental task, educating people about keeping our oceans and waterways clean and documenting what litters the shores—plastic bags, cigarette butts, straws, bottles, monofilament fishing line, shopping carts, and tires. Birds may ingest small pieces of trash, mistaking it for food, and obstruct their intestinal tracts, or they may become fatally entangled in fishing line. Your cleanup efforts will help the birds! Contact the Center for Marine Conservation at 202-429-5609 or www.cmc-ocean.org. In New York State, contact the American Littoral Society at 718-471-2166 or alsbeach@aol.com.

When to Go

Fall hawk flights are best seen from mid-September into late October, generally between 10:00 AM and 2:00 PM. American Kestrel, which contribute the greatest numbers of individuals, peak during these months. Merlin flights occur a bit later in the day; they are seen mostly between 2:00 and 6:00 PM, when they stop migrating and start hunting songbirds and small shorebirds. Osprey are seen from mid-September to early October, Northern Harrier from August into December, and Cooper's Hawk in October. These species as well as buteos and eagles peak at midday. Sharp-shinned Hawk are mainly morning migrants here, passing through between 9:00 AM and 1:00 PM. But on a day following a good flight of Sharp-shinned Hawk and American Kestrel, if the wind has continued overnight from the northwest, these birds of prey move through beginning with the first light. A sea breeze can blow in as early as 11:00 AM in August and September. This southerly breeze often occurs with light winds and reduces the numbers of migrants along the shore. Migrant Peregrine Falcon are observed from late September through mid-October. A pair that nests on the Marine Parkway (Gil Hodges Memorial) Bridge cruises the area year round. (See chap. 3, "Manhattan/Riverside Park," for more information on New York City Peregrine Falcon.)

Fall flights of diurnal songbirds begin in late July, an hour after daybreak, and continue for about two hours, led by Barn Swallow and Redwinged Blackbird. Tree Swallow are the most numerous diurnal songbird migrant from late September into October. In late October through mid-November, there may be spectacular flights of Northern Flicker, American Robin, and Common Grackle as well as a sprinkling of Eastern Bluebird and finches.

Nocturnal migrants can still be seen on the move for an hour or so after daybreak. Afterward, they can be found resting and feeding in the vegetation, where they are safe from hungry hawks.

Optimal Weather Conditions

Without question, the most exciting fall hawkwatching at Fort Tilden is on clear to partly cloudy days with northwest winds between 10 to 20 mph. In the spring of 1997, these fall conditions produced an unprecedented southbound flight of Chimney Swift, Eastern Kingbird, and Bank, Cliff, and Barn swallows. Ordinarily Cliff Swallow do not migrate along the Rockaway Peninsula, spring or fall.

Light north and northwest winds may also produce good numbers of migrating hawks, but they fly higher with these conditions. Southwest winds in the fall are the dread of eager birders; surprisingly, however, in late August 1994 such winds produced an unprecedented overland flight of 180 Black Tern.

Spring migration at Fort Tilden and Riis Park has not been explored fully. In nearby areas, southwest winds accompanied by early fog have produced impressive fallouts. Across the New York Bight at Sandy Hook (N.J.), the spring migration of hawks is quite good, but where they go from there is a mystery. A few, such as Osprey, harriers, and falcons, may end up at Fort Tilden.

Personal Safety

Riis Park, Fort Tilden, and Breezy Point are generally safe places to visit alone. As part of Gateway National Recreation Area, the National Park Service patrols them. However, it is more enjoyable to bird these areas with others.

In the warm weather, mosquitoes are pervasive. Places at Fort Tilden that are especially troublesome are the sheltered areas, such as the freshwater pond, the trails, and the southwest bunker. In the open areas, small biting flies are problematic near the beach, particularly in late August and early September. Striped mosquitoes thrive in the marsh at Breezy Point. Dog ticks are found in the grassy and brushy areas. Use repellent and enjoy the birds.

Poison ivy is plentiful. Long pants are strongly advised.

Getting There

The Metropolitan Transit Authority (MTA) puts out a free New York City subway map indicating major subway/bus connections, which can be obtained at subway station ticket booths. Detailed bus schedules can be picked up on board Queens buses. Or you can contact

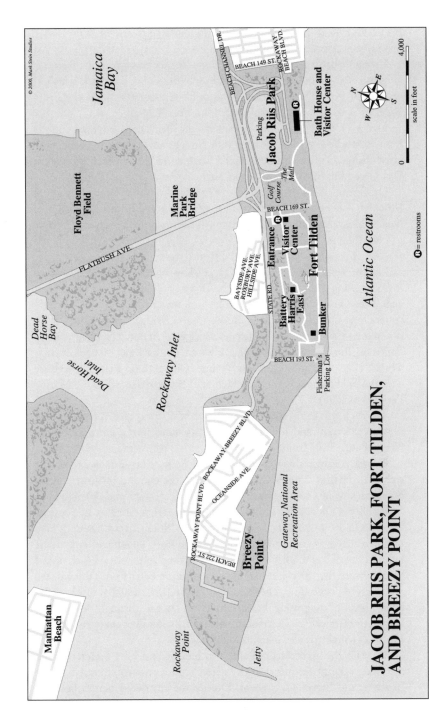

© 2000, Mark Stein Studios

Jamaica Bay

Floyd Bennett Field

Dead Horse Bay

Dead Horse Inlet

Rockaway Inlet

Manhattan Beach

Rockaway Point

Jetty

Breezy Point

Gateway National Recreation Area

FLATBUSH AVE.

Marine Park Bridge

ROCKAWAY POINT BLVD.

ROCKAWAY-BREEZY BLVD.

OCEANSIDE AVE.

BEACH 222 ST.

BEACH 193 ST.

Fisherman's Parking Lot

Bunker

Battery Harris East

Fort Tilden

STATE RD.

BAYSIDE AVE.
ROXBURY AVE.
HILLSIDE AVE.

Entrance

Visitor Center

BEACH 169 ST.

Golf Course

The Mall

Parking

Jacob Riis Park

BEACH 149 ST.

BEACH CHANNEL DR.

ROCKAWAY BEACH BLVD.

Bath House and Visitor Center

Atlantic Ocean

N
W   E
S

scale in feet

0   4,000

Ⓡ = restrooms

JACOB RIIS PARK, FORT TILDEN, AND BREEZY POINT

NYC Transit at 718-330-1234 or www.mta.nyc.ny.us for subway and bus information.

From Manhattan, the trip by public transportation to Fort Tilden is lengthy, taking well over an hour and sometimes two. Riis Park is a short walk from Fort Tilden. There is no public transportation to the tip of Breezy Point, which is several miles from Fort Tilden.

SUBWAY to BUS: From Manhattan, take the Queens-bound A subway train to Rockaway Park/Beach 116th Street station. (On weekends you must change to the S shuttle at Broad Channel.) From the station, take the Q35 Green bus line (718-995-1700) to the entrance of Fort Tilden.

Or from Manhattan, take the Brooklyn-bound 2 subway train to Brooklyn College/Flatbush Avenue, the last stop. From the corner of Nostrand Avenue, take the Q35 Green bus line south on Flatbush Avenue to Fort Tilden.

CAR: From Manhattan, take the Brooklyn Bridge over the East River and follow signs to the Brooklyn/Queens Expressway (Route 278) toward the Verrazano-Narrows Bridge. The Brooklyn/Queens Expressway becomes the Gowanus Expressway. The Gowanus Expressway (Route 278) splits off to the left to go over the Verrazano Bridge. Stay right (you do not want to go over the Verrazano Bridge to Staten Island) on Shore Parkway (the Belt Parkway). Continue on the parkway until Exit 11S, which brings you onto Flatbush Avenue. Go south on Flatbush Avenue over the toll bridge, Gil Hodges Memorial Bridge (also called the Marine Parkway Bridge).

To reach Riis Park, continue on the main roadway that veers left, then keep to the right and follow the Riis Park signs to the entrance on the right, about 1 mile from the bridge. There is a parking fee in summer.

To reach Fort Tilden, take the Breezy Point/Fort Tilden exit on the right. At the first traffic light, turn left into the entrance of Fort Tilden. Some parking lots require a seasonal permit ($25) from mid-April to mid-September. Others offer limited-time parking from April 15 to September 15. On-street parking is unrestricted on Beach 193rd Street, which can be reached by continuing 1 mile past the Fort Tilden entrance traffic light to the Silver Gull Club sign and making a left onto Beach 193rd Street. From this on-street parking area, you can enter Fort Tilden to the east. Before proceeding, check out the field to the west that offers wide-open views of migrating hawks. In late October through November, Northern Harrier and Sharp-shinned Hawk fly low over this strip of land. Flocks of songbirds also use this flight track.

To reach the tip of Breezy Point, continue on past Fort Tilden through the Breezy Point Cooperative, a "gated" residential community, to the Beach 222nd Street parking lot. During the restricted period between

April 15 to September 15, you may make arrangements to park. Group leaders or individual birders may obtain a one-day (same-day) parking permit by applying at Headquarters Building 1 at Fort Tilden, 9:00 AM to 4:00 PM, seven days a week. Birders should carry binoculars and a field guide when applying for the permit. For details, call the headquarters.

If coming from the Jamaica Bay Wildlife Refuge by car, go south on Cross Bay Boulevard through the community of Broad Channel. Cross over the toll bridge, the Cross Bay Veterans Memorial Bridge, and proceed west 3½ miles on Beach Channel Drive. To reach Riis Park, follow the signs. To reach Fort Tilden, continue past the Riis Park exit and keep right to the overpass marked Breezy Point–Fort Tilden, then make a left turn at the first traffic light into the Fort Tilden entrance.

For Additional Information on Jacob Riis Park, Fort Tilden, and Breezy Point

Jacob Riis Park/Fort Tilden Headquarters, 718-318-4300 and
   www.nps.gov/gate
National Park Service Rangers (lead tours), 718-318-4340
New York City Audubon Society (leads tours), 212-691-7483 and
   www.nycaudubon.org
American Littoral Society (leads tours), www.alsnyc.org
Resource persons: Ronald V. Bourque, Board of Directors and former President, New York City Audubon Society; Oscar W. Ruiz, New York City Audubon Society; and Steve Walter

Forest Park
Nesting   Spring Migration**   Fall Migration**   Winter
Park Lane South to Union Turnpike, Metropolitan Avenue to 98th Street

In the center of Queens sits Forest Park, City of New York/Parks and Recreation's 538 acres of parkland on the crest of Harbor Hills terminal moraine, which stretches from eastern Long Island to Queens, Brooklyn, and Staten Island. Woodhaven Boulevard, the Long Island Railroad, Metropolitan Avenue, Myrtle Avenue, and Interborough Parkway transect the park. The eastern portion, which includes North Forest and the Gully, hold the most interest for birders. The section to the west of Woodhaven Boulevard (not included on the map) is dominated by a golf course and other recreational facilities.

North Forest

The 72-acre North Forest portion of Forest Park can be entered from the intersection of Metropolitan Avenue and Park Lane South, where there is a footpath opposite Grosvenor Road. This section of the park is characterized by magnificent tall oak trees, which attract large numbers of migrating songbirds in spring and autumn. Take the path to Park Drive inside the park. Cross over the drive and enter a trail marked by two large boulders. There is a small depression approximately 100 yards on the right called the Water Hole. Look carefully because often it is obscured by vegetation. On a spring migration day, before the Water Hole dries up, stand near it and you will spot an amazing series of flycatchers, warblers, and other songbirds. The remainder of this wooded section of the park is worth exploring during migration periods. Because of its peculiar shape and numerous trails, it is one of the easiest parks in which to become disoriented.

The Gully

The 93-acre Gully, another good birding area, lies on the other side (south side) of the railroad tracks from which you entered. Follow the Park Drive Bridge (southern end of Park Drive) over the Long Island Railroad tracks to reach this section. The Gully's terrain is knob-and-kettle topography, with a mature overstory of oaks and hickory trees and an understory of flowering dogwood and mapleleaf viburnum. Red-bellied Woodpecker nest in this section of the park. Two of the area's glacial depressions worth investigating are the Gully (after which this section of the park was named) and the Horse Shoe.

When to Go

Spring migration usually peaks between May 5 and 25. It is best to go early in the morning between 7:00 and 11:00 AM. There is good viewing as the sun rises over the water. Scan the treetops at first light and listen for the early chorus of song. During spring migration, birding can be good also in the afternoon between 4:00 and 7:00PM.

Fall migration starts in late August and continues into early October after the passing of a cool or cold front.

Winter birding is not very productive, although wintering chickadees, nuthatches, sparrows, and juncos can be found.

Optimal Weather Conditions

Spring birding is best on warm days with light, southwest winds. Birding can also be quite good on a windless day if southwest winds blew during the previous night.

Fall birding is good on days with northwest winds.

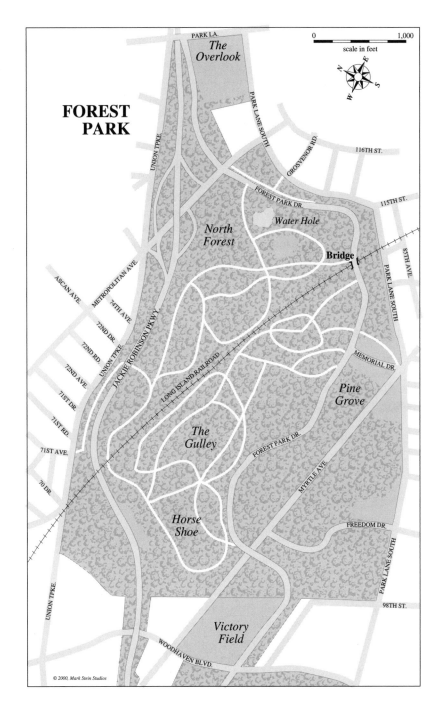

Personal Safety

The trails in Forest Park are not widely used. It is advisable to bird here with one or two other friends. There is a little poison ivy and, in summer, mosquitoes.

Getting There

The Metropolitan Transit Authority (MTA) puts out a free New York City subway map indicating major subway/bus connections, which can be obtained at subway station ticket booths.

SUBWAY: From Manhattan, take the Queens-bound E or F subway train to the Kew Gardens/Union Turnpike stop. Walk to Park Lane South and Metropolitan Avenue, where there is an entrance to the park.

CAR: From Manhattan, take the Queens Midtown Tunnel to the Long Island Expressway (Route 495). Follow it to Woodhaven Boulevard. Exit Woodhaven Boulevard at Myrtle Avenue. Take Myrtle Avenue east to Park Lane South. You will find places to park. Car theft and break-ins have occurred in this area.

For Additional Information on Forest Park

Queens Urban Park Rangers (lead tours), 718-846-2731

Resource persons: Don Riepe, Park Ranger, Gateway National Recreation Area, and Chapter Director, American Littoral Society; and Herb Roth, North Shore Audubon Society

Alley Pond Park

Nesting** Spring Migration** Fall Migration*** Winter**
Union Turnpike to Little Neck Bay, Cross Island Parkway, Easthampton Boulevard, 230th Street, 233rd Street, and Springfield Boulevard to Douglaston Parkway and Winchester Boulevard

Alley Pond Park is the most ecologically diverse park managed by the City of New York/Parks and Recreation in Queens. The northern border touches on Long Island Sound's Little Neck Bay. It contains an entire watershed; kettle ponds in a mature oak and beech forest on the terminal moraine, freshwater wetlands supported by groundwater seeps and artesian springs on the outwash plain, and abundant saltmarsh along Alley Creek and its confluence with Little Neck Bay. The two best birding areas are in Alley Wetlands and Upper Alley Woodlands.

Alley Pond Park's 635 acres are crisscrossed by Grand Central Parkway, Cross Island Parkway, Long Island Expressway, and the Long Island Railroad, slicing the park into many segments, some of which contain athletic fields, tennis courts, and playgrounds. The nationally recognized Alley Pond Environmental Center (APEC) is located just off Northern Boulevard in the Alley Wetlands section of the park. APEC offers educational programs to schoolchildren, teachers, and visitors, including birdwalks, nature hikes, and an annual Arline Thomas Urban Bird Arts Contest. Special events include an Arbor Day celebration, Halloween Happening, and Membership Day. APEC's publication *Alley Pond Park Trails* provides detailed information about the trail system. The Alley Wetlands meadows and old fields, on either side of the saltmarshes flanking Alley Creek, are nesting habitat for American Woodcock, vireos, Swamp Sparrow, and American Goldfinch. Eastern Bluebird are seen here in spring. In fall and winter, Common Snipe and American Tree Sparrow can be common. The Cattail Pond Trail from APEC leads to an observation deck overlooking Alley Creek and associated wetlands. In spring, Tree Swallow use nesting boxes situated in the saltmarshes. Great and Snowy egrets, Black-crowned Night-Heron, various sandpipers, and Belted Kingfisher congregate here in spring and in summer, after the breeding season. The avian convocation is joined by Great Blue Heron in the fall.

A larger, less accessible saltmarsh is situated at the confluence of Alley Creek and Little Neck Bay. Follow Joe Michael's Memorial Mile from APEC to search for nesting Saltmarsh Sharp-tailed Sparrow and Swamp Sparrow. In 1998, 14 acres of intertidal marsh were restored, in an area previously dominated by *Phragmites*. During construction, an Osprey platform was erected and, in the spring, was immediately occupied. The Osprey fledged chicks in 1998 and 1999. Until this time, Osprey had not been observed nesting on the north shore of Queens for 80 years or more. During the winter, Little Neck Bay is visited by wintering waterfowl, including Red-throated Loon, Common Loon, Horned Grebe, Northern Pintail, Canvasback, Greater Scaup, Bufflehead, Common Goldeneye, and Ruddy Duck. Aside from the usual sightings, the January 2000 Waterfowl Count included Great Cormorant, Green-winged Teal, and Red-breasted Merganser.

The Upper Alley (at the southern end of the park, west of Cross Island Parkway) comprises 100 acres of continuous forest canopy. Many trees here are 200 years old. This is the best spot in the park to look for spring and fall migrating songbirds. All the likely suspects can be expected, plus relative rarities such as Philadelphia Vireo, Prothonotary, Kentucky, and Connecticut warblers, and Yellow-breasted Chat. The trees and shrubs around the kettle ponds are good places to watch for Hooded and Wilson's warblers. In summer, breeders have included Wood Duck, Eastern Wood-Pewee, Red-eyed Vireo, Carolina Wren, Wood Thrush, American Redstart, and orioles.

Queens County Bird Club

The Queens County Bird Club was founded in September 1932 to observe and preserve the avifauna of Queens. The club sponsors monthly all-day field trips in and about New York City, and during migration, it runs mini-trips as well as weekend trips. In winter, club members take part in the Christmas Bird Count and the Waterfowl Count. The monthly newsletter, *News and Notes*, lists these activities. Meetings of the Queens County Bird Club are held at the Alley Pond Environmental Center on the third Wednesday of each month, except in July and August.

New York City Audubon Society Speaks Out

In 1998, the Board of Directors of New York City Audubon unanimously endorsed a bicycle route for the Cross Island Greenway that uses already paved residential streets outside Alley Pond Park. Their alternative countered the proposed greenway plan, which would have run through Alley Pond Park, causing major habitat destruction and fragmentation.

Personal Safety

It is best to bird with someone else or a group at Alley Pond Park. Poison ivy is found here and there throughout the park. It is not a problem if you stay on the trails. Dog ticks are prevalent from mid-April through June. Again, stay on the trails to avoid them. Mosquitoes breed in the wetlands June through September. They are usually not a problem on cool, dry days with wind.

Getting There

The Metropolitan Transit Authority (MTA) puts out a free New York City subway map indicating major subway/bus connections, which can be obtained at subway station ticket booths. Detailed bus schedule information can be picked up on board Queens buses. Or you can contact NYC Transit at 718-330-1234 or www.mta.nyc.ny.us for subway, bus, and train information.

SUBWAY to BUS: To reach Alley Wetlands from Manhattan, take the Queens-bound 7 to Flushing/Main Street, last stop. Take the Q12 bus from Stern's department store on Roosevelt Avenue toward Little Neck to the APEC bus stop at approximately 228th Street (a 20-minute ride).

TRAIN: To reach Alley Wetlands from Manhattan, take the Long Island Railroad from Penn Station to the Douglaston station. Hike south along Douglaston Parkway to Northern Boulevard. Take a right (west) on Northern Boulevard for about ¼ mile to APEC. Call 718-217-5477 for train schedule information.

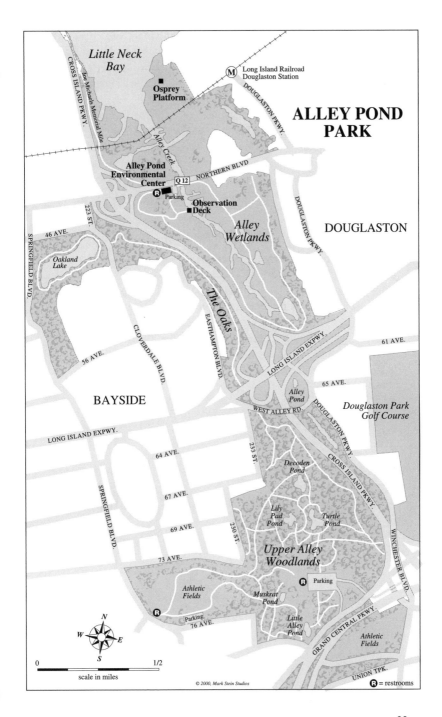

CAR: To reach Alley Wetlands from Manhattan, take the Triboro Bridge to Grand Central Parkway and then to the Cross Island Parkway North. Exit at Northern Boulevard East and look for the APEC parking lot immediately on the right. Parking is free. The lot is open from 9:00 A.M. to 4:30 P.M. daily, except some holidays.

To reach Upper Alley from Manhattan, take the Triboro Bridge to Grand Central Parkway and then to the Alley Park/Winchester Boulevard exit. Go left on Winchester Boulevard, then a quick left onto the park road. Follow the road to the parking lot (restrooms) on the right, which is open from 9:00 A.M. to 5:00 P.M. daily, except some holidays. Parking is free. Or go on to the parking lot (restrooms) off Springfield Boulevard and 76th Avenue.

For Additional Information on Alley Pond Park

Alley Pond Environmental Center (leads tours), 718-229-4000 and
    www.alleypond.com
Queens County Bird Club (leads tours), 718-229-4000
Queens Urban Park Rangers (lead tours), 718-846-2731
Resource persons: Aline Euler, Board of Directors, New York City Audubon Society, and Education Director, Alley Pond Environmental Center; Mike Feller, Natural Resources Group, City of New York/Parks and Recreation; and Larry Plotnick, Queens County Bird Club

Chapter Five

Staten Island

Staten Island is officially Richmond County, named in honor of the Duke of Richmond, King Charles II's illegitimate son. Giovanni da Verrazano discovered the island in 1524. Eighty-five years later Henry Hudson rediscovered it, giving it the name of Staaten Eylandt. Thousands of years before the colonists, Native Americans settled on Staten Island.

A number of famous naturalists are affiliated with Staten Island, including Henry David Thoreau, who spent the summer of 1843 here, entomologist and conservationist William T. Davis, botanist Nathaniel Lord Britton, landscape architect Frederick Law Olmsted (his Hylan Boulevard residence still stands), and ornithologist James Chapin.

Walking the Staten Island Greenbelt, a 3,000-acre network of second-growth forest in the island's center, you can experience "the healthiest forest ecosystem" in the entire city, as ranked by botanists and foresters for *Wild New York*. In addition to these thriving woodlands, Staten Island contains 2,000 acres of freshwater wetlands (the Staten Island Bluebelt), tidal marshlands, and 60 miles of waterfront, providing great diversity of avian habitat. On Christmas Bird Counts, Peregrine Falcon, Lesser Black-backed Gull, Glaucous Gull, Great Black-backed Gull, Great Horned Owl, and Marsh Wren have been sighted regularly. On a single day in May 1995, in 1996, and again in 1998, the Staten Island birdathon team, competing against New York City Audubon Society teams in each of the other boroughs, tallied the most species. (In 2000, the Staten Island team took second place with 162 species, only three less than Brooklyn's tally of 165 species—a birdathon record.)

In all seasons, but particularly during winter and spring migration, Staten Island offers excellent birding opportunities. Among the best places along the oceanfront are Great Kills Park, Wolfe's Pond Park, Mount Loretto Preserve, Long Pond Park, and Conference House Park; in the northwest corridor are Saw Mill Creek Park (Chelsea Marsh), Goethals Pond, Mariners Marsh Preserve, and Arlington Marsh; and mid-island is Clove Lakes Park.

Staten Island can be reached from Manhattan by a spectacular ferry ride (free of charge) on Upper New York Bay past the Statue of Liberty. Many bird species can be observed from the ferry. Express buses also run between the two boroughs.

Great Kills Park, Gateway National Recreation Area, and Great Kills Park, City of New York/Parks and Recreation

Nesting*   Spring Migration**   Fall Migration**   Winter**
Fairlawn Avenue to Miller Field, Hylan Boulevard and Great Kills Lane to Lower New York Bay

Great Kills Park, part of the Staten Island unit of Gateway National Recreation Area, covers 1,200 acres of woods, marshlands, dunes, and beaches that run along the south shore for more than two miles. Recreation areas include a marina, public beaches, public boat launch, fishing areas, model airplane field, nature trails, and numerous ball fields. The Beach Center (with restrooms) and its food concessions are open in the warm months, and a ranger station, with visitor information, is open year round. Educational programs for school groups are run from a recently constructed field station. Great Kills Harbor was created in the 1870s, when Crooke's Island was connected to the mainland using dredge material.

Great Kills Park is a very good place to bird, rain or shine. The Blue Dot and Orange trails are clearly marked. If following the Blue Dot Trail, look for Common Snipe along the stream edge to the west of the trail. The grassy areas around Parking Area A, the harbor's edge, and the ocean front, particularly at the mudflats (northern end), offer wonderful birding opportunities.

In mid-September into early October, investigate a grove of locust trees just north of the harbor (at the boat launch) for migrants, including vireos and warblers. In the spring, American Woodcock perform courtship flights on the path through the model airplane field, east of the baseball fields. During winter, Purple Sandpiper visit the jetties. Snowy Owl, Horned Lark, and Lapland Longspur are seen along the shoreline.

Along the shore and on the mudflats (where *Spartina* is taking hold again), gulls, ducks, wading birds, and shorebirds can be seen any time of year. In spring, egrets, waterfowl, plovers, American Oystercatcher, Red Knot, and gulls are regular visitors. Bring a scope to observe the shorebirds, and time your visit to the mud flats during low tide. Tide schedules can be obtained from the Sandy Hook Pilot (718-448-3900), Gateway National Recreation Area's Jamaica Bay Wildlife Refuge (718-318-4340), or from the National Oceanic and Atmospheric Administration (NOAA; www.opsd.nos.noaa.gov/tides/nyneWP).

The beach and rock jetty at the tip of Crooke's Point offer extraordinary views of the waters of Lower New York Bay as well as a sweeping vista that stretches from Manhattan to Brooklyn to Queens and south to New Jersey. Crooke's Point is another good place to set up your scope. The Great Kills Harbor is a good winter waterfowl viewing site for scaup, scoters, and others. In winter, Oldsquaw bob around in the harbor's inlet, and Snow Bunting are found in the open areas along the beach. Yellow-rumped Warbler winter in Crooke's Point bayberry thickets.

Two hundred and fifty acres of Great Kills Park are still managed by City of New York/Parks and Recreation. (In 1971, Parks and Recreation deeded the southern acreage to Gateway National Recreation Area.) You can enter the city parkland directly by turning east off Hylan Boulevard at Tysens Lane (several miles north of the Gateway entrance). Follow Tysens Lane to the end. Climb the sand dunes to reach the beachfront and mudflats that extend from the national park property. In September and October, investigate the city's weedy parkland on the west side of Grove Avenue between Agda Street and Ebbitts Street for fall migrants. Continue north to Gateway's Miller Field, a former U.S. Army base, which is another productive area during migration.

When to Go

If you are looking for migrating shorebirds, spring, particularly May, and again in mid-July through September are optimal times, especially at low tide. If you are interested in waterfowl, anytime in spring (April and May), fall (October and November), and most particularly, winter is productive. Fall and winter are also good times for raptors.

Optimal Weather Conditions

Fair weather (no precipitation) is best for wintering raptors, waterfowl, and shorebirds. For migrating songbirds, the conditions that favor fallouts, as described in chapter 3, "Manhattan/Central Park," are best.

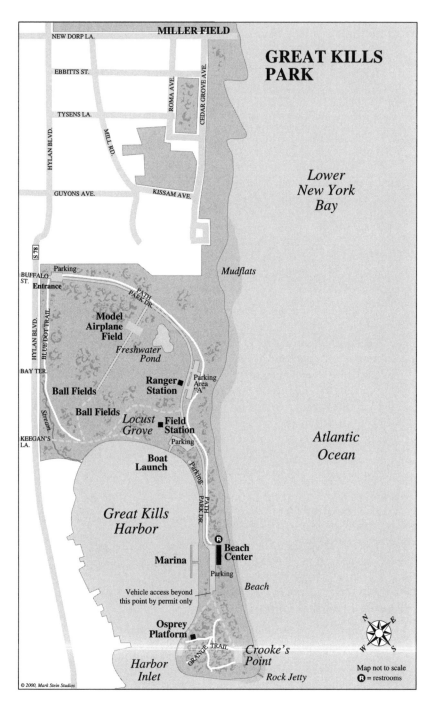

GREAT KILLS PARK

MILLER FIELD

NEW DORP LA.

EBBITTS ST.

TYSENS LA.

ROMA AVE.

CEDAR GROVE AVE.

HYLAN BLVD.

MILL RD.

GUYONS AVE.

KISSAM AVE.

Lower New York Bay

S 78

Parking

BUFFALO ST.

Entrance

Mudflats

PATH PARK DR.

HYLAN BLVD.

BLUE DOT TRAIL

Model Airplane Field

Freshwater Pond

BAY TER.

Ball Fields

Ranger Station

Parking Area "A"

Ball Fields

Locust Grove

Field Station

Parking

KEEGAN'S LA.

Strauss

Atlantic Ocean

Boat Launch

Parking

PATH PARK DR.

Great Kills Harbor

Ⓡ **Beach Center**

Marina

Parking

Vehicle access beyond
this point by permit only

Beach

Osprey Platform

ORANGE TRAIL

Crooke's Point

N

Harbor Inlet

Rock Jetty

Map not to scale

Ⓡ = restrooms

© 2000, Mark Stein Studios

Personal Safety

Joggers, walkers, and cyclists use the park and give the illusion of safety. However, some of the best birding areas are isolated, particularly along some portions of the beach, so it is best to bird with another person. Beware of dog ticks, poison ivy, and mosquitoes.

Getting There

FERRY to BUS: From Manhattan, take the Staten Island Ferry (718-815-2628) from the southern tip of Manhattan (Take the 1 and 9 subway line to South Ferry, the last stop in Manhattan) to St. George Terminal on Staten Island. From there take the Tottenville-bound S78 NYC Transit bus (D ramp) along Hylan Boulevard. (Call 718-979-0600 for schedule information.) Get off at the Great Kills Park entrance (at least a half-hour bus ride). From the entrance it is 2-mile walk to the tip of Crooke's Point.

BUS: From Manhattan, take the 1X Express bus that leaves from Carnegie Hall at 57th and 7th Avenue and goes to Staten Island. (Call 718-979-0600 for schedule information.) On Staten Island, this express bus follows Hylan Avenue to Richmond Avenue. Ask to be let off near the entrance to Gateway's Great Kills Park.

CAR: From Manhattan, take the Brooklyn Bridge over the East River and follow the signs to the Brooklyn/Queens Expressway (Route 278) to the Verrazano-Narrows Bridge. Follow Route 278, which becomes the Staten Island Expressway, over the bridge ($7.00 toll one way). Get off at the Hylan Boulevard exit and go south (left) on Hylan Boulevard for 5 miles to the park entrance, which is east of (opposite) Buffalo Street. Follow Park Drive for 1.5 miles to Parking Area A on the left (opposite the ranger station), where parking is free. Parking at Crooke's Point is by permit only.

For Additional Information on Great Kills Park

City of New York/Parks and Recreation, Staten Island Headquarters, 718-390-8000

Staten Island Institute of Arts and Sciences, Section of Natural History (leads tours), 718-727-1135

Staten Island Unit of Gateway National Recreation Area, Great Kills Park (leads tours), 718-987-6790

Staten Island Urban Park Rangers (lead tours), 718-667-6042

Resource persons: Howie Fischer and Scottie Jenkins

Wolfe's Pond Park

Nesting   Spring Migration*   Fall Migration**   Winter*
Holten Avenue to Luten Avenue and Irvington Street, Staten Island Railway
to Raritan Bay

During the early 1800s, the area of Wolfe's Pond Park was farmed by Joel
Wolfe, hence the name. Now it is a public park managed by the City of
New York/Parks and Recreation. The Department of Parks and Recreation built a playground (with restrooms) and is planning tennis courts,
leaving natural much of the 336 acres, which feature woodlands of maple,
oak, and beech, ponds, and a ¾-mile stretch of dunes and cobbled shoreline. Wolfe's Pond, a 16-acre body of freshwater perched above the Staten
Island water table, is only a short distance from oceanfront dunes. Legend
has it that oystermen dammed up a tidal inlet to create a place to wash
their catch. The pond is an ideal spot for night-herons, many duck
species, and Belted Kingfisher. Wood Duck can be seen here in the spring
and fall.

From the parking lot, cross the lawn to Wolfe's Pond. Walk north
along the pond's eastern edge (back toward Hylan Boulevard), checking
it for waterfowl and wading birds. Scan the shrubs and trees for migratory songbirds. Following an old roadbed that goes into the woods, you
enter a ravine created by the outflow from Acme Pond, a 5-acre body of
water on the north side of Hylan Boulevard. Staying on the south side of
Hylan Boulevard, take the trail to the left, which crosses a stream, and ascend the steep slope of the forested ravine to a ridge. From here you can
search the treetops in the ravine for songirds as well as scan Raritan Bay
for waterfowl.

Walk the beach area in winter to view loons and large rafts of Brant that
can be seen in the bay. The latter stay until the end of May, when they depart for their northern breeding grounds. A scope is recommended.

Cross Hylan Boulevard to stroll through an impressive mature forest
that started sprouting after the colonists abandoned farming on Staten Island. There is good birding both in the woodlands and at Acme Pond, but
dirt bikers disturb the tranquility, cause erosion, and destroy avian habitat. Rusty Blackbird frequent Acme Pond from late autumn through winter, and Fox Sparrow are here in winter. A small stream, where Common
Snipe are seen, runs from Eylandt Street and can be accessed from Tottenville High School on Chisholm Street.

Wood Duck breed at Bunker Ponds Park, also managed by City of
New York/Parks and Recreation, which is located opposite Intermediate

School (I.S.) 7 at the intersection of Huguenot Avenue and Hylan Boulevard. Make a side trip to Bunker Pond if you have time.

When to Go

In spring, songbird migration is good from April 1 to June 1, and in fall, from mid-August to early November. The best birding time of day is the early morning. Later, when there are lots of people in the park, wary species are frightened off.

During the winter as well as September and October, birding for waterfowl is good anytime of day, particularly after a storm.

Optimal Weather Conditions

For songbird migration weather, refer to Optimal Weather Conditions in chapter 3, "Manhattan/Central Park."

Personal Safety

Some parts of the park are isolated, so it is best to bird with others. Beware of dog ticks and poison ivy. Mosquitoes can also be a problem.

Getting There

FERRY to BUS: From Manhattan, take the Staten Island Ferry (718-815-2628) from the southern tip of Manhattan (take the 1 and 9 subway line to South Ferry, the last stop in Manhattan) to St. George Terminal on Staten Island. From there take the Tottenville-bound S78 NYC Transit bus (D ramp) along Hylan Boulevard. (Call 979-0600 for schedule information.) Get off at the Luten Avenue stop (about a 45-minute to one-hour ride). At the Luten Avenue stop, walk across Hylan Boulevard and go one block west to Cornelia Avenue. Walk south (left) on Cornelia Avenue to the park entrance on the right.

CAR: From Manhattan, take the Brooklyn Bridge over the East River and follow the signs to the Brooklyn/Queens Expressway (Route 278) to the Verrazano-Narrows Bridge. Follow Route 278, which becomes the Staten Island Expressway, over the bridge. Get off at the Hylan Boulevard exit and go south (left) on Hylan Boulevard for 6 miles to Cornelia Avenue. Turn left and you will see the park entrance on the right. Follow the park road to the last parking lot (no charge). Or you can continue south on the expressway to Route 440. Take 440 south, following the signs to Outerbridge Crossing/New Jersey. Get off at Bloomingdale Road. At the end of the exit ramp, turn left (south) on Bloomingdale Road and go 2 miles to Amboy Road. Turn left on Amboy Road and drive ¾ mile to Sequine Avenue. Make a right on Sequine Avenue. When you

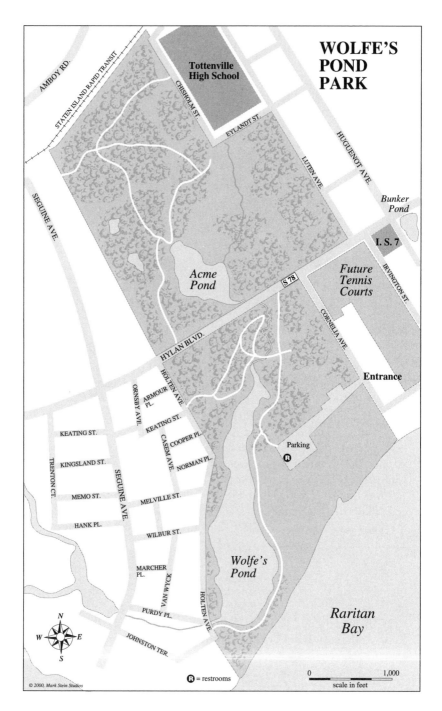

WOLFE'S POND PARK

Tottenville High School

Bunker Pond

I. S. 7

Acme Pond

Future Tennis Courts

Entrance

Parking

Wolfe's Pond

Raritan Bay

AMBOY RD.

STATEN ISLAND RAPID TRANSIT

CHISHOLM ST.

EYLANDT ST.

HUGUENOT AVE.

LUTEN AVE.

SEGUINE AVE.

IRVINGTON ST.

S 78

CORNELIA AVE.

HYLAN BLVD.

ORNSBY AVE.

ARMOUR PL.

HOLTEN AVE.

KEATING ST.

KEATING ST.

COOPER PL.

CASEM AVE.

NORMAN PL.

KINGSLAND ST.

TRENTON CT.

MEMO ST.

SEGUINE AVE.

MELVILLE ST.

HANK PL.

WILBUR ST.

MARCHER PL.

VAN WYCK

PURDY PL.

HOLTEN AVE.

JOHNSTON TER.

N
W   E
S

ℝ = restrooms

0   1,000

scale in feet

© 2000, Mark Stein Studios

reach Hylan Boulevard, turn left and drive ¾ mile to the park entrance. Take the park road to the last lot, where there is ample parking. From Brooklyn, follow the instructions above from the Brooklyn/ Queens Expressway. From New Jersey, go over the Arthur Kill on Outerbridge Crossing. After the toll booth, take Exit 1, Arthur Kill Road. Follow signs to Page Avenue, and follow it to Hylan Boulevard. Turn left onto Hylan Boulevard and follow it for about 3½ miles to Cornelia Avenue. Turn right on Cornelia Avenue. The park entrance is a short distance on the right.

For Additional Information on Wolfe's Pond Park

City of New York/Parks and Recreation, Staten Island Headquarters, 718-390-8000

Staten Island Institute of Arts and Sciences, Section of Natural History (leads tours), 718-727-1135

Staten Island Urban Park Rangers (leads tours), 718-667-6042

Wolfe's Pond Park, 718-984-8266

Resource persons: Howie Fischer; and Edward W. Johnson, Curator of Science, Staten Island Institute of Arts and Sciences

Mount Loretto Nature Preserve/Long Pond Park

Nesting** Spring Migration** Fall Migration** Winter*
Raritan Bay to Amboy Road, Page Avenue to Sharrott Avenue

Mount Loretto Nature Preserve

Mount Loretto, a large expanse of property overlooking Raritan Bay from a dramatic bluff, was owned in its entirety by the Archdiocese of New York. In 1998, after years of persistent lobbying by Staten Island–based Protectors of Pine Oak Woods, the Trust for Public Land acquired 194 acres on the south side of Hylan Boulevard (where the charred ruins of St. Elizabeth's Home for Girls stand), protecting a grassy bluff area and several ponds that were threatened by development. New York State Department of Environmental Conservation (NYSDEC) manages the property as a nature preserve. The acreage north of Hylan Boulevard, where the Church of St. Joachim and St. Ann (site of the baptism scene in *The Godfather*) and P.S. 25 are located, is still owned by the archdiocese. Both areas offer superb birding opportunities

In spring, visit the nature preserve acreage and look in the fields for Sora, Cliff Swallow, White-crowned Sparrow, Bobolink, and Neotropical migrants such as Orchard Oriole. It is hoped that Bobolink will once again stay to nest in the fields. Perhaps American Kestrel and Eastern Meadowlark will return to nest here as well. Rather than mow during nesting season, NYSDEC plans to cut the fields in August, after nestlings fledge. Black-billed Cuckoo, Yellow-billed Cuckoo, White-eyed Vireo, and Warbling Vireo nest in the wooded area on the western end of the property. In 1999, Cedar Waxwing nested in this woodland.

During autumn migration, Green-winged Teal, White-rumped Sandpiper, Pectoral Sandpiper, and swallows are found at the ponds. Wood Duck spend their eclipse molt period (late August to early September) in the wetland area to the west of Brown's Pond, and some nest regularly in the vicinity of the smaller pond also to the west of Brown's Pond. From August to October, Osprey, drawn by local dining opportunities, are common at the ponds.

Eastern Screech-Owl nest in dead oaks along the trail. Ring-necked Pheasant, Belted Kingfisher, Tree Swallow, and Yellow-breasted Chat nest nearby. Purple Martin, which nest at Lemon Creek to the east, are seen feeding in the area.

In the fall, scour the wooded bluff area for migrants and raptors.

From the bluff area in winter, scan the bay for Great Cormorant, Greater Scaup, Oldsquaw, and Common Goldeneye. These bluffs offer unparalleled views of Sandy Hook and Raritan Bay.

On the church/P.S. 25 side of Mount Loretto (north of Hylan Boulevard) in spring and summer, Cattle Egret are found regularly in the grassy area in front of the church, and on rare occasions, Buff-breasted Sandpiper are also found. Yellow-billed Cuckoo and Warbling Vireo are often sighted in the cottonwoods near Kenny Road.

From Sharrott Avenue you can enter a new site for the Mount Loretto Cemetery, where Yellow-breasted Chat have been seen in mid-May. It is suspected that they nest here.

Long Pond Park

West of the church/P.S. 25 section of Mount Loretto (west of Richard Avenue) is a newly dedicated City of New York/Parks and Recreation park (140 acres) with seven kettlehole ponds, the largest being 5-acre Long Pond. This area is excellent from late August through October for sighting autumn migrants, including large numbers of Fox, Lincoln's, Swamp, White-throated, and White-crowned sparrows, and for sighting Dark-eyed Junco from October to December. It is also a good spot to see migratory shorebirds and Wood Duck. From early May through late summer, Purple Martin and Northern Rough-winged Swallow conduct an energetic gleaning of air-borne insects over this area. Great Horned Owl, White-eyed Vireo, and Warbling Vireo breed here.

Protectors of Pine Oak Woods

Founded in 1972, Protectors of Pine Oak Woods is Staten Island's primary land conservation organization protecting its parks, natural areas, and wildlife. Besides its success in saving Mount Loretto Preserve, Protectors helped establish Long Pond Park as well as the Staten Island Greenbelt and Bluebelt. It publishes a newsletter that lists its activities, including nature walks to many of Staten Island's parklands.

When to Go

Early to mid-May, Bobolink arrive in the fields on the NYSDEC nature preserve side. The Chuck-will's-widow is a regular in June. Visit early in the morning for the best results, unless you want to see Common Nighthawk, which can be seen in good numbers soaring overhead in the evening, particularly in late August and September. Also in the evening you may be able to call in Eastern Screech-Owl.

Days from late August through October are excellent times to see a variety of migratory landbirds and raptors. In mid-October, the fields at Long Pond are alive with Yellow Warbler, Palm Warbler, and sparrows.

Optimal Weather Conditions

Cold fronts in early October produce great numbers of migrants. Hawk migration is quite good with northwest to west winds.

For songbird migration weather, refer to Optimal Weather Conditions in chapter 3, "Manhattan/Central Park."

Personal Safety

This area is relatively safe. Teens use the woods near Long Pond as a hangout but do not cause problems. Increased presence from New York City and New York State agencies may discourage them from congregating here. Nevertheless, it is recommended that you bird with others.

Poison ivy is prevalent, and ticks abound, so wear long pants. In a wet summer, mosquitoes are also plentiful.

Getting There

FERRY to BUS: From Manhattan, take the Staten Island Ferry (718-815-2628) from the southern tip of Manhattan (South Ferry is the last stop on the 1 and 9 subway line) to St. George Terminal on Staten Island. From there take the Tottenville-bound S78 NYC Transit bus (D ramp) along Hylan Boulevard to the P.S. 25 bus stop, one stop before Richard Avenue. (Call 718-979-0600 for schedule information.)

CAR: From Manhattan, take the Brooklyn Bridge over the East River

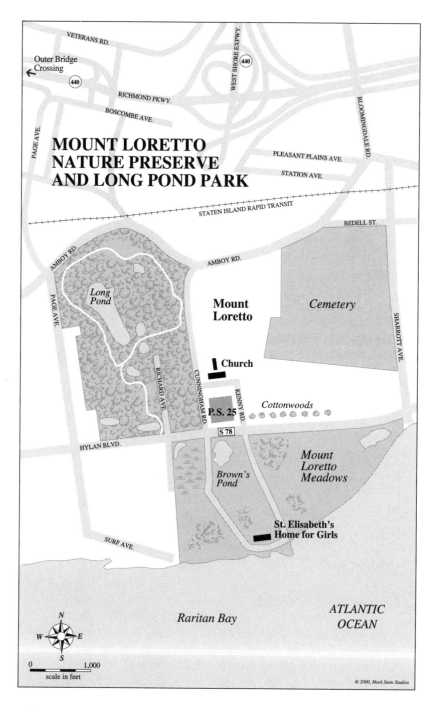

MOUNT LORETTO
NATURE PRESERVE
AND LONG POND PARK

VETERANS RD.

Outer Bridge
Crossing
440

440

WEST SHORE EXPWY.

RICHMOND PKWY.

BOSCOMBE AVE.

PAGE AVE.

PLEASANT PLAINS AVE.

STATION AVE.

BLOOMINGDALE RD.

STATEN ISLAND RAPID TRANSIT

BEDELL ST.

AMBOY RD.

AMBOY RD.

Long
Pond

PAGE AVE.

RICHARD AVE.

CUNNINGHAM RD.

Mount
Loretto

Cemetery

SHARROTT AVE.

Church

KENNY RD.

P.S. 25

Cottonwoods

S 78

HYLAN BLVD.

Brown's
Pond

Mount
Loretto
Meadows

St. Elisabeth's
Home for Girls

SURF AVE.

Raritan Bay

ATLANTIC
OCEAN

N
W   E
S

0   1,000
scale in feet

© 2000, Mark Stein Studios

and follow the signs to the Brooklyn/Queens Expressway (Route 278) to the Verrazano-Narrows Bridge. Follow Route 278, which becomes the Staten Island Expressway, over the bridge. Take Route 440 south, following the signs to Outerbridge Crossing/New Jersey. Get off at Page Road. At the end of the exit ramp, turn left (south) on Bloomingdale Road and go 2 miles to Amboy Road. Turn left on Amboy Road and take an immediate right on Sharrott Avenue. Drive ½ mile to Hylan Boulevard; turn right on Hylan Boulevard. Continue for 1 mile, past the meadows of Mount Loretto to just before Richard Avenue. Park on Richard Avenue close to Hylan Avenue.

From New Jersey, go over the Arthur Kill on Outerbridge Crossing. After the toll booth, take Exit 1, Arthur Kill Road. Follow signs to Page Avenue and follow it to Hylan Boulevard. Turn left onto Hylan Boulevard and follow it to Richard Avenue. Park on Richard Avenue close to Hylan Avenue.

For Additional Information on Mount Loretto Nature Preserve and Long Pond Park

City of New York/Parks and Recreation, Staten Island Headquarters, 718-390-8000

New York State Department of Environmental Conservation, 718-482-4900

Protectors of Pine Oak Woods (lead tours), 718-761-7496

Staten Island Institute of Arts and Sciences, Section of Natural Science (leads tours), 718-727-1135

Staten Island Urban Park Rangers (lead tours), 718-667-6042

Resource person: Howie Fischer

Conference House Park

Nesting*   Spring Migration**   Fall Migration***   Winter**
Raritan Bay and the Arthur Kill, Satterlee Street, Billop Avenue, Surf Avenue, and Richard Avenue

At the southern tip of Staten Island, where the Arthur Kill joins Raritan Bay, lies Conference House Park, a 254-acre parkland of dunes, beaches, a pond, freshwater wetlands, meadows, and wooded bluffs. The site is managed by the City of New York/Parks and Recreation. Its name is derived from a Revolutionary War peace conference held September 11, 1776, after the Battle of Long Island, in a stone manor house on the property. At the conference, Benjamin Franklin, John Adams, and Edward Rutledge refused to accept "clemency and full pardon" from the British without gaining independence for the colonies. Conference House (with restrooms), listed on the National Register of Historic Places, features seventeenth-century furnishings and a working kitchen. It is open to the public for a small admission charge from April through September, from Tuesday to Saturday. South of Conference House, on the bluffs overlooking the Arthur Kill, is an interesting landmarked Native American (the Algonquian Lenape) burial ground.

Start at the rolling lawns of Conference House (also known as Billopp House), where there are usually Northern Flicker, American Robin, and from time to time, Eastern Bluebird. From here, walk along the beach, scouting the forested edge and shoreline. In spring, the beach is a major mating site for horseshoe crabs. In late fall, from anywhere along the 1.5-mile beachfront, you may spot Red-throated and Common loons, Canvasback, Redhead, and Common Goldeneye in the waters of the Arthur Kill and Raritan Bay. In winter you will see Horned Grebe, Brant (in large numbers), Greater Scaup (formerly in large rafts, now somewhat diminished), Oldsquaw, Bufflehead, and Common Goldeneye. The beachfront offers scenic views across the bay to New Jersey's Atlantic Highlands. Have your scope handy.

Dune grasses along the shore are extremely fragile, so walk on the sand at the water's edge. In the fall, observe the grasses for dragonflies and butterflies, which may be perching there.

A stand of American hackberry, a berry-producing tree that attracts early fall migrants (vireos, warblers, and orioles) and butterflies (American snout, hackberry and tawny emperors), grows on the bluff just south of the lawn. Also inviting to migrants is a remnant coastal oak forest. This area is best investigated from Surf Avenue, an overgrown Works Progress Administration street constructed in the 1930s, that runs south toward the beach area. In early spring, walk around Surf Avenue, where Eastern Screech-Owl and Whip-poor-will are found. In June, another avian vocalist with a species name that is song-inspired, Chuck-will's-widow, can be found.

Walk back to the south side of Hylan Boulevard. Continue straight along the paved road that runs through the park and continue for two blocks to Finlay Street. During the peak of spring and fall migration, hundreds of vireos, warblers, and others gather at a little stream (one of the Twin Streams of the Lenape) on the east side of Finlay Street.

From mid-August through September, Eastern Kingbird form massive flocks along with a few Olive-sided Flycatcher. In October, impressive numbers of Northern Flicker, American Robin, and Purple Finch can be seen. In winter, Cedar Waxwing flock in the bittersweet. Wood

Thrush, Carolina Wren, and Eastern Screech-Owl nest in the larger wooded stands.

A freshwater wetlands and Wards Point Pond, fed by the Twin Streams of the Lenape, are located at the southernmost point. In early fall, this area is a good place for observing thrushes, warblers, orioles, and other Neotropical species in substantial numbers. Connecticut Warbler has been seen here in early September. Later in September and October, Sharp-shinned and other hawks are common.

Conference House Park is a particularly productive birding area in fall. Some refer to it as Little Cape May because it is the last bit of land jutting out into the water—Ward's Point. The effect is a bottleneck for birds flying south that are reluctant to cross water.

When to Go

Birding for migrants is best early in the morning, particularly April to mid-May and again in September and October. Sometimes birding can also be rewarding from 4:00 P.M. to dusk. Winter waterfowl can be seen December through January.

Optimal Weather Conditions

For viewing fall migrants, wait for cold fronts followed by northwesterly flows. Almost any weather is good for observing wintering waterfowl.

Personal Safety

It is wise to bird this quiet, isolated park with others. From time to time, numerous teenagers congregate here, which is a bit intimidating. Poison ivy is dense in the hackberry grove. Dog ticks are found in the brushy areas. Mosquitoes can be a problem.

Getting There

FERRY to BUS: From Manhattan, take the Staten Island Ferry (718-815-2628) from the southern tip of Manhattan (South Ferry is the last stop on the 1 and 9 subway line) to the St. George Terminal on Staten Island. From there, take the Tottenville-bound S78 NYC Transit bus (D ramp) along Hylan Boulevard. (Call 718-979-0600 for schedule information.) Get off at Craig Avenue (more than a half-hour bus ride), and walk one block south along Hylan Boulevard to Satterlee Street. The entrance is near the intersection of Satterlee Street and Hylan Boulevard, where there is a break in the wooden fence.

CAR: From Manhattan, take the Brooklyn Bridge over the East River and follow the signs to the Brooklyn/Queens Expressway (Route 278) to

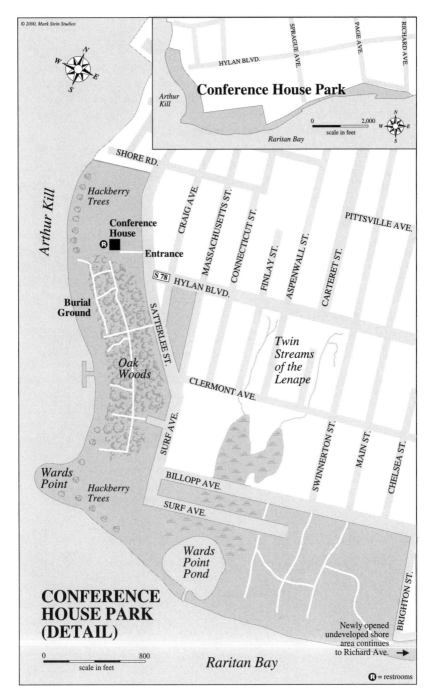

© 2000, Mark Stein Studios

Conference House Park

HYLAN BLVD.

SPRAGUE AVE.

PAGE AVE.

RICHARD AVE.

Arthur
Kill

0   2,000
scale in feet

Raritan Bay

Arthur Kill

SHORE RD.

Hackberry
Trees

Conference
House

ⓡ

Entrance

S 78 HYLAN BLVD.

Burial
Ground

CRAIG AVE.

MASSACHUSETTS ST.

CONNECTICUT ST.

FINLAY ST.

ASPENWALL ST.

CARTERET ST.

PITTSVILLE AVE.

SATTERLEE ST.

Oak
Woods

Twin
Streams
of the
Lenape

CLERMONT AVE.

SURF AVE.

Wards
Point

Hackberry
Trees

BILLOPP AVE.

SURF AVE.

SWINNERTON ST.

MAIN ST.

CHELSEA ST.

Wards
Point
Pond

**CONFERENCE
HOUSE PARK
(DETAIL)**

BRIGHTON ST.

Newly opened
undeveloped shore
area continues
to Richard Ave. ➜

0   800
scale in feet

Raritan Bay

ⓡ = restrooms

the Verrazano-Narrows Bridge. Follow Route 278, which becomes the Staten Island Expressway, over the bridge. Take Route 440 south, following the signs to Outerbridge Crossing/New Jersey. Get off at last exit in New York State, Arthur Kill Road. At the service road, turn right, go one block, and turn right again onto the overpass. Continue over the highway and turn right once more. Continue straight, and follow the curve onto Page Avenue. Stay on Page Avenue to Hylan Boulevard, and then go south to Satterlee Street. Park on the street. The entrance is near the intersection of Satterlee Street and Hylan Boulevard, where there is a break in the wooden fence.

Another good access point is to park at the south end of Brighton Avenue, parallel to Satterlee Road, about 10 blocks east. Bird your way along the trail to Ward's Point. In August and September, this is a wonderful place to look for migrating butterflies.

For Additional Information on Conference House Park

City of New York/Parks and Recreation, Staten Island Headquarters, 718-390-8000
Conference House, 718-984-6046
Conference House–Raritan Bay Conservancy, 718-356-6368
Staten Island Institute of Arts and Sciences, Section of Natural Science (leads tours), 718-727-1135
Staten Island Urban Park Rangers (lead tours), 718-667-6042
Resource persons: Howie Fischer; and Bonnie Petite, naturalist and President, Conference House Park–Raritan Bay Conservancy

Northwest Corridor
Fresh Kills Landfill to the Kill van Kull, Arthur Kill to South Avenue

The 12 square miles of Staten Island's northwest corridor are known historically as northfield. Residences are few. Human activity is limited almost entirely to industry, including, until closure in 2001, the world's largest active waste disposal area, the 3,000-acre Fresh Kills Landfill. Nevertheless, an astounding assemblage of wildlife exists in the northwest corridor's natural areas, particularly in the marshlands.

Long, long ago, Native Americans settled in the woodlands bordering these marshlands. In the seventeenth century, Dutch colonists settled nearby. Many local place-names are derived from the Dutch language, such as Achter Cull meaning "back creek," now known as the Arthur Kill.

Historical accounts report colonial farmers harvesting the salt meadow hay from the high marshes and then sending it by barge to Manhattan as feed for carriage horses. With the advent of the automobile, the value of this resource diminished and a demand for refined petroleum was created. The Arthur Kill and the Kill van Kull were dredged to open the way for ships serving the oil industry. Refineries sprang up on both Staten Island and New Jersey shores. The health of the Arthur Kill declined with repeated oil spills and discharge of industrial waste and raw sewage into the waterways. Fish populations diminished, and oysters suffered from disease that was followed by shellfish harvesting prohibitions. The Clean Water Act, passed in 1972, rescued the Arthur Kill by establishing water quality standards and mandating reduction of pollutant discharges. Dissolved oxygen levels in the water began to climb, and many species of fish returned. Three dredge islands, Prall's, Shooters, and Isle of Meadows, in the Kills became nesting sites of colonial wading birds such as Great Egret, Snowy Egret, Black-crowned Night-Heron, and Glossy Ibis. In 1985, a monitoring program, the Harbor Herons Project, was initiated by the New York City Audubon Society to track the birds' breeding success. Annually, researchers investigate 10 islands in the Kills, East River, Jamaica Bay, and Lower New York Harbor. Approximately one-quarter of the colonial wading bird population, from Massachusetts to Maryland, nest on these island refuges. In 1998, the Harbor Herons complex was awarded Important Bird Area status in New York State, classifying these islands as essential for sustaining naturally occurring heron populations.

By the early 1990s, the northwest corridor's 5,000 acres of open land were recognized as one of New York City's finest ecological treasures, containing some of the city's rarest botanical species and significant bird habitats. Within less than 10 years, nearly 1,000 acres have been put under protective covenants by the City of New York/Parks and Recreation and the New York State Department of Environmental Conservation. Historic ecotypes, such as tidal marsh, mature swamp forest, and oak barren/sandy hummock, are well represented in Saw Mill Creek Park (Chelsea Marsh)/Prall's Island, Goethals Pond, Mariners Marsh Preserve, and Arlington Marsh, which are included here.

Saw Mill Creek Park (Chelsea Marsh)/Prall's Island

Nesting***   Spring Migration**   Fall Migration**   Winter*
Chelsea Road to River Road, Prall's Creek to the West Shore Expressway (Route 440)

Saw Mill Creek Park, recently established by the City of New York/Parks and Recreation (111 acres) and the New York State Department of Environmental Conservation (5 acres), is located on the west-central shore of Staten Island in the section commonly known as Chelsea. The area was formerly called Merrelltown after Richard Merrell, who, at the time of the American Revolution, ran a sawmill in the creek. The park does not fit the traditional model. There is no supporting infrastructure: no restrooms, formal trails, or shelters. Along with Prall's Creek, a 2-mile diversion of the Arthur Kill, and the 80-acre city-owned, New York City Audubon Society–managed Prall's Island, it comprises one of New York City's finest natural areas. Slicing through the tract in a north–south direction is the formerly defunct, now-repaired, soon-to-operate CSX Railroad. Its elevated (trestled) railroad bed offers an excellent vantage from which to study birdlife without causing disturbance. How long the rail line will remain inactive or what restrictions will be placed on hikers and birders is uncertain.

Saw Mill Creek Park is primarily saltmarsh habitat, dominated by high marsh vegetation including salt meadow hay, spike grass, and black grass, with marsh elder scattered throughout. There are also linear strips of low marsh vegetation, such as smooth cordgrass and common reed, fringing the creeks and ditches. Common reed, often referred to as *Phragmites*, is present in areas of disruption, particularly along the southern boundary and along the entire length of the railroad embankment.

More than 140 bird species have been observed at Saw Mill Creek Park and Prall's Island since 1992, including such treats as Bald Eagle and Connecticut Warbler. Parks Department biologists, New York City Audubon members, and other volunteers have conducted Breeding Bird Surveys (55 species), Winter Bird Surveys, Christmas Bird Counts, Winter Waterfowl Counts, and Big Day (Spring Migration) Counts.

In the spring and summer you will see Great and Snowy egret, Little Blue Heron, Black-crowned Night-Heron, Yellow-crowned Night-Heron, Glossy Ibis, and on rare occasions, Tricolored Heron. American Bittern and Least Bittern can be seen, the former during autumn or spring migration. Great Blue Heron and Green Heron are common here also; the latter nests nearby. Frequently Northern Harrier course low over the tidal marsh in search of meadow voles and muskrats. In 1995 and again in 1996, these raptors were confirmed as breeding at a former industrial site a few hundred yards from the northern edge of the park. Occasionally you will spot a Peregrine Falcon, perhaps one from the pair nesting on Goethals Bridge. (See chap. 3, "Manhattan/Riverside Park," for additional information on Peregrine Falcon.)

If you venture down the railroad bridge embankment (avoid the tracks) and into the marsh, you may be rewarded by glimpses of Saltmarsh Sharp-tailed Sparrow and Seaside Sparrow. It is a treat to hear the faint metallic songs of these secretive sparrows. From 1992 to 1994, six or possibly seven pairs of each species bred in Saw Mill Creek Park. In and adjacent to the marsh, look for breeding Least Bittern, Red-tailed Hawk, Clapper Rail, Virginia Rail, Common Moorhen, Spotted Sandpiper, Fish Crow, Marsh Wren, and Swamp Sparrow. Frequent visitors include Forster's Tern, Least Tern, Black Skimmer, and an occasional Osprey. The nearby oak barrens occasionally yield some surprising finds: American Woodcock at dawn or dusk (courtship display) and Barn Owl in the evening. Willow Flycatcher, Brown Thrasher, Yellow Warbler, Common Yellowthroat, and Eastern Towhee are here also.

When to Go

May through July, breeding season, are excellent months to go. An early morning start, beginning at 5:30 A.M, will allow you to hear and see numerous species. However, most saltmarsh species continue to call throughout the day.

Winter is the time for waterfowl. Although less productive than Great Kills Park, Prall's Creek offers good views of Brant, Gadwall, American Wigeon, American Black Duck, Mallard, the teals, Northern Shoveler, Bufflehead, mergansers, and Ruddy Duck. Northern Harrier as well as Cooper's Hawk and Red-tailed Hawk are frequently seen in late fall and winter.

Despite an expansive mudflat at low tide, shorebird viewing is disappointing in both spring and fall migration.

Optimal Weather Conditions

Low cloud cover will sometimes insulate the area from distracting sounds from jets, cranes, power plants, and the like. Yet on a bright sunlit morning you can see as far as Prall's Creek, Prall's Island, and the Arthur Kill. Bring a scope for scanning the waters.

Any winter day holds promise. Do not be surprised by the stiff winter winds.

Personal Safety

If you decide to hike the marsh, be careful! Walking is difficult and hazardous. Wear rubber boots or waders. Do not try to walk across tidal ditches through the sucking mud. Use the narrow plank bridges, scattered here and there. They are hard to locate, so remember where they are for the walk back. Be watchful of electrical storms if you plan to walk the full half-mile out through the saltmarsh. It can be a long return journey through the rain.

Cell phones are an added comfort. Besides boots, wear a hat, sunscreen, and tick and mosquito repellent. Always take a friend or two to Saw Mill Creek Park. Chelsea Road has had the reputation of being an uncivil place, and illegal dumping persists.

Getting There

FERRY to BUS: From Manhattan, take the Staten Island Ferry (718-815-2628) from the southern tip of Manhattan (South Ferry is the last stop on the 1 and 9 subway line) to St. George Terminal on Staten Island. From there take the S46 NYC Transit bus (C ramp) to West Shore Plaza (40 minutes). (Call 718-97-0600 for schedule information.) Walk back (east) to the traffic light at the intersection of South Avenue and Chelsea Road. Walk north on Chelsea-Bloomfield Road to the first bend, where there is easy access up to the railroad berm. Look for the City of New York/Parks and Recreation emblem of a sycamore leaf.

Or continue on Chelsea-Bloomfield Road to Chelsea Bridge, from which you will command a good view of the marshes.

CAR: From Manhattan, take the Brooklyn Bridge over the East River and follow the signs to the Brooklyn/Queens Expressway (Route 278) to the Verrazano-Narrows Bridge. Follow Route 278, which becomes the Staten Island Expressway, over the bridge. Continue south on the Staten Island Expressway to the exit ramp to West Shore Expressway (Route 440), heading toward the Outerbridge Crossing. Once you are on Route 440, go about 1½ miles to Exit 8/South Avenue. Turn left at the stop sign at the end of the exit ramp onto Chelsea-Bloomfield Road (confusingly named and unmarked). You are at the park preserve. Chelsea-Bloomfield Road turns sharply to the right and then sharply to the left. Park on the right side of the road near the auto scrapyard and the bridge (Chelsea Bridge) over Saw Mill Creek. Walk back 400 yards to access the trail alongside the train line.

Or if you want to canoe the creek, follow Chelsea-Bloomfield Road to the Chelsea Bridge. Canoes can be launched from the embankment.

From New Jersey, take the New Jersey Turnpike to Exit 13/Goethals Bridge/Route 278 East. After the toll Plaza (toll $4.00), take the second exit to Route 440 South/West Shore Expressway. Go about 1½ miles to Exit 8/South Avenue and follow the directions above.

For Additional Information on Saw Mill Creek Park

City of New York/Parks and Recreation, Staten Island Headquarters, 718-390-8000

New York State Department of Environmental Conservation, 718-482-4900

Staten Island Urban Park Rangers (lead tours), 718-667-6042

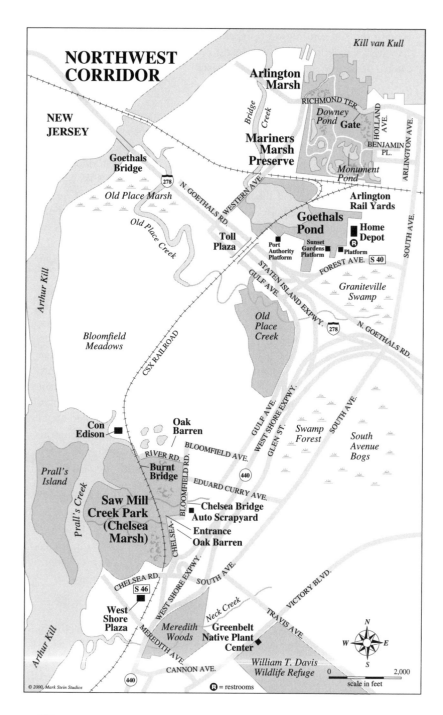

NORTHWEST CORRIDOR

Kill van Kull

Arlington Marsh

RICHMOND TER

Downey Pond

Gate

HOLLAND AVE.

ARLINGTON AVE.

BENJAMIN PL.

NEW JERSEY

Bridge Creek

Mariners Marsh Preserve

Monument Pond

Arlington Rail Yards

Goethals Bridge

N. GOETHALS RD.

N. WESTERN AVE.

278

Old Place Marsh

Goethals Pond

Home Depot

SOUTH AVE.

Old Place Creek

Toll Plaza

Port Authority Platform

Sunset Gardens Platform

Platform

ⓡ

S 40

FOREST AVE.

STATEN ISLAND EXPWY.

GULF AVE.

Graniteville Swamp

Bloomfield Meadows

Old Place Creek

N. GOETHALS RD.

278

CSX RAILROAD

GULF AVE.

WEST SHORE EXPWY.

GLEN ST.

SOUTH AVE.

Con Edison

Oak Barren

Swamp Forest

South Avenue Bogs

RIVER RD.

BLOOMFIELD AVE.

Prall's Island

Burnt Bridge

BLOOMFIELD RD.

440

Prall's Creek

Saw Mill Creek Park (Chelsea Marsh)

EDUARD CURRY AVE.

Chelsea Bridge Auto Scrapyard

Entrance Oak Barren

CHELSEA-

CHELSEA RD.

WEST SHORE EXPWY.

SOUTH AVE.

VICTORY BLVD.

S 46

Neck Creek

TRAVIS AVE.

N

W ✦ E

S

West Shore Plaza

Meredith Woods

Greenbelt Native Plant Center

MEREDITH AVE.

Arthur Kill

CANNON AVE.

440

William T. Davis Wildlife Refuge

0   2,000

scale in feet

© 2000, Mark Stein Studios

ⓡ = restrooms

Resource persons: Carl Alderson, Natural Resources Group, City of New York/Parks and Recreation; Catherine Barron, Treasurer, Mariners Marsh Conservancy; Robbin Bergfors, Natural Resources Group, City of New York/Parks and Recreation; and Scottie Jenkins

Goethals Pond

Nesting**   Spring Migration**   Fall Migration**   Winter
Route 278 service road north to the Travis Railroad and the Arlington Rail Yards to Forest Avenue and a Home Depot.

Goethals Pond is a relatively recent "natural" feature. The story begins well before the 1935 construction of Goethals Bridge, for which the preserve is named. In the 1880s, the Travis Rail Line split an unnamed creek, later known as Bridge Creek, and its associated meadows and marshes into an upper and lower system. Instead of railroad trestles like the ones built over Saw Mill Creek, an enormous earthen berm was constructed across the marshland, and two 5-foot-diameter concrete culvert pipes were installed to allow the ebb and flow of the creek. In 1892, Staten Island's famed naturalist, William T. Davis, made note in *Days Afield* that the rail line with trestle bridges, such as the one at Saw Mill Park, reshaped Staten Island's marshes and not always to their detriment. In contrast, the Bridge Creek culverts either collapsed, became choked with silt, or both, although they never entirely closed up; as a result, the upper system overflowed its banks, creating a shallow body of water, Goethals Pond. When the pond is full, it is no more than three feet deep. Saltwater intrusion is apparent by the brackish quality of the water and the occurrence of small patches of salt meadow hay. Although the pond level rises and falls, it is not related to the diurnal tides. Rainwater and runoff from nearby paved surfaces contribute to the inflow. Less is known about outflow through the restricted culverts. It is believed that most water escapes through evaporation. Between periods of rainfall, the pond becomes increasingly shallow. During extended dry periods, there are broad, open flats. *Phragmites* grow around the perimeter.

From 1992 through 1996, the New York State Department of Environmental Conservation (NYSDEC) took possession of 67 acres, including all of the pond and some surrounding forest land, to create the Goethals Pond Preservation Area.

Not until the 1970s did birders began to notice the pond's unique shorebird habitat and to make regular birding trips here. In the mid-1980s, migrating Black-necked Stilt were discovered. Goethals Pond made headlines in August 1992 when a single Roseate Spoonbill used the pond as its temporary haven, the northernmost site ever recorded for this species. By the time Roger Tory Peterson made the trek down from his Connecticut home, the bird had left for good. But Peterson was not disappointed; a Hudsonian Godwit and a Red Phalarope were among the day's sightings. Today a trip to the pond in late summer (during the August–September autumn migration) or in spring (when there is less activity) is sure to reveal Greater Yellowleg, Lesser Yellowleg, Solitary Sandpiper, Semipalmated Sandpiper, Least Sandpiper, both Short-billed and Long-billed dowitchers, Common Snipe, and Wilson's and Red-necked phalaropes. Among shorebirds, only Killdeer and Spotted Sandpiper are known to breed here.

Other warm season sightings include all of the heron species that nest on nearby islands; breeding waterfowl such as Gadwall and American Black Duck; breeding Red-tailed Hawk, Ring-necked Pheasant, Willow Flycatcher, Marsh Wren, Yellow Warbler, Common Yellowthroat, Eastern Towhee, Red-winged Blackbird, Baltimore Oriole, and American Goldfinch.

The number of species observed in recent winters has been disappointing. However, some species are dependable when the pond is not frozen. Among them are Canada Goose, Gadwall, American Black Duck, Mallard, Green-winged Teal, Hooded Merganser, numerous gulls, Great Horned Owl, and roosting Cooper's Hawk and Red-tailed Hawk.

When to Go

Some species of shorebirds seem to be constantly migrating throughout the spring and fall migration seasons. May is best for birdwatching spring migration. August and September are excellent for spotting shorebirds on the southward fall migration. Visiting Goethals Pond at any time could yield good results, but there are ways to improve your chances. Check the weather of the previous week or even month. Rain greatly affects the water level. Low water levels invite shorebirds. Mid-levels may encourage wading birds. If the water level is higher than one foot, watch for colonial waterbirds. They feed solo or in small numbers in the spring and become quite gregarious by the end of the breeding season.

Wintering waterfowl are numerous if the water is open and the level is high. Tides may play an indirect role as well. Shorebirds and some wading birds may relocate to the pond from nearby tidal marshes during daily high tides.

Optimal Weather Conditions

When the water level is low in winter, the pond ices over easily. The Winter Waterfowl Count in January has generally been disappointing. Rain greatly affects the water's depth, so it is best to consult last week's weather. Differing water heights will affect birds' use during migration.

Personal Safety

This field trip site is not dangerous unless you decide to walk out across the pond in hopes of retrieving a shopping cart from mid-pond. How did it get there? The mud is the sticky, sucking kind. Stay to the edges. There are three safe viewing locations: the Home Depot observation platform, the Sunset Gardens observation area, and Port Authority Goethals Bridge building viewing area, so do not test the water or the ice to see that special bird. Wear sunscreen, hat, and tick and mosquito repellent.

Cell phones are an added comfort. Just as a precaution, take a buddy or two. You can always stay within view of your car.

Getting There

FERRY to BUS: From Manhattan, take the Staten Island Ferry (718-815-2628) from the southern tip of Manhattan (South Ferry is the last stop on the 1 and 9 subway line) to St. George Terminal on Staten Island. From there take the S40 NYC Transit bus (D ramp) to the 24-hour Home Depot (with restrooms) on Forest Avenue. (Call 718-979-0600 for schedule information.) Walk along Forest Avenue to the left (west) side of Home Depot. The NYSDEC has provided an elevated viewing platform with good views overlooking the east end of the pond. The heavily fenced and gated parking area is sometimes closed.

Or continue on the bus or walk from Home Depot to the Port Authority Toll Plaza at Goethals Bridge. Walk to the rear of the parking lot to the right of the Administration Building. The west end of pond can be viewed from the tall evergreen trees on the embankment behind the parking lot.

Or you can walk a short way back toward the mobile home community of Sunset Gardens. Turn left down any street to the back of the neighborhood. There is a viewing trail at ground level at mid-pond to the right rear.

CAR: From Manhattan, take the Brooklyn Bridge over the East River and follow the signs to Brooklyn/Queens Expressway (Route 278) to the Verazzano-Narrows Bridge. Follow Route 278, which becomes the Staten Island Expressway, over the bridge. Take the Staten Island Expressway to the South Avenue exit. Stay on the service road through the South Avenue intersection. Continue on to the intersection of Forest Avenue. Turn right at the stop sign and proceed a short distance to the Home Depot parking lot. At the far left entrance is the NYSDEC-provided elevated viewing platform overlooking the pond. The fenced and gated parking area is sometimes closed. Or follow the bus route/walking directions to the other viewing locations.

From New Jersey, take the New Jersey Turnpike to Exit 13, Goethals Bridge/Route 278 East. After the toll plaza, take the first exit for Forest Avenue on the right. Continue down the ramp and make an immediate left onto Forest Avenue. Go under the expressway and proceed a few hundred yards to Home Depot. Follow the directions above.

For Additional Information on Goethals Pond

New York State Department of Environmental Conservation, 718-482-4900

Resource persons: Carl Alderson, Natural Resources Group, City of New York/Parks and Recreation; and Catherine Barron, Treasurer, Mariners Marsh Conservancy

Mariners Marsh Preserve/Arlington Marsh

Nesting** Spring Migration** Fall Migration*** Winter*
Arlington Rail Yards to the Arthur Kill, Western Avenue to Holland Avenue

Mariners Marsh Preserve

Located south of Richmond of Terrace, the 107-acre Mariners Marsh Preserve is an atypical urban park. Previously used for mining fill material and other industrial activities, the park is now a jumble of old fields, diverse forests with pin oak and sweetgum, swamps, marshes, wet meadows, dug-out ponds, trails, and concrete ruins. Although the area is not pristine, it provides very good birding opportunities. Mariners Marsh Preserve is managed by the City of New York/Parks and Recreation with the Mariners Marsh Conservancy, a nonprofit conservation group established specifically to create and look after this preserve. The Conservancy publishes a detailed map of the preserve.

North of Richmond Terrace to the west of the ball fields is Arlington Marsh, a 40-acre cordgrass saltmarsh owned by New York City Economic Development Corporation. When Arlington Marsh is not too wet, access can be had to the center of the marsh, to the Arthur Kill, and to some mudflats, where excellent birding opportunities are found. Together, Mariners Marsh Preserve and Arlington Marsh comprise a major metropolitan birding site. It should be noted that although

Mariners Marsh is parkland, the contiguous Arlington Marsh does not currently have protected status and may be subject to alteration and loss of natural habitat.

Mariners Marsh Preserve, a birding site for all seasons, is relatively easy to bird. Simply walk the mile-long trail, it provides the best access to all the habitats and is comfortable for walking and birding at whatever pace you wish. If you are primarily interested in migratory or nesting songbirds, proceed directly to the forested and brushy areas (pin oak and sweetgum forests and their edges). If you are interested in waterbirds, go to Monument and Downey Ponds, where Pied-billed Grebe, egrets, herons, Green-winged Teal, Canvasback, Virginia Rail, and Belted Kingfisher forage. Approach the ponds quietly so you will not disturb the birds' feeding. For snipe and woodcock (December through March in most years), walk the edge of the baseball fields.

Nesting species include American Bittern, Virginia Rail, Common Moorhen, American Woodcock, Willow Flycatcher, Marsh Wren, Wood Thrush (in the area), Yellow Warbler, Eastern Towhee, Swamp Sparrow, and Baltimore Oriole. Mariners Marsh Preserve is near Harbor Heron nest sites on islands in the Arthur Kill and Kill van Kull. These wading birds feed in the ponds and marsh.

Veery and Hermit Thrush are seen during spring migration, as are 16 species of warbler (look in the pin oak swamp). Eastern Bluebird show up in late autumn and can be present in winter. Chipping, Vesper, Lark, Savannah, Lincoln's, Swamp, and White-throated sparrows and others make stopovers from autumn into early winter.

During fall, hawk migrants, including Sharp-shinned Hawk, Coopers Hawk, Broad-winged Hawk, and Merlin, fly through. Northern Harrier, Red-tailed Hawk, American Kestrel, and Peregrine Falcon (nest on Goethals Bridge) are seen regularly. Barn Owl (nest in nearby bridges) and Great Horned Owl are seen occasionally.

Arlington Marsh

Arlington Marsh is the last tidal marsh on Staten Island's north shore. You can enter the marsh by following a pipeline right-of-way north to a small westward path through the *Phragmites*. It leads to mudflats that attract a diversity of birdlife. In spring and summer, egrets, herons, and ibis, flying in from their island refuge nests, forage in the mudflats along with a few sandpipers. Part of the attraction of the marsh for these wading birds are the thousands of fiddler crabs working the rich peat beds that have been built up over the last 5,000 years. Marsh Wren, Saltmarsh Sharp-tailed Sparrow (occasional nesters), and Swamp Sparrow can be found here also. From March through autumn, Double-crested Cormorant come and go along the Arthur Kill. Barn Swallow nest in the wrecks, where there are crevices and overhangs.

Fall through early spring, Pied-billed Grebe and dabbling and diving ducks, American Wigeon, Green-winged Teal, Canvasback, Ring-necked Duck, and Hooded Merganser feed in the saltmarsh.

Migrants, especially waterfowl and sparrows, linger into the winter because of the quality of the saltmarsh, thanks once again to the Clean Water Act of 1972. In the dead of winter, wildlife numbers decline at both Mariners Marsh and Arlington Marsh, although waterfowl, hawks, and White-throated and American Tree sparrows are present.

When to Go

During nesting season and late spring migration, early morning (6:00 to 10:30 AM) is best for observing singing birds. If you wish to witness woodcock flight/song displays, come just before sunset and be prepared to stay until 30 minutes after sunset. Try the edge of the larger fields and clearings. For birding the marsh across Richmond Terrace, low tide is best; that is when you will have access and when you may see species such as rails and shorebirds on the mudflats. Sparrows will be in the vegetation nearby.

Optimal Weather Conditions

For songbird migration weather, refer to Optimal Weather Conditions in chapter 3, "Manhattan/Central Park."

Personal Safety

The preserve and Arlington Marsh are isolated; you will not see many people. It is recommended that you bird with others.

Dog ticks and mosquitoes are present, as is poison ivy. The trails are usually damp and muddy. Wear boots and bring insect repellent.

The CSX Railroad (refer to the Saw Mill Creek Park above) at the south end of Mariners Marsh Preserve may become active again, which likely will restrict birding and hiking activity.

Getting There

FERRY to BUS: From Manhattan, take the Staten Island Ferry (718-815-2628) from the southern tip of Manhattan (South Ferry is the last stop on the 1 and 9 subway line) to St. George Terminal on Staten Island. From there take the S48 NYC Transit bus (C ramp) to the Holland Avenue stop closest to Richmond Terrace. (Call 718-979-0600 for schedule information.) Walk to the corner of Holland Avenue and Richmond Terrace and turn left. Walk approximately 100 yards to the Mariners Marsh Preserve gate on the left side of Richmond Terrace.

CAR: From Manhattan, take the Brooklyn Bridge over the East River and follow the signs to Brooklyn/Queens Expressway (Route 278) to the Verrazano-Narrows Bridge. Follow Route 278, which becomes the Staten Island Expressway, over the bridge. Take the Staten Island Expressway to the South Avenue exit. Go right on South Avenue and continue to Richmond Terrace. Go left until Mariners Marsh Preserve is on the left (the old baseball fields are obvious); the entrance has a gate.

From New Jersey, take the Staten Island Expressway to Forest Avenue (first exit). Continue to the stop sign and go left under the expressway; take the next left onto the service road. Go past Port Authority facilities and then right onto Western Avenue. At end of Western Avenue, make a right onto Richmond Terrace. Go 200–300 yards to the baseball fields; the Mariners Marsh Preserve gate is on the right.

For Additional Information on Mariners Marsh Preserve and Arlington Marsh

City of New York/Parks and Recreation, Staten Island Headquarters, 718-390-8000
Mariners Marsh Conservancy (leads tours), 718-448-7827
Staten Island Urban Park Rangers (leads tours), 718-667-6042
Resource person: Howard Snyder, President and founder, Mariners Marsh Conservancy, and former Vice President, New York City Audubon Society

Clove Lakes Park

Nesting   Spring Migration**   Fall Migration**   Winter
Victory Boulevard to Forest Avenue, Brookside Avenue, Slosson Avenue, Royal Oak Road to Clove Road

Clove Lakes Park was created in the 1930s by filling in marshland and damming up a brook that ran to the Kill van Kull. Almost half of its 198 acres are devoted to recreation, with ball fields, a playground (restrooms), and boating facilities. The other half comprises Brooks Pond, Martling Pond, Clove Lake, streams, and 100 acres of hilly woodlands. Paved pedestrian roads encircle the lakes, and an informal network of dirt trails winds through the woods. The City of New York/Parks and Recreation manages Clove Lakes Park. The park's name is derived from the Dutch word *kloven*, meaning "stream-cut valley." An elegant restaurant, the Lake Café, overlooking Clove Lake, serves lunch and dinner year round.

Birding is particularly good during spring migration, especially if you are looking for warblers. Spring mornings, it is possible to see 15–20 warbler species, including Cerulean, Prothonotary, Louisiana Waterthrush (early in spring), Kentucky, and Mourning (late in spring).

For observing spring (and fall) migrants, start at Martling Avenue, head east to the eastern edge of Martling Pond and then the hillsides until you reach Clove Lake. Cross over the large stone bridge and head back, working the western side of the stream and its brushy areas, an excellent place for Connecticut Warbler and Lincoln's Sparrow. If you have time, walk west to the vicinity of the fire tower; Indigo Bunting have been seen here in spring. When you reach Martling Avenue, cross over the concrete bridge, stopping for a moment to search the eye-level willows for migrants. Continue on and work the stream to Brooks Pond. Follow along the pond to another stream, working the banks and treetops, until you reach Forest Avenue. In spring, this woodland patch attracts large numbers of warblers. Cross the stream and work the other side on your way back to Martling Avenue.

Waterfowl can be seen during fall migration as well as spring migration. In summer, there are wading birds, and in winter, songbirds, waterfowl, and hawks.

When to Go

For observing spring songbirds, it is best to go from before dawn until around 10 A.M. From April 1 to June 1, with April 25 to May 25 being the peak time. Early morning is also the best time to view waterfowl. Shy species such as Wood Duck tend to be scared away by the crowds of people who show up later in the morning and afternoon.

For birding fall migrants, visit the park from mid–August to early November, early in the day through midmorning, when the birds are most active.

Optimal Weather Conditions

For songbird migration weather, refer to Optimal Weather Conditions in chapter 3, "Manhattan/Central Park."

Personal Safety

It is a good idea to bird with at least one other person, although the park is considered safe. Watch out for dog ticks, particularly in May and June, and poison ivy.

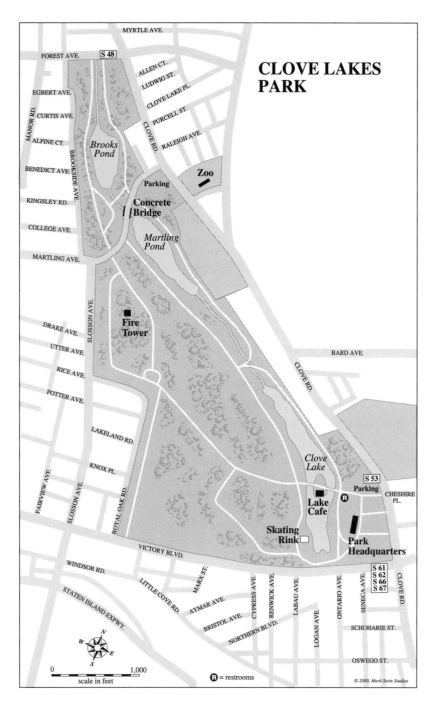

CLOVE LAKES PARK

MYRTLE AVE.

FOREST AVE. **S 48**

ALLEN CT.

LUDWIG ST.

CLOVE LAKE PL.

PURCELL ST.

RALEIGH AVE.

EGBERT AVE.

MANOR RD.

CURTIS AVE.

ALPINE CT.

BENEDICT AVE.

KINGSLEY RD.

COLLEGE AVE.

MARTLING AVE.

BROOKSIDE AVE.

CLOVE RD.

Brooks Pond

Zoo

Parking

Concrete Bridge

Martling Pond

SLOSSON AVE.

DRAKE AVE.

UTTER AVE.

RICE AVE.

POTTER AVE.

Fire Tower

BARD AVE.

CLOVE RD.

LAKELAND RD.

KNOX PL.

FAIRVIEW AVE.

SLOSSON AVE.

ROYAL OAK RD.

Clove Lake

S 53

Parking

CHESHIRE PL.

Ⓡ

Lake Cafe

Skating Rink □

Park Headquarters

VICTORY BLVD.

WINDSOR RD.

STATEN ISLAND EXPWY.

LITTLE COVE RD.

MARK ST.

AYMAR AVE.

BRISTOL AVE.

CYPRESS AVE.

RENWICK AVE.

NORTHERN BLVD.

LABAU AVE.

LOGAN AVE.

ONTARIO AVE.

SENECA AVE.

CLOVE RD.

S 61
S 62
S 66
S 67

SCHOHARIE ST.

OSWEGO ST.

N
W   E
S

0 ———————— 1,000
scale in feet

Ⓡ = restrooms

© 2000, Mark Stein Studios

Getting There

FERRY to BUS: From Manhattan, take the Staten Island Ferry (718-815-2628) from the southern tip of Manhattan (South Ferry is the last stop on the 1 and 9 subway line) to St. George Terminal on Staten Island. From there take S61, S62, S66, or S67 NYC Transit bus (A ramp) to Victory Boulevard. (Call 718-979-0600 for schedule information.) Ask the driver to let you off at the ice skating rink. From here, walk into the park. Or take one of these buses to Slosson Avenue and walk the ¾ mile to Martling Avenue, which cuts through the park. Or take the S48 NYC Transit bus (C ramp) to Forest Avenue and Clove Road.

BUS: From Bay Ridge, Brooklyn, take S53 from 95th Street and 4th Avenue (the N and R subway stop) to the Cloves Lake stop at Cheshire Place.

CAR: From Manhattan, take the Brooklyn Bridge over the East River and follow the signs to Brooklyn/Queens Expressway (Route 278) to the Verrazano-Narrows Bridge. Follow Route 278, which becomes the Staten Island Expressway, over the bridge. Take the Clove Road exit. Stay on the service road until you reach Clove Road. Take a right on Clove Road and follow it through three traffic-light intersections. On the left, opposite Cheshire Place, turn into the parking lot (no charge). The lot is often jammed. Or take the Slosson exit off of Route 278. Make a right turn onto Slosson Avenue. Go approximately 1 mile to Martling Avenue. Turn right and park.

For Additional Information on Clove Lakes Park

City of New York/Parks and Recreation, Staten Island Headquarters (located at Cloves Lakes Park, 718-390-8000

Staten Island Institute of Arts and Sciences, Section of Natural Science Section (lead tours), 718-727-1135

Staten Island Urban Park Rangers (lead tours), 718-667-6042

Resource persons: Howie Fischer; and Edward W. Johnson, Curator of Science, Staten Island Institute of Arts and Sciences

Chapter Six

Nassau County, Long Island

Harlequin Duck

Nassau County, a densely populated area classified as "metropolitan" by the United States Census Bureau, is located due east of New York City. The Atlantic Ocean lies to the south and Long Island Sound to the north. Despite encroaching development, the ocean, bays, beaches, and salt-marshes remain healthy habitats for marine and land birds. Extraordinary birding experiences can be found on the Atlantic Ocean side at Jones Beach State Park and Point Lookout. Inland of these barrier beaches lies Hempstead Lake State Park, one of Long Island's important places for wintering waterfowl. The barrier beaches and Hempstead Lake have been designated Important Bird Areas by the National Audubon Society, which emphasizes their significance for avian species.

Jones Beach State Park
Nesting**   Fall Migration***   Spring Migration*   Winter***

Jones Beach, 2,400 acres managed mainly by the New York State Office of Parks, Recreation, and Historic Preservation, is recognized as one of the best birding areas in the United States. Following the vision of Robert Moses in its design, the park is a haven for millions of people from the end of May to the beginning of September (and an admission fee is charged from Memorial Day to Labor Day). They come to enjoy one of the finest beaches in the world. For the rest of the year, the park is a magnet for people looking for open space, the beauty of the natural world, and birds. Jones Beach should be high on a list for all birders at all times. Even in midsummer, when crowds swarm to the beach, the West End offers good birdng. In fall, the sightings of migratory raptors and songbirds are renowned, and the adjoining sea offers great sightings of gannets and scoters. Bring your scope, and you are sure to have a productive excursion.

The Jones Beach experience starts at the southern portion of the Meadowbrook Parkway, as you leave the body of Long Island and start the 3-mile drive across the causeway to the beach. A vast, fecund saltmarsh fills much of the area between the "mainland" and the great barrier island, which protects the marsh from the Atlantic. The beauty and significance of the marsh eluded most Americans until late in the twentieth century, when people began to understand that its flat, monotonous vegetation produced more food per acre than the most fertile farmland. Much of the food produced in the marsh moves into the surrounding open water and eventually to the ocean. The saltmarsh is the source of food for fish and invertebrates that attract the birds we observe in the marsh, in the waterways, and on the beaches.

At the end of the causeway, Jones Beach State Park extends east and west for 6½ miles. While many of the East Coast and Gulf of Mexico Coast barrier islands are degraded by extensive development and are exposed to erosion, Jones Beach maintains its beauty and its magnificent dune fields through the management practices of New York State Office of Parks. Each year the park accommodates 6–7 million people. Most come in the summer to enjoy the beach; others come during the less crowded months to soak up the salt air and to walk among the dunes.

The dunes ripple off to the ocean and bay sides of the parkways (Bay Drive and Ocean Parkway). They are held in place by beach grass and other seaside plants. The more sheltered dunes grow beach heather (*Hudsonia*), seaside goldenrod, and bayberry. Toward the east end of the park, some of the dune areas have evolved into extensive dense vegetative masses that include cherries and junipers. This vegetation invites insects and a variety of mammals, including meadow voles, rabbits, and foxes.

The parkways are defined by substantial plantings of Japanese black pine (now dying and soon to be replaced with native plantings) and grassy borders, both of which attract birds. Along these parkways (which have become a major commuter route) are public parking areas and roadways to special destinations such as the park police headquarters, the Coast Guard Station, the boardwalk, and the Boardwalk Restaurant and Terrace.

The great excitement of Jones Beach lies in the variety of birds to be found. It is a model migrant trap with a huge saltmarsh on one side and the ocean on the other. Land birds converge in enormous numbers, having arrived at the edge of a landmass with only a narrow strip of suitable habitat. Gulls, terns, waders, and waterfowl are lured by tidal flats and by the food-rich confluence of the bay and the ocean. Shorebirds feed over a wide area at low tide and crowd into the few suitable roosts at high tide. Experienced birders combine tide schedules with traditional activity patterns of migrant land birds to determine where and when the biggest and best concentrations of birds will occur. Of course, there is also the element of luck.

Try the following for a typical fall or winter car trip. As you travel south across the causeway (Meadowbrook Parkway), you will get your first impression of avian possibilities. The lawns on either side of the roads are good feeding areas for migrating Northern Flicker and American Robin. The thickets bordering the saltmarshes provide good feeding sites for arboreal migrants. Since you may not stop here to look, be satisfied that it is only a preview.

At the end of the Meadowbrook Parkway, go west (right) on Bay Drive toward the west end of Jones Beach State Park. Watch for more doves, flickers, and robins between the road and the Japanese black pines and on the median strip. There are often Canada Goose grazing. Once in a while a Snow Goose joins in, and if there are puddles, Mallard, teals and Northern Pintail can be seen here.

Pull into the Coast Guard Station (with restrooms) area on the right, a few hundred yards short of West End Field 2 parking lot (on the left). Turn right to park in the small public parking area near the large shelter. To the northeast in the cove is an island (Short Beach) and beach favored by all manner of shorebirds and gulls at high tide; they are often joined by cormorants (whose number may include a Great Cormorant or two), thousands of Brant (in winter), and a few ducks.

Leave the cove's edge and go south on the walk across the lawn and the parkway. Check the tree line on the north side of West End Field 1 parking lot for fall and winter migrants.

Return to the small parking lot and this time walk west, following the line of large Japanese black pines, toward the Coast Guard Station and Jones Inlet. For many fall songbird migrants, this is the last suitable habitat at the western end of the island, making the area an unusually rich birding corner. Most of the regular migrants are to be expected, along with an occasional Western Kingbird, Clay-colored Sparrow, Dickcissel, and other surprises.

Beyond the cluster of black pines is a trail leading west into a magnificent dune field and to Jones Inlet and the ocean. The trip out to the inlet and back around the Coast Guard Station parking lot takes more than an hour but is worth the time. Birding the dunes is not so predictable as birding the pines. The dune field is where Northern Harrier hunt and into which the Sharp-shinned Hawk and Merlin are likely to chase their prey. The area is also a haven for Eastern Meadowlark, Savannah Sparrow, and other grassland birds. In winter, there are occasional Short-eared Owl, Horned Lark, and flocks of Snow Bunting.

The trail from the Coast Guard Station is a favorite for people on their way to fish, so it goes directly to the bay's edge. A walk around the riprap and the beach of the inlet leads finally to the boulders of the long jetty, which was built to protect Jones Inlet from natural breakthroughs by the Atlantic Ocean. There is usually a lot of bird activity in the inlet. (Much of this activity is better observed from the opposite shore. See the section on Point Lookout below.) Look for loons, grebes, cormorants, gulls, and terns, and on the beach, for occasional shorebirds. In winter, survey the jetty for Purple Sandpiper. You can also get a passing look at westbound migrants as they move on from Jones Beach.

It is possible to return to West End Field 2 parking lot and thence back to the Coast Guard Station by either walking back east across the dune field or continuing to the mouth of Jones Inlet and then turning east along the Atlantic Ocean beach (Short Beach) and back to West End Field 2 from the ocean front. The latter route, longer and sandier, offers the chance to see more sandpipers, gulls, and terns as well as gannets, occasionally jaegers (mostly Parasitic), and offshore migrants such as loons (both Red-throated and Common), Horned Grebe, and scoters (all three species) in October and November.

Once back in West End Field 2, bird the clumps of Japanese black pines on the way back to the Coast Guard Station parking lot.

The central area of the park is the next stop. Drive east on Ocean Parkway past the traffic circle and the magnificent Water Tower and into Parking Field 6 on the right. Park at the western end and proceed to the 1½-mile-long boardwalk to scan the gulls on the beach and ocean. There are restrooms and food available here. Be certain to search the top of the Water Tower's east face. You will see whitewash at key places (even if you do not see the birds) that are the favorite roosts for local Peregrine Falcon (see chap. 3, "Manhattan/Riverside Park" for more information about these raptors). The plantings around the parking fields and the buildings attract migrants and resident birds. There is a tunnel under Ocean Parkway to Zach's Bay. In the fall, shorebirds accumulate in the bay, and in winter, there are likely to be ducks worth seeing.

Theodore Roosevelt Nature Center

The Theodore Roosevelt Nature Center, located at West End Field 1 parking lot, is a recent addition to Jones Beach State Park. (The expansive paved area is currently being removed.) The center includes an indoor museum and outdoor displays, both of which provide information about the flora and fauna of the barrier beach ecosystem. Stop in to check the nature log, where daily bird sightings are recorded, and add your own observations.

Special Notes

Jones Beach State Park provides ample parking in Fields, 2, 4, 5, 6, and 10 and West End Field 2, but only 4, 6, and 10 and West End 2 are available off season, that is, after Labor Day to Memorial Day. Field 10, known as the Fishing Station, permits fine views of East Bay. Scan the area thoroughly for harbor seals, which winter here.

During Piping Plover (endangered species) and Least Tern nesting season (April–September), the dunes are out of bounds. Obey the signs by staying well out of the nesting areas.

Optimal Weather Conditions

Northwest winds favor fall bird migration, whereas warm southwest winds are best for spring migration. Great ocean sightings often coincide with nasty, rainy conditions and strong east winds. Be prepared and dress warmly. Early morning birding is best. Fall migrant land birds (robins, waxwings, sparrows, finches, blackbirds, etc.) fly in large quantities from sunrise to 8:30 AM in October, while raptors tend to pass through beginning around 9:00 AM from mid-September throughout October. Flickers and swallows can be seen all day long.

Personal Safety

Jones Beach State Park is patrolled periodically by the police, making it quite safe. Nevertheless, it is always a good idea to bird with others. Mosquitoes can be bothersome in the warm months. Dog ticks are common.

Getting There

CAR: From Westchester, the Bronx, Manhattan, and northern Queens, take the Triboro Bridge to Grand Central Parkway east to Meadowbrook Parkway south or the Throgs Neck Bridge to Whitestone Bridge to Grant Central Parkway east to Meadowbrook Parkway south to Jones Beach.

From Brooklyn and southern Queens, take the Shore/Belt Parkway to the Southern State Parkway east to Meadowbrook Parkway south to Jones Beach.

For Additional Information on Jones Beach State Park

Jones Beach State Park, 516-785-1600
New York City Audubon Society (leads tours), 212-691-7483, and www.nycaudubon.org

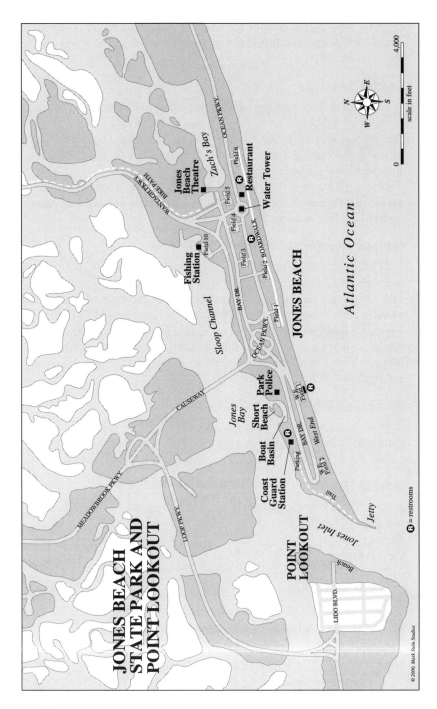

JONES BEACH
STATE PARK AND
POINT LOOKOUT

MEADOWBROOK PKWY.

LOOP PKWY.

CAUSEWAY

Sloop Channel

Jones Bay

BAY DR.

WANTAGH PKWY.

BIKE PATH

Zach's Bay

OCEAN PKWY.

Jones Beach
Theatre

Field 6

Field 5

Fishing
Station

Field 10

Field 4

Restaurant

Water Tower

Field 3

Field 2

BOARDWALK

®

JONES BEACH

Field 1

OCEAN PKWY.

Park
Police

Short
Beach

®

W.E.
Field 1

®

Boat
Basin

®

Parking

Coast
Guard
Station

BAY DR.

West End

W.E.
Field 2

Trail

Atlantic Ocean

POINT
LOOKOUT

Jones Inlet

Jetty

Beach

LIDO BLVD.

® = restrooms

© 2000, Mark Stein Studios

N
W   E
S

0   4,000
scale in feet

New York State Office of Parks, Recreation, and Historic Preservation,
Long Island Regional Office, 516-669-1000 and www.nysparks
Theodore Roosevelt Nature Center, Jones Beach State Park,
516-679-7254
Resource persons: Annie McIntyre, environmental educator,
Theodore Roosevelt Nature Center, Jones Beach State Park; Peter
Rhoades Mott, Board of Directors and former President, New York City
Audubon Society; and Herb Roth, North Shore Audubon Society

Point Lookout

Nesting   Fall Migration**   Spring Migration*   Winter**

Point Lookout is located on the western side of Jones Inlet; Jones Beach
State Park is on the eastern side. The inlet attracts large numbers and a
variety of grebes, sea ducks, and gulls during the late autumn and winter
months and can be viewed easily from Point Lookout. For birders wish-
ing to see Harlequin Duck, one of the most resplendent seabirds to be
found in out area, Point Lookout is the place. Bring a scope.

The best viewing of the late fall/winter gull spectacles is at the water's
edge of Point Lookout's town beach. Outgoing tides and an emergent
sand bar regularly attract a horde of gulls representing more species than
can be seen in any other place in the metropolitan area. Sharp-eyed lar-
iphiles sometimes find Little Gull, and on two recent occasions they
found the coveted Ross's Gull. Double-crested and Great cormorants,
Brant, and American Black Duck are also found.

Loons, grebes, and diving ducks feed in the inlet. Harlequin Duck are
also regular visitors and can be seen sleeping and preening on the jetties
along the oceanfront beach. King and Common eiders and occasional
shorebirds, including Purple Sandpiper, are found on the jetties.

To reach the oceanfront beach, walk to the right through a small dune
field along the inlet until you reach houses at the end of the field and the
street. Walk south on the street and through the gates onto the town
beach. Out-of-town birders are permitted on the municipal beach during
winter.

Getting There

Take the Meadowbrook State Parkway to Loop Parkway. (The loop
crosses saltmarsh and waterway, where there is a lot to see.) At the traffic
light, turn left onto Lido Boulevard, obeying the 15 mph speed limit, and
go through the town of Point Lookout. Continue almost to the end. When
you reach the post office, look for a parking spot on the street. Most side
streets are for resident parking only. Please observe the parking restric-

tions. After parking, walk east on Lido Boulevard to its end and then go through the town park pedestrian gate. Proceed to Jones Inlet.

For Additional Information on Point Lookout

New York City Audubon Society (leads tours), 212-691-7483 and www.nycaudubon.org
Resource person: Peter Rhoades Mott, Board of Directors and former President, New York City Audubon Society

Hempstead Lake State Park

Nesting*   Fall Migration**   Spring Migration***   Winter***

Hempstead Lake State Park covers 903 acres of forest, ponds (East, West, and South), Hempstead Lake, and marshes surrounded by suburban homes and busy roads. The park was originally part of the Brooklyn water supply system. In 1925, the bodies of water and surrounding open lands were given over to the New York State Office of Parks, Recreation, and Historic Preservation. Southern State Parkway divides the park into two distinct areas; the northern section, which has limited access, and the southern section, which has numerous recreational facilities such as picnic areas, bridle paths, tennis courts, playgrounds, archery range, ball fields, and hiking/nature trails. The main feature is 1-mile-long, ½-mile-wide Hempstead Lake with its surrounding deciduous forest (in the southern section). It is the lake and forest that attract the birds and the people who watch them. Affirming its significant avian habitat, the National Audubon Society designated Hempstead Lake State Park a New York State Important Bird Area in 1998.

Walking the trails through the woodlands provides excellent birdwatching opportunities during winter and spring migration. The park supports flycatchers, vireos, swallows, warblers, and other migrants passing through. In winter, you can expect to see woodpeckers, chickadees, nuthatches, sparrows, cardinals, and other winter visitors. Sharp-shinned and Cooper's hawks as well as Peregrine Falcon can be seen hunting here. Eastern Bluebird and Rusty Blackbird visit the lake, and more than once, Bald Eagle were sighted here.

Hempstead Lake is an important wintering location for waterfowl. The population begins to build in late August and peaks in winter, reaching several thousand birds. The lake is an excellent location to see Common Merganser. Other species that can be seen are Gadwall, American Wigeon, American Black Duck, Mallard, Northern Shoveler, Northern Pintail, Canvasback, Lesser Scaup, Hooded Merganser, and Ruddy Duck.

Seventeen species of shorebird have been seen at the northern end of the lake. They are most plentiful when the water level drops. Snipe can be observed in the marshy area in the northeast corner. In summer, Great and Snowy egrets stalk along the shore. Great Blue Heron arrive to scan the shallows in the fall and winter. In late summer, large numbers of Common and Forster's terns feed and bathe in the lake.

Begin birdwatching at either Parking Lot 1 (with restrooms) or Parking Lot 3 (with restrooms). The route is circular and passes both parking lots, allowing birdwatchers to start at either location. From Parking Lot 1, proceed south through a picnic area, toward the tennis courts. The picnic area is shaded by oak trees, an ideal habitat for woodland birds. South of the tennis courts is another picnic area bordered to the west by Schodack Pond. Although this pond is sometimes dry, Wood Duck are found here, especially in the trees at the pond's north end. Take the path that follows the pond's shoreline to the south toward South Pond. Mallard can be seen on this pond but rarely any other species. Follow the shoreline, turning north, and you pass McDonald Pond. Continue north a short distance to the dam, crossing East Lake Road. Climb a small hill to the top of the dam. From the top of the dam you can see numerous waterfowl on Hempstead Lake. This is an excellent location to set up a scope.

Proceed west along the dam to an access point. The lake was once a reservoir and is surrounded by a chain-link fence. Opposite Parking Lots 1 and 3 are openings in the fence to provide access to the lake. Follow the lakeshore, scanning the lake and the woods. Exit the lake at the access point opposite Parking Lot 1. If you are parked in Lot 3, turn south and walk through the picnic area back to your car.

Birders also walk along East Lake Road. The shoulder along this roadway is wide, allowing for pedestrians, but beware—it is an active thoroughfare, with autos, bicyclists, in-line skaters, and joggers competing for the same space.

It is also possible to bird north of the Southern State Parkway at East and West Ponds. The ponds are usually dry and thus not worth the trip. Many more species are seen in the park south of Southern State Parkway. If you wish to investigate this area, cross the traffic circles at either Eagle Avenue or Peninsula Boulevard. Be careful making these crossings.

Personal Safety

Do not bird alone in Hempstead Lake State Park. It is best to bird in a group. Hiking is prohibited on the bridle paths.

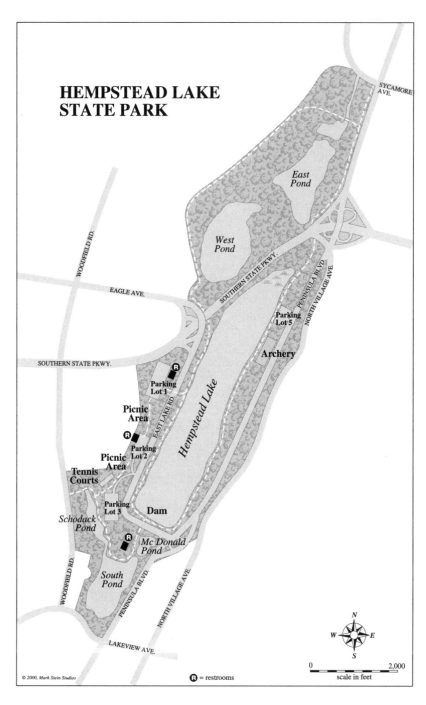

HEMPSTEAD LAKE
STATE PARK

SYCAMORE AVE.

East Pond

West Pond

WOODFIELD RD.

SOUTHERN STATE PKWY.

EAGLE AVE.

PENINSULA BLVD.

NORTH VILLAGE AVE.

Parking Lot 5

SOUTHERN STATE PKWY.

Archery

Ⓡ Parking Lot 1

EAST LAKE RD.

Hempstead Lake

Picnic Area

Ⓡ Parking Lot 2

Picnic Area

Tennis Courts

Parking Lot 3

Dam

Schodack Pond

Ⓡ *Mc Donald Pond*

WOODFIELD RD.

South Pond

PENINSULA BLVD.

NORTH VILLAGE AVE.

LAKEVIEW AVE.

N
W ✦ E
S

© 2000, Mark Stein Studios

Ⓡ = restrooms

0 ————— 2,000
scale in feet

Getting There

CAR: From Brooklyn and southern Queens, take the Shore/Belt Parkway to the Southern Parkway east to Exit 18 South. Take East Lake Road into Hempstead Lake State Park. Turn right into Parking Lot 1 or continue south to Parking Lot 3.

From Westchester, the Bronx, and northern Queens, take the Throgs Neck Bridge or Whitestone Bridge to the Cross Island Parkway. Then take Southern State Parkway east to Exit 18 South. Follow the directions above.

From Manhattan and the Bronx, take the Triboro Bridge to Grand Central Parkway east to the Southern State Parkway east to Exit 18 South. Follow the directions above.

For additional Information on Hempstead Lake State Park

Hempstead Lake State Park, 516-766-1029
New York State Office of Parks, Recreation, and Historic Preservation, Long Island Regional Office, 516-669-1000 and www.nysparks
Resource person: Tom Torma, South Shore Audubon

Chapter Seven

Westchester County, New York

Beyond the northern border of the Bronx are several good birding locations that are only a short ride from New York City. Even the most insular urbanites will be tempted by these birding sites.

The four recommended sites are Westchester County parks that attract large numbers of birds in all seasons. The Edith G. Read Wildlife Sanctuary and the Marshlands Conservancy, both in Rye, provide excellent opportunities to see migrating and wintering waterfowl (on Long Island Sound), nesting and migrating marsh birds, and migrating songbirds and hawks. Lenoir Preserve and Sprain Ridge Park, two inland sanctuaries with forest, brushland, and open fields, are advantageous sites for observing nesting songbirds, migrating hawks, and wintering birds (at feeders). Local Audubon chapters (see Appendix 1, "Metropolitan Birding Resources") offer field trips to these parks. The parks themselves offer numerous nature programs.

These Westchester sites are easily accessible by car from New York City. The Lenoir Preserve can be reached by public transportation.

Edith G. Read Wildlife Sanctuary at Playland Park, Rye

Nesting*   Spring Migration**   Fall Migration**   Winter***

Located on the north shore of Long Island Sound (not far from the Connecticut border), the Edith G. Read Wildlife Sanctuary, managed by the Westchester County Department of Parks, Recreation, and Conservation and designated an Important Bird Area, offers wonderful opportunities to bird in a variety of habitat. The sanctuary comprises 170 acres of uplands, wetlands, lawns, informal gardens, intertidal zone (rocky and sandy), an 80-acre lake, a ½ mile of shoreline, and open water where 290 species have been recorded. The sanctuary is part of Playland Park (with restrooms), an immense 273-acre amusement park complete with roller coasters, merry-go-rounds, an ice-skating rink, and a bathing beach. (Adjacent to the beach, the rehabilitated boardwalk, which juts out into the Sound, provides a good spot for observing sea ducks and gulls.)

Although some songbirds (Yellow Warbler) and waterbirds nest in the area, the site is known primarily for autumn and spring migrants and winter birds. During late spring and summer, Great and Snowy egrets and Black-crowned Night-Heron may be seen foraging around the edges of Playland Lake and in the intertidal areas along Long Island Sound. Listen for the night-heron's hoarse "wok" call. These waders feed at dusk and before dawn (and through the night). In summer you may also see American Oystercatcher, gulls, terns (mostly Common Tern), and Black Skimmer feeding along the shore. Bring a scope to observe them closely.

Autumn hawkwatching during migration periods is very rewarding here. From mid-September through mid-October, the procession of hawks includes Osprey, Northern Harrier, Sharp-shinned, Cooper's, Broad-winged, and Red-tailed hawks, American Kestrel, and even Merlin and Peregrine Falcon. These raptors are often flying at low altitudes, affording excellent views. On some fall days, Osprey (also known as fish hawks) will hover over Playland Lake. More often they feed over the Sound, especially if menhaden (fish of the herring family) are abundant. Watching Osprey catch a large menhaden is exhilarating. Plunging from 50 feet or more above the water and making a terrific splash as it hits the surface feet first, the bird grabs the slippery fish with its talons, positioning the prey so it creates the least amount of wind resistance, and then flies off to a perch to devour the meal. Sometimes you may see these hawks in migration carrying their catch.

After mid-October and into November, Northern Harrier, Red-shouldered and Red-tailed hawks, and an occasional Bald Eagle are seen flying parallel to the shoreline.

From September to early November, in the forested patches of the sanctuary and around Playland Lake, migrating songbirds (flycatchers, vireos, and warblers) may be abundant, especially after a cold front has passed through. Investigate the edges of the brush and open fields for sparrow species. Check also the mudflats at low tide for migratory shorebirds, although this area is not known as an important shorebird stopover.

During autumn (especially after October 15) and into winter, waterfowl and other waterbirds may be numerous. Watch from anywhere along the shoreline of the Sound, including the boardwalk at Rye Beach. Greater Scaup can be numerous, with more than 5,000 (sometimes as many as 10,000) gathered together. You may also see Red-throated and Common loons, scoters, Bufflehead, and Red-breasted Merganser.

After Labor Day, the row boats are hauled from Playland Lake, so there is no water activity here to disturb bird populations. You are likely to see Pied-billed Grebe, American Wigeon, American Black Duck, Canvasback, and Hooded Merganser feeding in the lake. Foraging around the lake's edges, you may see Great Blue Heron and a late-to-leave Black-crowned Night-Heron or two. Each evening, just after sunset, the entire raft of ducks takes flight from Playland Lake to forage on the open waters of the Sound. With orange-red highlights of the setting winter sun as a backdrop, the sight and sound of these multitudes on the wing are breathtaking.

Through the winter, sparrows are found around the grassy areas because they use the brush as a cover of safety. Hawks, usually Red-tailed (but sometimes Red-shouldered), can be seen on most days as they hunt over the open areas. Sharp-shinned and Cooper's hawks also frequent the park, usually looking for the small birds mentioned above. Check the feeding stations on the northeast side of the Visitor Center (with restrooms) for resident and wintering species.

Off the shore in winter, you may see loons, Horned Grebe, Brant, scaup, Oldsquaw (the Read Sanctuary logo), Bufflehead, and Red-breasted Merganser. In some years, Red-necked Grebe have been seen, but it is very rare. Check the shore for Ruddy Turnstone, Purple Sandpiper, and other shorebirds. If the lake is not frozen, scan it with your scope for the wintering ducks.

Visitor Center

The Visitor Center is staffed Wednesday through Sunday, 10:00 A.M. to 4:00 P.M., where brochures, bird lists, and maps are available. A list of current bird sightings is posted outside the building.

Personal Safety

The park police patrol the area regularly. All the same, it is best to bird with others. In season there may be dog and deer ticks and, infrequently, mosquitoes. There is some poison ivy. The winds coming off Long Island Sound and across the lake can be bitter, so dress warmly.

Getting There

CAR: Take I-95 (New England Thruway) north to Exit 19. Follow signs to Playland Parkway. Take Playland Parkway about 1½ miles into Playland Park. Go through the Playland gates and follow signs to the

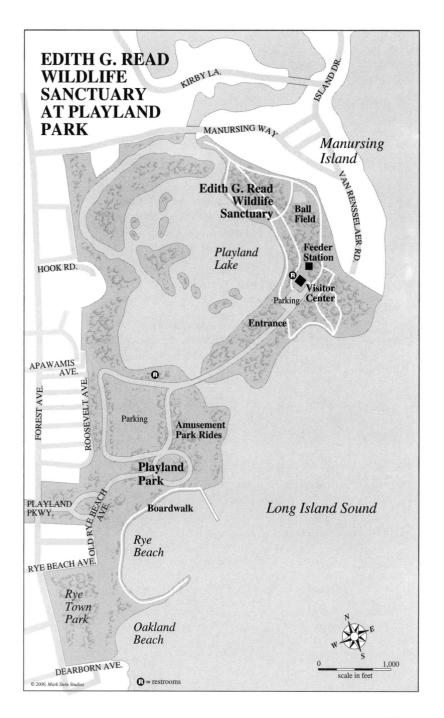

EDITH G. READ WILDLIFE SANCTUARY AT PLAYLAND PARK

KIRBY LA.

ISLAND DR.

MANURSING WAY

Manursing Island

Edith G. Read Wildlife Sanctuary

Ball Field

VAN RENSSELAER RD.

Playland Lake

Feeder Station

HOOK RD.

Ⓡ

◆ **Visitor Center**

Parking

Entrance

APAWAMIS AVE.

FOREST AVE.

ROOSEVELT AVE.

Ⓡ

Parking

Amusement Park Rides

Playland Park

PLAYLAND PKWY.

OLD RYE BEACH AVE.

Boardwalk

Long Island Sound

Rye Beach

RYE BEACH AVE.

Rye Town Park

Oakland Beach

N E W S

0   1,000
scale in feet

DEARBORN AVE.

© 2000, Mark Stein Studios

Ⓡ = restrooms

147

Read Sanctuary, which is located on Manursing Island beyond the amusement park complex. Parking is permitted at the Visitor Center.

TRAIN: Take Metro-North (800-METRO-NORTH or 212-532-4900) from Grand Central Station in Manhattan to the Rye station. Taxis are available that will take you to Playland Park. May through Labor Day, the Bee-line 75 bus shuttles between the Rye station and the park. Call 914-682-2020 for schedule information.

For Additional Information about the Edith G. Read Wildlife Sanctuary at Playland Park

Read Wildlife Sanctuary (leads tours), 914-967-8720
Westchester County Department of Parks, Recreation, and Conservation, 914-242-PARKS and www.westchestergov.com
Resource person: Jeff Main, Curator, Read Wildlife Sanctuary

Marshlands Conservancy, Rye

Nesting**   Spring Migration**   Fall Migration***   Winter***

A short distance from the Read Sanctuary is Marshlands Conservancy, another delightful Westchester County Department of Parks, Recreation, and Conservation park that is a true wildlife sanctuary, not recreational parkland. Marshlands is designated a New York State Important Bird Area (290 species recorded) mainly because of its extensive and healthy saltmarsh habitat. Aside from the saltmarsh, Marshlands Conservancy comprises upland forest, a large, annually mowed meadow, a woodland pond, and ¼ mile of frontage along Milton Harbor (in Long Island Sound), totaling 160 acres.

Start at the Marshlands Conservancy headquarters building (with restrooms, saltwater aquaria, and changing exhibits) and follow the trail along the meadow and down a hill to the causeway that is bordered by the saltmarsh. The trail circles Marie's Neck, a tidal island along the shore of Milton Harbor. Roundtrip on this trail is 1½ miles.

The *Spartina alterniflora* saltmarsh hosts nesting populations of Clapper Rail, Marsh Wren, and Saltmarsh Sharp-tailed Sparrow. From spring through autumn, Great Blue Heron, Great and Snowy egrets, and Black-crowned Night-Heron are readily seen feeding in the marsh. In August, dozens of egrets are seen roosting in the trees of the saltmarsh islands. Osprey have nested successfully here on a platform since 1999.

Great Horned Owl have nested at Marshlands since 1980 and can be found roosting year round. The uplands also support nesting American Woodcock, Yellow-breasted Chat, and Orchard Oriole.

In March, New York City Audubon runs special late afternoon field trips to Marshlands to watch woodcock (sometimes known as timber-doodles) performing their courtship ritual in the open meadow. The Parks Department offers free guided natural history walks every weekend of the year, including a series of six birdwalks during spring migration.

Autumn and spring migration of songbirds at Marshlands can be spectacular. In spring, the larger trees, especially the oaks, attract numerous warblers. Thirty species of warbler have been seen, along with many other species such as vireos, gnatcatchers, thrushes, tanagers, sparrows, and orioles. The best times are between May 1 and 25, with the peak coming in the middle of this period. The tidal flats in and at the edge of the salt-marsh attract migratory shorebirds, and the forests and thickets attract migratory owls (especially in autumn). Rarities show up at Marshlands periodically and have included White Ibis, Wood Sandpiper, and Yellow-headed Blackbird.

In autumn and winter, the migrating waterbirds are similar to those seen on the open water at the Read Sanctuary. The best place to view these species is from the shore of Milton Harbor. Bring a scope to scan the waters.

During fall migration, superb hawk flights can be seen from the top of the meadow. In winter, hawks (the same species as at the Read Sanctuary) hunt the edge of the marsh and upland fields, where various winter sparrows can be found.

Personal Safety

There are no safety concerns at Marshlands. In season, you may want insect repellent for the mosquitoes and no-see-ums. Stay on the trails to avoid dog and deer ticks.

Getting There

CAR: Take I-95 north to the Playland Parkway, Exit 19. Get off the ramp and take the first right. At the T, make a left, and then make a right at the next T onto Old Boston Post Road, which turns into Route 1 (Boston Post Road). Proceed 1 mile to the Conservancy entrance on the left, just past the Rye golf club.

TRAIN: Take Metro–North/New Haven line (800-METRO-NORTH or 212-532-4900) from Grand Central Station in Manhattan to the Harrison station. Then take a taxi (914-835-3400) to the Marshlands Conservancy in Rye.

If you wish to walk the 1 mile to the Conservancy, leave the train sta-

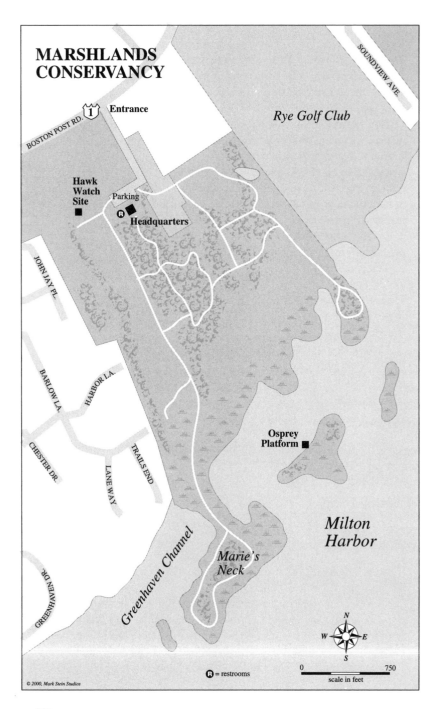

MARSHLANDS CONSERVANCY

Entrance

BOSTON POST RD.

Rye Golf Club

SOUNDVIEW AVE.

Hawk
Watch
Site ■

Parking

Ⓡ ■ Headquarters

JOHN JAY PL.

BARLOW LA.

HARBOR LA.

CHESTER DR.

TRAILS END

LANE WAY

GREENHAVEN DR.

Osprey
Platform ■

Milton
Harbor

Greenhaven Channel

Marie's
Neck

N
W   E
S

Ⓡ = restrooms

0   750
scale in feet

© 2000, Mark Stein Studios

tion by walking left on Halstead Avenue, right on Oakland (just beyond the shopping center), and then left on Park, following it to Route 1 (Boston Post Road). Cross Route 1 and walk right until you see the brown and yellow Marshlands Conservancy sign on the left.

For Additional Information on Marshlands Conservancy

Marshlands Conservancy (leads tours), 914-835-4466
New York City Audubon Society (leads tours), 212-691-7483 and www.nycaudubon.org
Westchester County Department of Parks, Recreation, and Conservation 914-242-PARKS and www.westchestergov.com
Resource persons: Alison Beall, Curator, Marshlands Conservancy; and Thomas W. Burke, Greenwich Audubon Society

Lenoir Preserve, Yonkers

Nesting   Spring Migration**   Fall Migration**   Winter*

With a mere 39 acres, the Lenoir Preserve seems too small to be a notable birding site. However, its location on top of a ridge near the Hudson River makes this preserve a good site for birding during migration. Managed by the Westchester Department of Parks, Recreation, and Conservation, this park includes native hardwood forest with some important specimen trees, as well as fields and lawns. The Lenoir Preserve maintains a nature center (with restrooms) that includes natural science interpretive exhibits.

The best birding at Lenoir is during autumn migration, although spring migration of songbirds can also provide good sightings. From early September through November, songbirds of many species stopover at the preserve. Bird the site by following the well-groomed trails, stopping to look upward for migrants flying overhead and in the surrounding trees. Many species of warbler can be seen here, along with vireos, thrushes, orioles, and others. The best time for songbirds is early morning. Although these birds rarely leave the preserve during the daytime, they move deeper into the woods as the day goes on, making it difficult to observe them. Aside from the woodlands, check the field edges for Northern Flicker and sparrows.

In October and early November, flocks of waterfowl, Blue Jay, and American Robin can be seen flying down the Hudson Valley, especially when winds are from the west to north after a cold front. Hawks soar on the updrafts above the west-facing hillside, affording watchers some eye-level and underside views of these raptors. From mid-September through November, thousands of hawks pass over the preserve. These include common species such as Sharp-shinned Hawk and Red-tailed

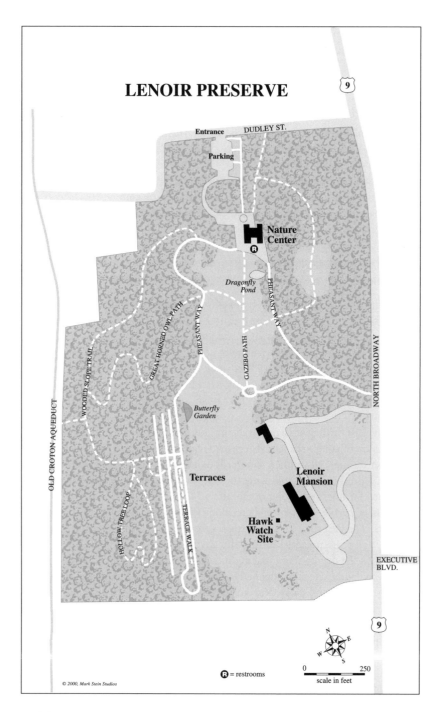

LENOIR PRESERVE

Entrance   DUDLEY ST.

Parking

Nature Center

Dragonfly Pond

PHEASANT WAY

GREAT HORNED OWL PATH

PHEASANT WAY

GAZEBO PATH

WOODED SLOPE TRAIL

OLD CROTON AQUEDUCT

Butterfly Garden

Terraces

HOLLOW TREE LOOP

TERRACE WALK

Lenoir Mansion

Hawk Watch Site

NORTH BROADWAY

EXECUTIVE BLVD.

R = restrooms

0   250
scale in feet

© 2000, Mark Stein Studios

152

Hawk and even Bald Eagle. Hawkwatches are held in back (west) of Lenoir Mansion.

In winter, the feeders at Lenoir Preserve attract many seed-eating birds such as various sparrow species (White-throated and others), juncos, and goldfinches. Look in the conifers near the nature center for Red-breasted Nuthatch.

For insect aficionados, a butterfly garden is maintained in the preserve and usually hosts several species during summer and early autumn. In addition, a dragonfly pond is maintained near the nature center that is active in warm months.

Personal Safety

Lenoir Preserve is a safe area to bird, but it is always better to go out with a friend or two.

Getting There

CAR: Take the Henry Hudson Parkway north. It becomes the Saw Mill River Parkway at the city limits. Go north to Exit 9, Executive Boulevard. Go straight ahead on Executive Boulevard, up the hill to the T, which is North Broadway (Route 9). Go north (right) on North Broadway for about ¼ mile and turn left onto Dudley Street. The parking lot for Lenoir Preserve is a few hundred yards farther on the left.

SUBWAY to BUS: From Manhattan, take the 1 and 9 Bronx-bound subway to its end at 242nd Street in the Bronx. From there, take the 1 or 2 bus up Broadway into Yonkers. At Getty Square, switch to the 6 bus, which runs up North Broadway to Dudley Street.

For Additional Information on Lenoir Preserve

Lenoir Preserve, 914-968-5853 and www.co.westchester.ny.us/
   parks/lenoir
Westchester County Department of Parks, Recreation, and
   Conservation 914-242-PARKS and www.westchestergov.com
Hudson River Audubon Society of Westchester (leads tours)
   914-237-9331 and www.audubon.org/chapter/ny/hudsonriver
Resource person: Michael Bochnik, Hudson River Audubon Society
of Westchester

Sprain Ridge Park, Yonkers

Nesting**   Spring Migrtion***   Fall Migration***   Winter*

The Sprain Brook area in Yonkers includes part of a ridge that luckily is too steep to be turned into housing developments or shopping centers. As a result, Sprain Ridge Park has become a major wildlife sanctuary in southern Westchester County. The area consists of a series of open spaces and remnant forests that runs north–south through Westchester into the Bronx and serves as a significant wildlife corridor for animals and plants dispersing and migrating between upstate New York and New York City. Species such as Wild Turkey undoubtedly make their way to the Bronx parks via this ridge.

Sprain Ridge Park is a Westchester County Parks, Recreation, and Conservation holding that includes approximately 278 acres of mature hardwood forest, grassy areas, an overgrown power-line right-of-way, and recreational facilities (with restrooms). The system of trails is ideal for birding because they are wide and go through rich habitat.

Sprain Ridge is one of the better places in lower Westchester County to seek out nesting songbirds. Look for Brown Thrasher, Prairie Warbler, Eastern Towhee, and other brush nesters along the power-line trail. (The low wet woodlands used to be home to Kentucky Warbler.) Forest nesters include Pileated Woodpecker, White-eyed Vireo, Warbling Vireo, Red-eyed Vireo, Veery, Wood Thrush, Blue-winged Warbler, Chestnut-sided Warbler, and Black-and-white Warbler, along with the occasional Ovenbird, Scarlet Tanager, Rose-breasted Grosbeak, and Orchard Oriole. In addition to songbirds, Wild Turkey are common here. Great Horned Owl nest in the park, and in the 1980s, Ruffed Grouse nested here.

During spring migration, the large oak and other trees attract north-bound songbirds and provide them with good foraging opportunities. From early to mid-May, a good birder searching the entire area may see two dozen species of warbler as well as other Neotropical species. Unlike city parks, where birds concentrate in limited woodlands, these birds spread over a large area and therefore require more work to find. They flit about in the treetops, often deep in the woods and out of sight.

Sprain Ridge Park is also a very fine birding site during autumn migration. From early September through October, songbirds drop into this strip of green. After early October, brushy areas can be excellent for many sparrow species as well as kinglets, Yellow-rumped Warbler, and juncos. The best migration birding is after a cold front has passed.

Hawks, including more than a dozen species, migrate along the ridge in autumn. Sharp-shinned and Cooper's hawks will fly low over the trees and along the edge of the forest in search of songbirds. Broad-winged Hawk soar at higher altitudes. Later in autumn, Red-tailed Hawk glide along the ridge, sometimes stopping to hunt. There will also be an occasional Osprey, Northern Harrier, and Red-shouldered Hawk.

The best way to bird the site is to head toward the east side of the park, where the power-line trail is located. From the swimming pool parking lot, go back past the pool to the entrance road. From here take the paved fire road to the left up into the forest. Proceed up the hill and find the wide dirt trail on the left. Follow the trail southward to the power-line trail and bird along it. This trail will eventually bring you back into forest. The trail merges back to the dirt and gravel fire road. Turn right to head back.

In fall and winter, the pines and cedars in the southern part of the park should be checked for owls such as Great Horned and Northern Saw-whet. There will also be sparrows and other winter birds (Red-breasted Nuthatch at times), including the occasional Red-tailed Hawk.

The sunny edge of the power-line trail is best at first light because large numbers of migrants congregate in this habitat to be in the sun. The sun also warms up insects, food for the migrants. Later the migrants disperse into the forest.

Special Notes

The power-line trail is steep, and erosion combined with stones make footing difficult in places. Recent and ongoing trail construction has reduced the problem, but still take care. Plans to use the trails for mountain biking and the illegal presence of motorized off-road vehicles present an obvious hazard to birders and may reduce the suitability of the trail for birding. However, go early before bikers appear.

Park access in summer is restricted to Westchester residents with a park pass (because of the swimming pool). At this time you may wish to use the State Thruway access (which is unofficial and not sanctioned by the parks department or the authors). Located at the back of a rest area on the New York State Thruway (Route 87), north of Tuckahoe Road, is a steep path that leads into the park.

Personal Safety

Take the usual precautions to combat ticks and poison ivy.

Getting There

CAR: Take the Bronx River Parkway north. Stay left after leaving the Bronx and take the Sprain Brook Parkway north to Jackson Avenue in Yonkers. After exiting, turn left onto Jackson Avenue and go about ½ mile to the park entrance on the left.

For Additional Information on Sprain Ridge Park

Sprain Ridge Park, 914-478-2300 and www.co.westchester.ny.us/parks/sprdg

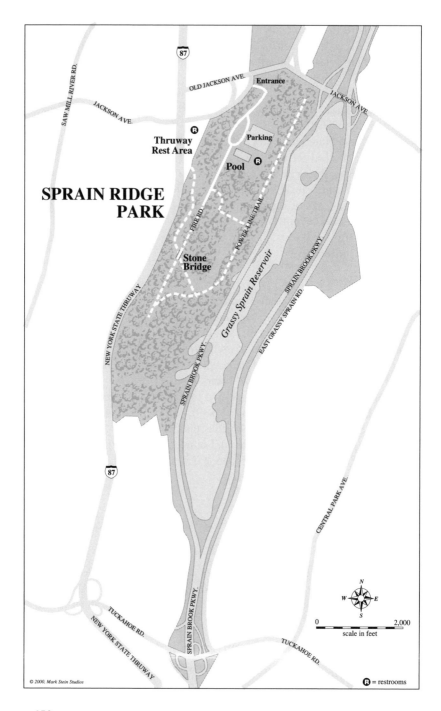

87

SAW MILL RIVER RD.

JACKSON AVE.

OLD JACKSON AVE.

Entrance

JACKSON AVE.

Ⓡ

**Thruway
Rest Area**

Parking

Pool Ⓡ

SPRAIN RIDGE
PARK

FIRE RD.

POWER LINE TRAIL

**Stone
Bridge**

Grassy Sprain Reservoir

SPRAIN BROOK PKWY.

EAST GRASSY SPRAIN RD.

SPRAIN BROOK PKWY.

NEW YORK STATE THRUWAY

87

CENTRAL PARK AVE.

SPRAIN BROOK PKWY.

TUCKAHOE RD.

NEW YORK STATE THRUWAY

TUCKAHOE RD.

N
W E
S

0   2,000
scale in feet

© 2000, Mark Stein Studios

Ⓡ = restrooms

Westchester County Department of Parks, Recreation, and
    Conservation, 914-242-PARKS and www.westchestergov.com
Hudson River Audubon Society of Westchester (leads tours),
    914-237-9331 and www.audubon.org/chapter/ny/hudsonriver
Resource person: Michael Bochnik, Hudson River Audubon Society
of Westchester

Chapter Eight

Snowy Owl

Nearby Sites in New Jersey

Until New York birders venture over the bridges or through the tunnels to New Jersey's wonderful places to watch migrants as well as nesting and wintering birds, they see little reason to cross the Hudson River. Visiting these sites rounds out the metropolitan birding experience.

Despite its dense human population and its relatively small area, New Jersey hosts numerous natural treasures such as the Pine Barrens (see chap. 9, "Great Birding Day Trips"), the Highlands, and Cape May. For birding information in the state, the New Jersey Audubon Society is a longtime leader. Established in 1897, New Jersey Audubon administers sanctuaries throughout the state and sponsors hundreds of birding field trips. For information on birding trips to Cape May, access www.capemaytimes.com, which has links to the Cape May Bird Observatory web site. National Audubon Society chapters located in New Jersey also sponsor field trips. After birding the areas discussed in this chapter—Liberty State Park, Hackensack Meadowlands, and Sandy Hook—explore other prime birding areas with these local birding organizations (see Appendix 1, "Metropolitan Birding Resources").

Liberty State Park, Hudson County
Nesting Spring Migration** Fall Migration** Winter**

Liberty State Park is a jumble of large open fields, saltmarsh, shallow cover, pine groves, jetties and other structures and is managed by the New Jersey Department of Environmental Protection's Division of Parks and Forestry. Covering 1,122 acres, the park provides excellent birding opportunities, particularly for observing wintering owls. It also attracts large numbers and types of waterfowl, shorebirds, and gulls while affording fine views of the Statue of Liberty and the Manhattan Skyline. Close to Manhattan, it can be reached easily by ferry, bus, or car.

Records show that between 75 and 80 species of waterbirds have been sighted in Liberty State Park, including large numbers of wintering waterfowl, rails, and migratory shorebirds as well as egrets and herons. Migrating songbirds find refuge in the park's pine groves. Barn, Long-eared, and Northern Saw-whet owls and occasional Great Horned and Short-eared owls also inhabit these groves during migration and sometimes in winter. Liberty State Park is one of the best places in the area to see Snowy Owl, which survive on the rats and large birds, including waterfowl, that the site provides. Although these midwinter Arctic visitors prefer the open spaces, such as the jetties and other man-made structures, they also perch in the pines. Do not approach them too closely (for observing or photographing). If spooked, they will cease to frequent this park.

Northern Harrier, Horned Lark, and Snow Bunting are found in the open fields, as are a plethora of sparrows.

Start at the Visitor Center (restrooms). Scope the nearby open water and jetties for Horned Grebe, cormorants (both Double-crested and Great), geese, ducks, and gulls (including Little Gull in some years). Particularly in winter, search the jetties and other structures for Purple Sandpiper and Snowy Owl. Also in winter, look along the edges of the water for shorebirds. During migration, many gull species and waterfowl (including Brant, American Wigeon, Green-winged Teal, Canvasback, scaup, all three scoters, Bufflehead, Common Goldeneye, and Ruddy Duck) gather in the waters just off the shore.

Survey Caven Cove with your scope. The following species have been seen at Caven Pier (now off limits) and may be seen in or near the cove: Purple Sandpiper, Black-headed and Bonaparte's gulls, Horned Lark, Lapland Longpur, and Snow Bunting. Also check the saltmarsh to the left of the Visitor Center.

Next go toward the Environment Center on Freedom Way. From here, check the pine groves for owls (in winter) as well as songbirds (during autumn and spring migration). White-crowned Sparrow and more common sparrows can be seen here during migration. Walk the Hudson riverfront and train your scope on the water toward Liberty Island for waterfowl and gulls.

Liberty State Park's rare sightings include Eared Grebe, Eurasian Wigeon, Little Gull, Black-headed Gull, Ivory Gull, Snowy Owl, Boreal Chickadee, and Common Redpoll.

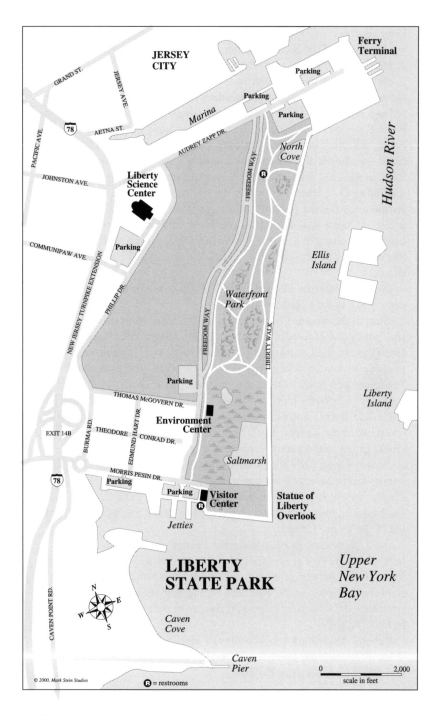

JERSEY CITY

GRAND ST.

JERSEY AVE.

78

AETNA ST.

PACIFIC AVE.

JOHNSTON AVE.

Liberty
Science
Center

COMMUNIPAW AVE.

Parking

NEW JERSEY TURNPIKE EXTENSION

PHILLIP DR.

AUDREY ZAPP DR.

Marina

Parking

Parking

Parking

Ferry Terminal

Parking

North Cove

ℝ

FREEDOM WAY

FREEDOM WAY

Hudson River

Ellis Island

Waterfront Park

LIBERTY WALK

Parking

THOMAS McGOVERN DR.

BURMA RD.

THEODORE

EDMUND HART DR.

CONRAD DR.

EXIT 14B

Environment Center

Saltmarsh

Liberty Island

MORRIS PESIN DR.

78

Parking

Parking

ℝ

Visitor Center

Statue of Liberty Overlook

Jetties

CAVEN POINT RD.

N E W S

LIBERTY STATE PARK

Caven Cove

Upper New York Bay

Caven Pier

0   2,000
scale in feet

© 2000, Mark Stein Studios

ℝ = restrooms

When to Go

The months of October through May provide fine birding opportunities. The best season is winter, although late autumn and early spring are also very good. Any time of day is good for birding at Liberty State Park. Tide can be important for shorebirds, with half tides or low tides providing mudflat availability. Breeding birds are scarce here. Gadwall, Clapper Rail, and a few other species, including foraging herons and egrets, however, can be seen here in late spring through early autumn.

Optimal Weather Conditions

Except for its implications for human comfort, weather is not a primary factor in successful birding here. Waterfowl and many of the other birds of interest are not materially affected, unlike the birders.

Personal Safety

Although this is a state park with security patrol, it is not a good idea to bird here alone. Follow advisories and stay out of areas marked hazardous. Brisk winter winds blow off the water from November through March, so dress warmly.

Getting There

FERRY: From Manhattan, ferries run directly to the ferry terminal at Liberty State Park. Call 800-53-FERRY for information.

PATH to BUS: Free bus service from the Colgate Ferry/Grove Street PATH station runs every half hour from 7:30 AM to 6:30 PM.

CAR: Take the Jersey City Exit 14B off the New Jersey Turnpike Extention (Route 78), not far from the Holland Tunnel. Turn left after the toll booth and follow signs for the park. Park at the Visitor Center.

For Additional Information on Liberty State Park

Liberty State Park 201-200-1000

New Jersey Audubon (leads tours), 908-204-8998 and www. njaudubon.org

Resource person: Richard Kane, Vice President, New Jersey Audubon Society

Hackensack Meadowlands/Richard W. DeKorte Park, Bergen County

Nesting*   Spring Migration**   Fall Migration***   Winter**

The Hackensack Meadowlands, traversed by busy highways that include the New Jersey Turnpike and by railroad lines, is a vast complex of wetlands, both fresh and tidal marsh, tidal creeks, the Hackensack River, various ponds, and small stands of trees. Once a productive wetland, it suffers from years of filling and draining for roadways, shopping centers, industrial areas, landfills, and residential buildings. Today, through an extensive system of dikes, the Hackensack Meadowlands Development Commission (HMDC) monitors and controls the water movement.

Surprisingly good birding exists in the Meadowlands' 2,000 acres. Start at the HMDC Environment Center (with restrooms). Before venturing out, check the birdwatchers' bulletin (in the lobby) for recent sightings and obtain an area map. While at the center, you may also wish to visit the world's only Garbage Museum. Start your birdwalk at the Lyndhurst Nature Reserve. Scan the tidal flats for shorebirds, ducks, and gulls in the Sawmill Creek Wildlife Management Area. Bring a scope because viewing distances are great.

Back at the Nature Reserve entrance, go south on the Transco Trail, walking toward the turnpike. The tidal marsh to the right and the Kingsland Tidal Impoundment to the left host herons, egrets, ducks, rails, shorebirds, gulls, and terns in the appropriate seasons. Follow the Transco Trail for approximately 1 mile to railroad (active) tracks. You may go left and continue the loop back to the Environment Center, stopping to scan where possible. Or at your own risk, follow the railroad tracks south to the Hackensack River. Scan the marshes and landfills as you go. As a third option, follow the Marsh Discovery Trail, a 1-mile trail that crosses Kingsland Tidal Impoundment. It is a fine place to observe marsh birds at close range.

Raptors can be observed in the marshes and landfill back at Valley Brook Avenue. Next drive from the Environment Center parking lot for 1.25 miles to Clay Avenue (second street on the right) and turn right. After approximately ¼ mile on Clay Avenue, turn left, after the *Phragmites*, into a parking lot. Park on the left. Scan the tidal area for migrant shorebirds (in spring and autumn).

The Kearny Marshes nearby also offer some fine birding. However, because of the dangers of the active railroad tracks, we suggest that readers visit only at their own risk. Details can be found in William Boyle's *Guide to Bird Finding in New Jersey* (see "Suggested Readings").

Several local cemeteries in this area offer good birding in some years. Hillside Cemetery in Lyndhurst on Orient Way and Rutherford Avenue (Route 17) is excellent for sighting winter songbirds. Holy Cross Cemetery in North Arlington on Schuyler Avenue is another possibility. Arlington Cemetery in Kearny on Belleville Pike and Schuyler Avenue can also be excellent for songbirds in winter. These cemeteries should also be checked for owls; in some years, Long-eared Owl and others have roosted in conifers at these locations.

When to Go

The best birding occurs in autumn, spring, and winter. Migrants, such as shorebirds, can be very numerous from September through October. Later in autumn, waterfowl arrive by the thousands and many remain throughout the winter.

Winter birding is very rewarding. Among the species tallied in the Lower Hudson Christmas Bird Count (Lyndhurst, North Arlington, and Kearny Meadowlands areas) are Least Bittern, Great Egret, Rough-legged Hawk, Merlin, Peregrine Falcon, Virginia Rail, many different gulls (including Iceland, Lesser Black-backed, and Glaucous gulls), Barn and Short-eared owls, Lapland Longspur, and Snow Bunting.

Good opportunities in summer include nesting rails, moorhen, coot, waterfowl, and some songbirds.

Optimal Weather Conditions

Good to excellent birding is available in any weather.

Personal Safety

Do not bird alone. It is safer to bird with a group of friends. Cars should be locked with valuables out of sight. Exercise extreme caution in viewing sites near railroad tracks. Mosquitoes are plentiful in the hot months.

Getting There

CAR: Route 3 west (accessible from the Lincoln Tunnel, New Jersey Turnpike, Garden State Parkway, Route 21, and Route 46) to the Route 17 South exit (just past Giants' Stadium). Follow the ramp over Route 3 to the bottom of hill at the light. Turn left at the light and proceed ahead onto Polito Avenue (large motels/hotels are on both sides of road). Go ½ mile on Polito Avenue through a traffic light to a stop sign. Turn left on Valley Brook Avenue and go 1½ miles to a railroad track; continue straight ahead, bearing left to the last HMDC parking lot.

Additonal Information on Hackensack Meadowlands/Richard W. DeKorte Park

Hackensack Meadowlands Development Commission/DeKorte Park 201-460-8300

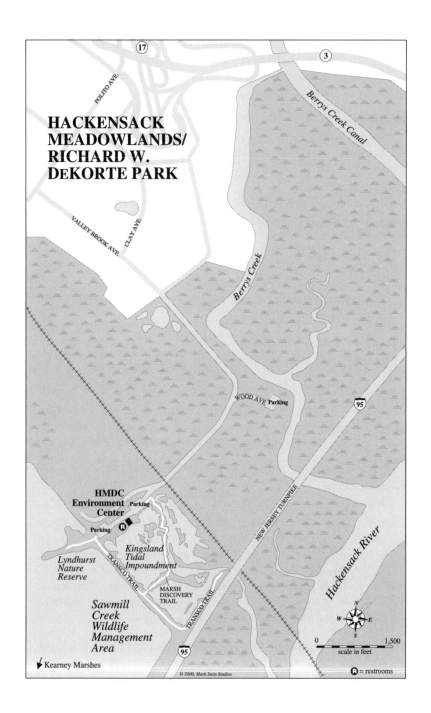

HACKENSACK MEADOWLANDS/ RICHARD W. DeKORTE PARK

POLITO AVE.

VALLEY BROOK AVE.

CLAY AVE.

Berry's Creek Canal

Berrys Creek

WOOD AVE. Parking

95

HMDC
Environment
Center Parking

Parking

Ⓡ

Kingsland
Tidal
Impoundment

Lyndhurst
Nature
Reserve

TRANSCO TRAIL

MARSH
DISCOVERY
TRAIL

TRANSCO TRAIL

NEW JERSEY TURNPIKE

Hackensack River

Sawmill
Creek
Wildlife
Management
Area

95

Kearney Marshes

© 2000, Mark Stein Studios

N
W E
S

0   1,500
scale in feet

Ⓡ = restrooms

New Jersey Audubon (leads tours), 908-204-8998 and www. njaudubon.org

Resource persons: Pete Bacinski, Sanctuary Director, Sandy Hook Nature Center; New Jersey Audubon Society; James Bangma; and Don Smith

Sandy Hook, Gateway National Recreation Area, Monmouth County

Nesting**   Spring Migration***   Fall Migration***   Winter***

Sandy Hook is a narrow peninsula that extends northward for approximately 6½ miles. Its name reflects its shape, which is constantly changing from the action of wind and waves. To the west of this sandy spit is Sandy Hook Bay, and to the east is the Atlantic Ocean. Three city boroughs, Brooklyn, Queens, and Staten Island, are visible from the tip of Sandy Hook.

Sandy Hook is managed by the National Park Service's Gateway National Recreation Area and encompasses approximately 1,665 acres of maritime forest, saltmarsh, weedy fields, second-growth forest (including a gorgeous holly forest), freshwater wetlands, open beach, bay, and ocean. There are also large parking lots (for summertime beachgoers), concession areas, Park Service buildings, historic gunnery embankments, the oldest operating lighthouse in the United States, the landmark Fort Hancock, and a Coast Guard Station. Sandy Hook's 6 miles of beach are prime swimming and sunbathing destinations in the warmer months, when it becomes extremely crowded. Birding on summer weekends is not recommended, except very early in the morning. A fee is charged for beach parking and beach access from Memorial Day to Labor Day.

Area maps are available at the Visitor Center (with restrooms), built in 1894, where a logbook of recent wildlife sightings is kept.

Birding at Sandy Hook is excellent year round. For winter birding (December through February), start by visiting the Bayberry Beach, Chokecherry Beach, and Seagull's Nest parking lots. All three are on the right side of the road beyond the entrance. Look along the beach and out over the ocean for loons (Red-throated and Common), Horned Grebe, Northern Gannet, sea ducks, and gulls. On rare occasions, Red-necked Grebe can be seen from this beach. Next, walk across the road to the boardwalk at Spermaceti Cove. Frequently there will be thousands of Greater Scaup, along with lesser numbers of Bufflehead, Common Goldeneye, and Red-breasted Merganser. The sandbar at the opposite end of Spermaceti Cove hosts Peregrine Falcon, gulls, and even harbor seals, which appear as large, motionless lumps.

Drive to Horseshoe Cove and park just beyond the intersection of Hartshorne Drive and Atlantic Drive. Aside from the same species as those seen at Spermaceti Cove, Horned Grebe, Common Goldeneye (100 or so gathered together), and in some years, Eared Grebe (rare) and Barrow's Goldeneye may be seen here. Red-throated and Common loons, Great Cormorant, and various gulls may also be present.

Take Atlantic Drive to the North Beach parking area. From the observation deck, look out over the ocean and beach for gulls (including an occasional Iceland, Lesser Black-backed, and Glaucous), and farther south look for Horned Lark, Lapland Longspur (rare), and Snow Bunting. On the ocean there will be loons, grebes, gannets, and some sea ducks.

Continue to the end of Atlantic Drive; make a left and then a right to a stop sign. Go left, back onto Hartshorne Drive, and park toward the passenger ramp for the ferry terminal. This area is called the Auditorium by birders. Look out toward the water for Oldsquaw, Bufflehead, Common Goldeneye, and Red-breasted Merganser, and look on the rocks for Purple Sandpiper and harbor seals. Rarities at this location have included Pacific Loon and Harlequin Duck.

An interesting array of winter birds can be seen here and there in the recreation areas. Some not mentioned above include Merlin, which roost in the groves of trees, as well as Carolina Wren and Hermit Thrush.

During spring, begin at Plum Island (Bayberry Beach parking area), starting early before the crowds, or head to the north end of Sandy Hook. At Plum Island, check for marsh birds, raptors, and songbirds. The saltwater marsh hosts herons, egrets, and Clapper Rail. The grove of taller vegetation is the best area for songbirds, including migrants such as flycatchers, vireos, and warblers.

From the Visitor Center, cross the road and bird the boardwalk in Spermaceti Cove for herons, egrets, waterfowl, raptors, shorebirds, and terns. Morning light is best. Next go to the maintenance area by turning right out of the Visitor Center onto Hartshorne Drive. After passing Horseshoe Cove (on the left), continue straight through a forest (on a one-lane road). Go right at the stop sign and then left into the Guardian Park parking lot, where you will see a Nike missile in the field. Walk back along the road through the forest. Walk the National Park Service vehicles-only road through the woods, birding as you go, and then return to the maintenance area. This is one of the best places in New Jersey for observing spring-migrating songbirds. Slowly work this area for cuckoos, vireos, kinglets, thrushes, warblers, sparrows, and most other songbirds. In May, Nashville, Bay-breasted, Worm-eating, Mourning, and Wilson's warblers may be seen. Try other roads with trees in this area for songbird migrants.

From Guardian Park, proceed to where the road ends at the dirt parking lot (K-Lot). Here there are paths into the gunnery embankments. Raptors and songbirds are common here. On the North Pond Loop Trail, you may see Pied-billed Grebe, American Bittern, night-herons, Wood Duck, Sora, Common Moorhen, and snipe. From the K-Lot you can also see hawks in spring migration.

Sandy Hook is one of the best places to watch spring migration of hawks. From mid-March through early May, approximately 5,000 migrants are counted as they pass through Sandy Hook. The most common species include Northern Harrier, Sharp-shinned and Cooper's hawks, Red-shouldered and Red-tailed hawks, American Kestrel, Merlin, and Peregrine Falcon. Rarities include Swallow-tailed Kite and Bald Eagle. The customary hawkwatch is conducted from a hilltop (on top of the concrete bunkers) about 200 yards east of the lighthouse (just across the road). Although this hill gives a commanding view, migrating hawks can be seen hunting almost anywhere on Sandy Hook.

Fall migration can also be spectacular from any of the sites discussed above. At the western edge of E-Lot, rare fall visitors can sometimes be seen, including Philadelphia Vireo and Clay-colored Sparrow, along with more common species. Also try The Garden (an old vegetable garden), located between Hudson, Knox, and South Bragg Roads, just north of the lighthouse. This emerging wooded area attracts large numbers of songbirds, including such rarities as Philadelphia Vireo, Connecticut Warbler, Mourning Warbler, and Clay-colored Sparrow and the hawks that prey on them. Bird the North Beach parking area edges for Vesper Sparrow, Lark Sparrow, and Dickcissel.

In summer (June through August), birding at Plum Island can be quite good. Egrets (Great and Snowy), Green Heron, Clapper Rail, and Common and Least terns are seen, along with early migrating shorebirds. Spermaceti Cove and Horseshoe Cove are good places to search for the same species. Sometimes Brown Pelican are found in these areas. On the oceanfront at the North Beach Observation Deck, you may see Common and Least terns as well as the endangered Piping Plover. (All nest nearby. Stay out of areas that are cordoned off.) From the North Pond observation deck and the Loop Trail, look for Least Bittern, egrets, herons, various ducks and terns, and Black Skimmer. Several species of songbirds nest locally, including Willow Flycatcher, Marsh Wren, Brown Thrasher, Yellow Warbler, Eastern Towhee, and Swamp Sparrow. Other nesting birds include American Woodcock, Whip-poor-will, Eastern Kingbird, Yellow-breasted Chat, and Boat-tailed Grackle.

New Jersey Audubon Sandy Hook Nature Center

In 2001, the New Jersey Audubon Society is opening a Sandy Hook birding and nature center, which is housed in one of the National Park Service buildings near Guardian Park at the southern end of Fort Hancock. This center serves as the focus for birding at Sandy Hook and provides a bird sightings list as well as natural history information. We suggest that you check in at the new center for information about birds and a schedule of field trips.

Personal Safety

Birding is safe in the Sandy Hook unit of Gateway National Recreation Area. However, we recommend that you bird with others because lone birders have encountered awkward and offensive situations. Poison ivy is abundant. In season, both dog and deer ticks and mosquitoes are present.

Getting There

CAR: Take the New Jersey Turnpike south to the Garden State Parkway south to Exit 117. Follow Route 36 about 12 miles to the entrance of the Gateway National Recreation Area.

For Additional Information on Sandy Hook

Gateway National Recreation Area, Sandy Hook District,
    732-872-5970 and www.nps.gov/gate/
Monmouth County Audubon Society (leads tours),
    www.audubon.org (New Jersey chapter in Monmouth County)
New Jersey Audubon Society (leads tours), 908-204-8998 and
    www.njaudubon.org
Sandy Hook Visitor Center, 732-872-5900 and 732-872-0115
Resource person: Scott Barnes, teacher-naturalist, Sandy Hook
Nature Center, New Jersey Audubon Society

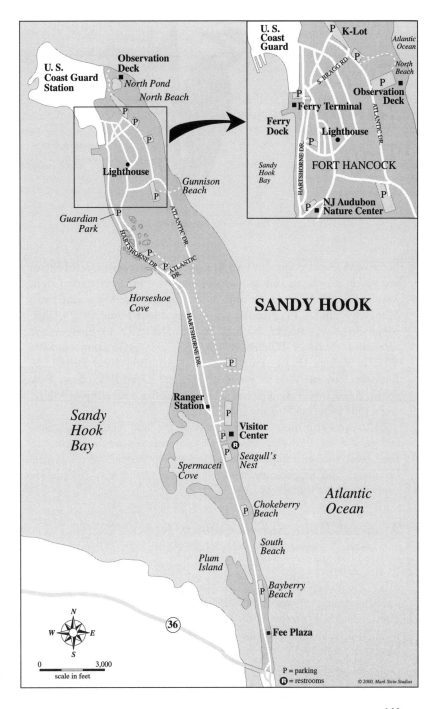

U. S.
Coast Guard
Station

Observation
Deck

North Pond

North Beach

P
P
P

P

Lighthouse

Gunnison
Beach

Guardian
Park

P

ATLANTIC DR.

HARTSHORNE DR.

P
P

ATLANTIC
DR.

Horseshoe
Cove

HARTSHORNE DR.

P

SANDY HOOK

Ranger
Station

P

Visitor
Center

P
P
R

Seagull's
Nest

Sandy
Hook
Bay

Spermaceti
Cove

Chokeberry
Beach

P

Atlantic
Ocean

South
Beach

Plum
Island

Bayberry
Beach

P

Fee Plaza

N
W   E
S

0   3,000
scale in feet

36

P = parking
R = restrooms

© 2000, Mark Stein Studios

U. S.
Coast
Guard

K-Lot

Atlantic
Ocean

North
Beach

S. BRAGG RD.

P
P

P

Observation
Deck

P

ATLANTIC DR.

P

Ferry Terminal

Ferry
Dock

Lighthouse

FORT HANCOCK

Sandy
Hook
Bay

HARTSHORNE DR.

P

P

NJ Audubon
Nature Center

P

Chapter Nine

Pileated Woodpecker

Great Birding Day Trips

Some of the most important bird habitats in northeastern United States are within a two- to two-and-a-half-hour drive (in light traffic) from Manhattan. We have chosen nine public nature preserves as day trips: Montauk Point (N.Y.), Doodletown Road and Iona Island (N.Y.), Slide Mountain (N.Y.), Wallkill National Wildlife Refuge (N.J.), Shawangunk Grasslands National Wildlife Refuge (N.Y.), Great Swamp National Wildlife Refuge (N.J.), Pine Barrens (N.J.), Brigantine District of Forsythe National Wildlife Refuge (N.J.), and Island Beach State Park (N.J.). Aside from ease of access, these areas offer a diversity of habitat and a wide variety of bird species.

When you visit these areas and frequent the local restaurants, stores, and gas stations, let the business people know that you are there to bird in their local wildlife refuges. Reinforcing the connection between their businesses and neighboring nature preserves strengthens community support of these wilderness areas.

Montauk Point, Suffolk County, New York
Nesting** Spring Migration** Autumn Migration*** Winter***

At the easternmost tip of Long Island, about a two-and-one-half-hour drive (130 miles) from Manhattan, Montauk Point, a 14-mile peninsula, stretches from Amagansett, Long Island, to the Atlantic Ocean. The Point, where the currents of Block Island Sound and Long Island Sound meet, is a famous location for anglers (surf casters) and birders. Both Montauk Point State Park and the adjoining Camp Hero State Park, which are managed by the New York State Office of Parks, Recreation, and Historic Preservation, are part of a 6,000-acre Important Bird Area designated by the National Audubon Society.

At the Point near the lighthouse, from mid-September through October, migrating Osprey, Sharp-shinned Hawk, American Kestrel, Merlin, and Peregrine Falcon can be seen. These raptors can also be seen over the dunes and brush, hunting shorebird and songbird migrants, as well as along the saltmarshes and beaches. In the thickets and forests, the fallout of thrushes, warblers, and sparrows, which come in off the ocean at dawn, can be spectacular.

Birding opportunities from October through early spring are also spectacular. During the fall migration season, it is likely that as many as several million birds pass Montauk, including loons, waterbirds, waterfowl, hawks, shorebirds, gulls, and terns. The waters off Montauk Point and the lighthouse host one of the largest wintering aggregations of waterfowl along the eastern seaboard. At one time, more than 20,000 ducks have been observed, including Greater Scaup, Common Eider, all scoter species, Oldsquaw, and Red-breasted Merganser. The occasional King Eider, Harlequin Duck, and Common Goldeneye have also been seen here. Other seabirds include loons, Northern Gannet, and alcids (mostly Razorbill and the occasional Dovekie). Patient and cold-tolerant gull watchers may spot Little, Black-headed, Bonaparte's, Iceland, Lesser Black-backed, and Glaucous gulls as well as Black-legged Kittiwake. The best viewing spots are the lighthouse point and Shagwong Point, near the tip of the peninsula. On the rocks and around the harbor jetties below lighthouse point, Purple Sandpiper are usually found.

During this same period, Lake Montauk (the harbor), Fort Pond, and other bodies of water host many species of ducks and geese, including Horned Grebe, cormorant, scaup, and Bufflehead. These waters also offer a safe haven for migrating egrets and herons as well as such shorebirds as Black-bellied Plover, Ruddy Turnstone, and Dunlin.

In midwinter, check the sand dunes and open areas, including marshes, for Northern Harrier, Rough-legged Hawk, Snowy Owl, and Short-eared Owl. The dunes and grassy fields also host Horned Lark, Lapland Longspur (rare), and Snow Bunting.

In summer, the beaches are crowded with vacationers. All the same, birders may see a variety of beach and saltmarsh nesting species and migrants that include Blue-winged Teal, Osprey, Northern Harrier, Northern Bobwhite, Piping Plover, Common Tern, Least Tern, and Whip-poor-will.

A scope is recommended. Restrooms are available at Montauk State Park.

Personal Safety

Deer ticks abound. Take the necessary precautions.

Getting There

CAR: Take the Long Island Expressway (I-495) east to Exit 70; then take Route 111 to the Sunrise Highway east (Route 27). Montauk Point State Park is at the eastern end of the highway. The Long Island Railroad runs as far as Montauk, but if you wish to move from location to location within the wildlife area, a car is a necessity.

For Additional Information on Montauk Point State Park

Montauk Point State Park, 631-668-2461

Doodletown Road/Iona Island, Rockland County, New York

Nesting***   Spring Migration*   Fall Migration*   Winter*

Doodletown Road and Iona Island, another New York State Important Bird Area managed by the New York State Office of Parks, Recreation, and Historic Preservation, is a one-hour drive north from Manhattan. Part of the Bear Mountain State Park at Stony Point, the 1,650-acre area consists mainly of deciduous forest with smaller areas of tidal marsh, grassland, and brush. Doodletown, an abandoned town, gives the road (more accurately, the trail) and the area its name. The park hosts a large number of rare and threatened plant and animal species, including timber rattlesnake.

Nesting warblers (and a few migrants in spring) and other woodland birds are the site's main attraction. From late April through June, birding is excellent, with May and early June being best. Listen and look for Golden-winged Warbler, Cerulean Warbler, Louisiana Waterthrush, Kentucky Warbler, and Hooded Warbler. There have been more than a dozen nesting pairs of Cerulean Warbler here. Around Doodletown Road and in the forests nearby, you will find Ruby-throated Hummingbird, Pileated Woodpecker, Acadian (and other) Flycatcher, vireos (several species), Blue-gray Gnatcatcher, Wood Thrush, Scarlet Tanager, and many other nesting songbirds as well as a few nesting hawks.

Iona Island is a good spot for observing waterbirds and marsh birds, including nesting species such as Least Bittern, Virginia Rail, Sora, and Marsh Wren. Migrants include Double-crested Cormorant, American Bittern, Osprey, Northern Harrier, and Belted Kingfisher. Several swallow species forage over the marshes and open water that can be seen from the accessible causeway. In winter, Bald Eagle (sometimes Golden Eagle), other hawks (Red-tailed and Rough-legged), and waterfowl frequent the island.

After birding the Doodletown Road and Iona Island complex, you may wish to explore other portions of Bear Mountain State Park and nearby Harriman State Park, where forests abound with nesting songbirds. A portion of the Appalachian Trail, which stretches from Georgia to Maine, runs through these parks.

Personal Safety

Deer and dog ticks are present, along with other insect pests and poison ivy.

Getting There

CAR: Drive north on the New York Thruway over the Tappan Zee Bridge. A couple miles after crossing the Tappan Zee Bridge, take the Palisades Interstate Parkway north to the Perkins Drive/Bear Mountain State Park exit. Follow the road along the mountainside to a small traffic circle. Take the first right and go downhill until you come to a Yield sign at Route 9W. Continue south on 9W for 100 feet to a parking place on the roadside, just before the entrance to Iona Island Road. The blue-blazed trail (old Doodletown Road) is 20 feet north of the concrete rail bridge.

For Additional Information on Doodletown Road and Iona Island

New York State Office of Parks, Recreation, and Historic Preservation, 914-889-4100

Slide Mountain, Ulster County, New York

Nesting*** Spring Migration Fall Migration Winter

The closest boreal forest areas to New York City are in the high peaks of the Catskill Mountains. The highest mountain (4,204 feet above sea level) in New York State south of the Adirondacks is Slide Mountain in Oliverea, New York. Here you will be surrounded by dense stands of fragrant, cool balsam fir that still convey the same sense of remoteness noted by naturalist John Burroughs in 1885. Slide Mountain, part of the New York State Catskill Forest Preserve, is managed by New York State Department of Environmental Conservation.

Even from the car park to the beginning of the firs, birding opportunities are good, especially for northern forest species. Stop frequently and listen for Black-throated Blue and Black-throated Green warblers,

American Redstart, and Ovenbird. The lower elevation forests are, at times, home to Broad-winged Hawk, other hawks, and Barred Owl as well as bobcat and black bear. There are also Ruffed Grouse and Pileated Woodpecker along with the more common species found in deciduous woodlands.

Five thrush species can be found on Slide Mountain and the surrounding hillsides. Wood Thrush can be found below the car park (in the forests at the bottom of the mountain and along Route 28). From the car park upward, listen and look first for Veery, farther up for Hermit Thrush, and farther still, from pine forest to just below the summit, Swainson's Thrush. The most difficult species to see and hear is Bicknell's Thrush, a New York State species of special concern formerly considered a race of the Gray-cheeked Thrush. Bicknell's Thrush prefer to be at least 3,800 feet above sea level and in the densest part of the balsam forest. They sing most commonly at dawn and dusk (even in darkness). To see or hear Bicknell's Thrush in daylight, find a place at the side of the trail (hiking off the trail is not permitted) with good visibility into the forest. Make yourself comfortable and be prepared to wait a few hours. Be alert and you may see this thrush foraging on the forest floor. If you are really adventurous, try to find Bicknell's Thrush on one of the other nearby peaks.

From the beginning of the dense conifers, listen carefully for Black-poll Warbler, which usually are very common and sing throughout the day. Also present in this forest habitat are Yellow-bellied Flycatcher (just below the summit), Magnolia Warbler, Yellow-rumped Warbler, White-throated Sparrow, and Dark-eyed Junco. Yellow-bellied Flycatcher perch on the snags, although they are usually heard before they are seen. Northern Saw-whet Owl probably nest at elevations from 3,600 feet and downslope. At the summit of Slide Mountain, you will find spectacular views from large rock outcroppings surrounded by thick fir forest.

A similar array of species can be seen at Hunter Mountain and the nearby Blackheads, whose name refers to their dark-appearing peaks. Hikes to the top of Table, Rocky, Lone, Friday, and Wittenberg mountains are difficult and the views obscured, although there may be rewarding thrush sightings.

Special Note

The trail up Slide Mountain is steep and rocky, so take your time. If you are seeking Bicknell's Thrush, which sing both in the gray light of dawn and again at dusk, be extremely careful hiking up or down in the darkness. Going off trail above 3,500 feet and camping are illegal.

Getting There

CAR: Drive north on the New York State Thruway to Kingston (Exit 19). Go west on Route 28 through Phoenicia to Big Indian (Route 47). Turn left toward Oliverea and continue up the road for several miles. The Slide Mountain parking area, which often fills up, is situated on the left-hand side not far after a small reservoir and dam adjacent to a large house. The drive from New York City is about two and a half hours, more if there is traffic. Other ascents of Slide Mountain are possible, but they are longer than the climb suggested here.

For Additional Information on Slide Mountain

New York State Department of Environmental Conservation, 607-652-7741

Wallkill National Wildlife Refuge, Passaic County, New Jersey

Nesting***   Spring Migration**   Autumn Migration*   Winter*

Wallkill, the newest national wildlife refuge in New Jersey, is managed by the U.S. Fish and Wildlife Service. Plans are afoot that include increasing public access. We can look forward to more trails, interpretive signs, and a refuge headquarters. Already available is a checklist of 200 species that can be observed in the refuge's riparian and upland forests, swamps, marshes, ponds, rivers, and grasslands. Wallkill promises to be one of the great birding spots in the region, primarily during nesting season.

Visit from spring through early summer, when songbirds, hawks, owls, and others are nesting. American and Least bitterns, Wood Duck, and Hooded and Common mergansers nest in or near the refuge, as do King Rail, Virginia Rail, Sora, Common Moorhen, and Spotted Sandpiper. Grassland birds, including Upland Sandpiper, Savannah Sparrow, Grasshopper Sparrow, and Bobolink, can be seen in the open fields. About 18 species of warbler nest here, including Cerulean, Prothonotary, Worm-eating, Kentucky, and Hooded; in some years, Sedge Wren does also. Woodpeckers, flycatchers (Alder, Willow, and Least), vireos (including Yellow-throated), and swallows (all eastern species) are also abundant.

The best way to bird the Wallkill is to walk the main trail, an old railroad bed, stopping regularly to look and listen. Spend 20 minutes at a stop. Patience will be rewarded. You must wait for the rails and bitterns to call from the swamp before you can locate them. Beaver and muskrat may appear also. To see grassland birds, go to the meadow area and wait quietly at the edges. Focus on the taller vegetation, where they will perch. In some of these open areas, a scope is helpful.

There are several good birding sites near the Wallkill National Wildlife Refuge. You may wish to visit High Point State Park, Wawayanda State Park, Ringwood State Park, and the Pequannock Watershed. Refer to Boyle's *A Guide to Bird Finding in New Jersey* for detailed information (see "Suggested Readings").

Personal Safety

Parking is currently limited, although there are plans for expansion. Care should be taken when birding along the roads (either on foot or in your car) because traffic moves quickly along these narrow, country thoroughfares.

Getting There

CAR: Wallkill National Wildlife Refuge is located in Wantage, New Jersey, 90 minutes from northwest Manhattan. Take US Route 80 west to Route 15 north. Continue on Route 15 to Route 94 and then to Route 23. Proceed 3 miles on Route 23 to Route 565 and go north. The parking area is only 500 feet on the right on Route 565 after you turn off Route 23.

For Additional Information on Wallkill National Wildlife Refuge

Wallkill National Wildlife Refuge, 973-702-7266
Resource person: Elizabeth Herland, Refuge Manager, Wallkill National Wildlife Refuge

Shawangunk Grasslands National Wildlife Refuge, Ulster County, New York

Nesting***   Spring Migration*   Fall Migration*   Winter**

A short distance north from the Wallkill National Wildlife Refuge, over the New York border to Shawangunk, New York, is a newly designated wildlife refuge, formerly the site of a military airbase. When Galeville Airport was declared surplus by the U.S. Department of Defense in 1994, discussions ensued about the fate of this healthy grassland. The National Audubon Society, the Trust for Public Land, the town of Shawangunk, the U.S. Fish and Wildlife Service, members of New York State Congress, the New York State Department of Corrections, and the governor all took an interest. In 2000, this New York State Important Bird Area, with a total 650 acres, became the Shawangunk National Wildlife Refuge. It is managed by the U.S. Fish and Wildlife Service.

Plans are in the works for public facilities, including parking and observation areas. In May 2000, when the refuge officially opened to the public, the first bird species checklist was made available.

For years, even while the airbase was functioning, birders visited the area in spring and summer to see nesting grassland species, including Northern Harrier, Upland Sandpiper, Vesper Sparrow, Savannah Sparrow, Grasshopper Sparrow, Henslow's Sparrow, Bobolink, Eastern Meadowlark, and possibly Short-eared Owl.

In winter, Northern Harrier, Red-tailed Hawk, Rough-legged Hawk, American Kestrel, Short-eared Owl, and Horned Lark are present, as is Northern Shrike. The location of this refuge is just north of Wallkill, New York, not to be confused with the Wallkill National Wildlife Refuge in New Jersey. While at Wallkill National Wildlife Refuge, inquire about directions to Shawangunk.

Getting There

CAR: Take the New York Turnpike north to the Route 84 Exit. Go west on 84 to Exit 5 (Route 208); go north, following the Wallkill into village of Wallkill. At a T, turn left and travel for one block, then turn left onto Bruyn Turnpike. Take a right onto Hoagerburgh Road. The entrance to the refuge is 1 mile on the right.

For Additional Information on Shawangunk National Wildlife Refuge

Shawangunk National Wildlife Refuge, 973-702-7266 (Wallkill, N.J., National Wildlife Refuge)

Resource person: Elizabeth Herland, Refuge Manager, Wallkill National Wildlife Refuge

Great Swamp National Wildlife Refuge, Morris County, New Jersey

Nesting***   Spring Migration***   Autumn Migration**   Winter*

Located within an hour's drive of New York City, the Great Swamp National Wildlife Refuge, managed by the U.S. Fish and Wildlife Service, provides special birding opportunities. The 7,400-acre refuge includes the swamp (through which birders can walk on an elevated boardwalk), marshes, upland forests, and grassy fields.

Spring is the best time to bird this refuge, when you can see both nesting birds and migrants. Take your time exploring the following areas: the the Wildlife Observation Center, with its trails and boardwalk through swamp and ponds; Pleasant Plains Road, including grassland and field birding; the Laurel Trail from the Morris County Outdoor Education Center adjacent to the refuge; Woodland Road, a trail through field and marsh; Old Meyersville Road, with a trail, swamp, and fields; and the Primitive Access.

Starting at the Wildlife Observation Center on Long Hill Road, walk the trails and boardwalks, from which you may see waterbirds (Great Blue Heron, Green Heron, Virginia Rail, Wood Duck—often overhead, the teals, Hooded Merganser, and some migrant ducks) and songbirds (Gray Catbird, Common Yellowthroat, and Swamp Sparrow). Some birds are visible along the edges of the ponds, and others are best observed from the observation blinds.

Along Pleasant Plains Road, you may find Red-tailed Hawk, American Kestrel, swallows (Tree, Northern Rough-winged, Bank, and Barn), Eastern Bluebird, Savannah Sparrow, Grasshopper Sparrow, Bobolink, and Eastern Meadowlark.

The Old Meyersville Road trail is a good location for observing Least Bittern, Red-shouldered Hawk, Ruffed Grouse, King Rail (rare), and songbirds such as Least Flycatcher, other flycatchers (Acadian Fly-catcher, Willow Flycatcher, and Eastern Phoebe), and Marsh Wren.

From the Woodland Road trail, you pass wetlands that attract migrating shorebirds as well as Wood Duck, Virginia Rail, and Sora, and you pass through forest that attracts upland species such as Veery and Baltimore Oriole.

The Primitive Access area off Long Hill Road is an excellent place for observing both waterfowl (in the open water) and forest species, including Wood Duck, American Woodcock, Northern Flicker, Pileated Wood-pecker, Eastern Kingbird, White-eyed Vireo, Brown Creeper (rare), Blue-winged Warbler, Yellow Warbler, American Redstart, and Rose-breasted Grosbeak. Red-headed Woodpecker has been common in the past.

Bathrooms are at several locations, including refuge headquarters (where maps can be obtained) and the Morris County Outdoor Education Center (adjacent to the refuge). Scopes are helpful in a few locations.

Personal Safety

Ticks are present in the refuge. Take the necessary precautions. You may find some bird species while driving along the narrow country roads. Keep your eyes on the road. There can be significant traffic in this suburban neighborhood.

Getting There

CAR: The Great Swamp is located 7 miles south of Morristown, New Jersey. Take the 78 Exit off the New Jersey Turnpike. Going West on

I-78, take Route 24 toward Morristown. Exit at Morris Avenue in Summit, which leads to River Road. Go left on River Road (first left) to Chatham and follow it to Fairmount Avenue. Then go left onto Meyersville Road to Meyersville. Go right on New Vernon Road and then follow the signs to the Great Swamp National Wildlife Refuge.

For Additional Information about Great Swamp National Wildlife Refuge

Great Swamp National Wildlife Refuge, 973-425-1222

Pine Barrens, Burlington County, New Jersey

Nesting***   Spring Migration   Fall Migration   Winter

Despite their stark, arid appearance and sandy roads, which can suck the tires off your car, the Pine Barrens of New Jersey offer a multitude of birding experiences. Similar to the sandy, acidic soil habitat found on Long Island, the Pine Barrens cover more than one million acres and spread across seven New Jersey counties (or 20% of New Jersey's total land mass).

In 1983, the United Nations designated this vast ecosystem an International Biosphere Reserve, protecting it for the future. The best birding areas are managed by the New Jersey Department of Environmental Protection, Division of Parks and Forestry. We suggest birding in the Burlington County area of the Pine Barrens.

The habitats to visit include oak forest with few pines, oak–pine forest with some dwarf oaks beneath, pitch pine barrens, and the Atlantic white cedar swamps. There are also a few marshes here and there that, in some cases, used to be cedar swamps. All may be included in a one-day adventure. You need not go to specific locations, because there is representative habitat scattered throughout this immense, far from barren, area.

During autumn and winter, most of the nesting birds have gone south, and migrants generally do not stop over in large numbers. The best time to visit is from early or mid-May through mid-June, before the heat of summer bakes the barrens. You should make a point of seeing the full spectrum of habitat: mature oak forest, mature pine forest, pine–oak forest, cedar swamp, and of course the stunted pine plains. The smell of pine and cedar, especially on hot days, makes your adventure memorable.

The best way to bird the barrens is to find a parking place and walk the asphalt or dirt roads, or even the sandy fire trails that run throughout the forests and swamps. You may wish to start at the stunted pine plains (on Routes 72 and 539 north of Warren Grove, N.J.), where there are no trees taller than 8 feet, to experience the plains' beauty and to observe the specific avifauna they host. The species are few, so you need not spend much time here. Park along a hardtop road and walk down the perpendicular dirt fire roads. Walk as far as a ½ mile, and you will be surrounded by stunted pines and scrub oaks. Look and listen for Brown Thrasher, Prairie Warbler, and Eastern Towhee.

Next, explore the taller pine–oak forests within Lebanon State Forest, where there is a great diversity of pine barren nesters. Again, park along a hardtop road, this time near the park headquarters building (with restrooms). Walk and listen (the traffic is usually so sparse that the forest is quiet) for Carolina Chickadee, Brown Thrasher, Pine, Prairie, and Black-and-white warblers, Ovenbird, and Scarlet Tanager. Also investigate the oak forests and cutover areas, where there may be Red-headed Woodpecker, White-breasted Nuthatch, Eastern Bluebird, Wood Thrush, and Summer Tanager. Broad-winged Hawk can be seen soaring over the forest with their young later in the summer. Wild Turkey are becoming common here.

Evenings in the barrens can be good times to observe (and listen to) Common Nighthawk and Whip-poor-will. Eastern Screech-Owl are common. Barred and Northern Saw-whet owls are known to nest in a few places, but these locations are kept secret for fear the owls will be harassed by eager birders.

Early morning is best, although on cool days, nesting birds will sing throughout the day.

Lebanon State Forest's cedar swamps and other wetlands host Acadian Flycatcher, Black-throated Green Warbler, Northern Waterthrush, and Canada Warbler as well as Green Heron, Ruffed Grouse, Virginia Rail, and American Woodcock. Try the swamps in the Whitesbog area, located at the northern end of the state forest about 3 miles east of Browns Mills off Route 530 (the sign says Conservation and Environmental Studies Center) or 1¼ miles east on Route 530 from Route 70. Narrow paved roads run through forest and cedar swamp, abandoned cranberry bogs, blueberry fields, and streams. Late winter into early spring, a few waterfowl species are present, including Tundra Swan, Wood Duck, both teal species, Northern Pintail, and Hooded Merganser.

Aside from Lebanon State Forest, you may also wish to try Wharton State Forest, which offers the same types of habitat. It is southwest of Lebanon State Forest, a bit farther from New York City.

Special Note

The Lebanon State Forest headquarters building (just off Route 72 south of the intersection with Route 70) provides interpretive information and detailed maps of the forest.

Personal Safety

Insect repellent is advised. Deer ticks abound. Stay on the wide sandy fire roads so you do not brush up against vegetation, minimizing your chances of picking up ticks.

Getting There

CAR: Take the New Jersey Turnpike south to Exit 11 to the Garden State Parkway; then take the Garden State Parkway south to Exit 88. Go west on Route 70 to Route 72. Turn left on Route 72 and go south/east for about 4 miles. The entrance to Lebanon State Forest is on the left, on an asphalt road. It is east of Hedger House, N.J., which can be found on area maps.

For Additional Information on the Pine Barrens

Pinelands Commission, 609-894-9342
Lebanon State Forest, 609-726-1191

Brigantine Division of Forsythe National Wildlife Refuge, Atlantic County, New Jersey

Nesting**   Spring Migration***   Fall Migration***   Winter***

In all seasons, the Brigantine Division of the Forsythe National Wildlife Refuge (managed by the U.S. Fish and Wildlife Service) in Oceanville, New Jersey, provides some of the best wetlands and water birding in the East. More than 300 species of birds have been recorded at Brigantine, including many rarities. In addition, the panoramic views of the marsh, back bays, and even Atlantic City casinos make for a wonderful day. Physically, this wilderness area is part of the outer reaches of the Pine Barrens.

To bird Brigantine, drive the 8-mile wildlife loop road. Start by parking in the lot. Sign in and pay at the self-serve station. There is a small fee per car; special passes are available from the U.S. Fish and Wildlife Service. Check the sightings sheet and obtain a checklist and other literature in the building (with restrooms) adjacent to the fee payment table. The sightings sheets will tell you which birds have been seen lately and where they were seen (a grid map shows the exact locations). Before getting back into the car, look through the nearby forest edge for songbirds, especially during spring and autumn migration. A trail leads a short distance into the forest. If there is evidence of migrant fallout from the previous night, take some time to bird the trail.

During breeding season, look for Chipping Sparrow that nest next to the parking lot. The lawns along the road to the wildlife loop host Killdeer, meadowlarks, and other grassland birds.

Drive down the road to the wetlands and wildlife drive. At the bottom of the first hill is a pullout that provides an introductory view of the wetlands. Clapper Rail may be heard here.

In a short distance, the road splits. Straight ahead you will find a nice pond and a viewing tower. Waterfowl and terns (sometimes Caspian) can be seen at this stop, depending on the season. After stopping briefly at the pond, continue on the main wildlife drive out onto the marsh. Drive slowly and scan for birds. Stop frequently by pulling out of the middle of the road (out of traffic). You can get out to look or set up your scope anywhere, as long as you pull over to the side. There are several designated pullouts around the loop that provide parking for many cars and even buses. The best way to bird the impoundments and adjacent saltwater marshes and bays is to drive slowly while looking for rafts of ducks or flocks of shorebirds. The birds are fairly used to people, but you should still avoid slamming car doors and making quick movements. Look before getting out of your car so you do not startle the birds. The sloughs and freshwater wetlands on the interior of the drive (to your left) host a different set of bird species from the saltmarsh and open saltwater. This is where more than one set of eyes pays off.

Summer birding is a bit slower, although some shorebirds are always present. Marsh Wren, Saltmarsh Sharp-tailed Sparrow, and Seaside Sparrow nest in or near the wildlife drive and usually can be heard singing, especially in spring and summer. Clapper Rail are abundant in the saltmarshes from spring through early autumn, and Virginia Rail can sometimes be seen within the impounded wetland areas during migration. There are rumors that Black Rail nest within the impoundment; the habitat appears suitable for this elusive species. Peregrine Falcon have nested in the nesting/platform box in the impoundments about 1 mile out onto the marsh (on your left). Egrets, herons, and ibis are always present. Look carefully for Black-crowned Night-Heron and possibly Yellow-crowned Night-Heron roosting in the brushy impoundment.

The Brigantine Division of Forsythe is one of the best places in New Jersey to see migrating shorebirds, in part because of management of the wetlands. The refuge manager and staff have done a marvelous job making Brig birder-friendly. Autumn migration starts in late June with the arrival of a few shorebirds. (The avid birders arrive then as well.) By mid-July, migration is in full swing. In August, a trip is extremely worthwhile. The presence of shorebirds outside the dike in tidal areas is best when mudflats are exposed, so you may wish to check the tide schedule (www.opsd.nos.noaa.gov/tides or Jersey shore newspapers).

Freshwater/brackish areas inside the dike can produce excellent birding at any time, although water levels are changed for waterfowl and shore-birds, according to season and refuge management. The shorebirds are too numerous to list; you can expect almost everything, including Black-bellied Plover, Semipalmated Plover, both yellowlegs, Spotted Sand-piper, Least Sandpiper, and Short-billed Dowitcher. The uncommon shorebirds include Hudsonian Godwit, Western Sandpiper, and Buff-breasted Sandpiper.

Late autumn, after mid-October, is a great time for waterfowl, raptors, and shorebirds. Within the impoundments and outside, you will find enormous rafts of waterfowl, with Snow Goose and Brant the most nu-merous, followed by American Black Duck, Northern Shoveler, North-ern Pintail, Green-winged Teal, Bufflehead, and Coot. Although Dunlin are the most numerous shorebirds, you may also find godwits and Red Knot. With your scope, scan through the shorebirds and hone your bird-ing skills. Aside from the uncountable numbers of waterfowl and shore-birds, you will find Bald Eagle, Merlin, and Peregrine Falcon. Northern Harrier and Red-tailed Hawk are common. And there may also be an oc-casional Short-eared Owl.

Winter is an ideal time for sighting waterfowl and raptors. Snow Goose by the thousands winter in Forsythe, along with Brant, American Black Duck, and other waterfowl. Great Blue Heron are here year round. Short-eared Owl may be about at anytime, especially when it is cloudy. Northern Harrier are present throughout the year and nest nearby. Bald and Golden (rare) eagles are present. Often Bald Eagle perch on the ground in the middle of the central impoundment, sometimes right on the mud. They are also seen perched in the tree line to the north as you leave the wetlands portion of the wildlife drive. Peregrine Falcon, which nest on hacking platforms within the central impoundment, often spend the winter here. Red-tailed Hawk soar everywhere. Dunlin winter in signifi-cant numbers here, along with Black-bellied Plover. In very cold weather, the ponds freeze over, causing many waterfowl to leave. The saltwater species—outside the impoundment—generally stay.

At any time of year, the fields and forests at the end of the loop drive can be productive. The nesting box in the open field (on your left as you go up a slight incline at the end of the loop drive) hosts Barn Owl and bluebirds, and grassland songbirds frequent the fields during migration.

Special Note

One of the best ways to see raptors at Brigantine is to be alert for large flocks of birds taking off. When a Bald Eagle, Northern Harrier, Merlin, Peregrine, or Short-eared Owl flies low over the marsh, they make the other birds nervous. Tight flocks of flying shorebirds or waterfowl indicate such apprehension and may be an indication that a raptor is nearby. Search the sky above or adjacent to the flocks.

Equipment

A spotting scope is a necessity. Viewing from automobile windows can be a great way to get good views and save time. A window mount for the scope comes in very handy when birding this area.

Personal Safety

In season, deer ticks are abundant in grassy and brushy areas. In the warm months, gnats, flies, and mosquitoes are prevalent. Apply insect repellant around your ankles if you plan to go into the brush or grass.

Drive with caution along the dike loop; the sides are steep and there are no curbs. Stay off the road when looking through your binoculars or scope,.

The wildlife loop road is closed for a few weeks each autumn to allow hunting. Call ahead for the dates of hunting season.

Getting There

CAR: Take the New Jersey Turnpike south to Exit 11 for the Garden State Parkway. Go south on the Garden State Parkway to Exit 48 (Absecon and Route 9) just past the Mullica River bridge. Go south on Route 9 for about 4½ miles until you arrive at Great Creek Road about 1 mile south of Smithville. A sign to Forsythe National Wildlife Refuge will be obvious along the road at that intersection. Go left and follow the main road into the refuge, about 1 mile. The entrance fee is $3.00 per vehicle, unless you have a Duck Stamp or other such pass for National Wildlife Refuges.

For Additional Information on Forsythe National Wildlife Refuge

Forsythe National Wildlife Refuge, 609-652-1665

Island Beach State Park, Ocean County, New Jersey

Nesting*   Spring Migration**   Fall Migration***   Winter*

Island Beach State Park in New Jersey is a bit farther than Jones Beach on Long Island and is an equally productive birding area for species found in ocean, dune, and marsh habitat. Located halfway between Manhattan and Cape May in Seaside Park, Island Beach can be reached before 8:00 AM by a birder who has left Manhattan at 6:00 AM, allowing for many hours of birding. Island Beach, physically an outermost reach of the Pine Barren wilderness, is a barrier island of sand jutting out into Barnegat Bay Inlet.

It is primarily an autumn birding site. The park is managed by the New Jersey Department of Environmental Protection, Division of Parks and Forestry.

Birding Island Beach State Park is relatively easy. Drive the north–south road (basically the only road) and look for raptors both on telephone poles and coursing the dunes. Park in the designated parking areas, from which you can access the boardwalks and trails that cross the dunes to the beach. Look out past the surf and along the dunes. Seabirds and water-fowl will be found from the beach area out toward the sea. Landbirds will be either moving inland or, in the case of hawks, moving parallel to the dune or water. In the fall, for a prolonged view, look north (to your left as you face the ocean) to sight arriving birds.

The best time for birding Island Beach coincides with the autumn runs of striped bass and bluefish, so you will share the beaches and parking areas with die-hard anglers. The birding starts in late summer with shore-birds and songbirds. By mid-September, thousands of hawks are moving through. The Jersey shore is a highway for falcons, and by the end of September, numerous Peregrine Falcon come through along with American Kestrel and Merlin. Osprey and Northern Harrier can be seen as well. Songbirds are in the dunes (observe them from the boardwalks), brush, and wet forests. The trees and bushes are sometimes dripping with tired migrants.

The peak time for birding at Island Beach State Park is from mid-October through the first two weeks of November. You will see loons (mostly Red-throated), Horned Grebe, thousands of Northern Gannet, cor-morants, scoters (all three species), Oldsquaw, Red-breasted Merganser, and other migrating and feeding waterbirds. On some days more than a thousand Red-throated and Common loons pass close to shore and over-head. Gannets of all ages are sometimes just beyond the surf, diving into the water from more than 100 feet up. They are trying to catch elusive baitfish, which are also migrating or trying to elude predatory fish. Gulls of several species and Caspian, Royal, Common, and Forster's terns join the melee.

Jaeger, mostly Parasitic with an occasional Pomarine, are not uncom-mon in late October through mid-November. They are present mostly when the fish runs occur and gannets, gulls, and terns are chasing baitfish close to shore. Watch for a slightly different-looking "gull" chasing other birds, trying to take their prey. On rare occasions, Black-legged Kittiwake and rare gulls mix in with the usual gulls and terns. The surf line usually has plenty of Sanderling, with the occasional Dunlin, Black-bellied Plover, and Semipalmated Plover. At the end of November, birding op-portunities taper off, although there are still birds to be seen throughout the winter.

In late October and November, walk the beach from the last parking lot southwest toward the jetty, about 1 mile. There will be anglers and dune buggies assembled here. Bird the jetties, the channel, and the dunes back from the jetty. Harlequin Duck is a regular in late autumn and most winters. Eider, mostly Common, and some other interesting ducks can be present in winter. Also in winter, Purple Sandpiper will be on the jetty if they are anywhere. Anglers can spook them, but they will always come back to the rocks. Be extremely careful on the jetty; large waves and slippery rocks make it hazardous. Also, watch the jetty and dunes for Horned Lark, Savannah Sparrow, Snow Bunting, and other grassland/open ground songbirds that stop off during migration or for the winter. These birds also attract Northern Harrier, Merlin, and Peregrine Falcon.

In autumn, walk to the blinds on the inland side of the island via trails from the main road. On the way out, watch for songbirds and hawks (Sharp-shinned Hawk and Merlin) hunting for songbirds. Yellow-rumped Warbler are the most numerous in late autumn along with Palm Warbler, White-throated Sparrow, and Dark-eyed Junco. Short-eared Owl hunt the marshes and dunes at dawn and dusk. Late in autumn and on into winter, Snowy Owl are visitors to the dunes, telephone poles, snow fencing, jetty, and even small trees.

Scan the open water of the back bays in late autumn for American Black Duck, Ring-necked Duck, and Bufflehead. Harriers hunt the marsh regularly, as do Peregrine Falcon. In summer there will be herons, Osprey, Clapper Rail, shorebirds, most of the terns, and other nesting birds.

Also watch for Rough-legged Hawk over the dunes and marshes in late autumn and winter. Northern Harrier may be the most common raptors during late autumn and winter. Horned Lark, Snow Bunting, and other winter songbirds can be found at times.

Bring a scope as well as good shoes for walking on the soft sand. Primitive restrooms are located at several of the parking areas, including the one at the end of the road. There is a fee to get into the park, payable at the main gate. In summer, the park is packed with beachgoers.

Personal Safety

There are ticks, and in warm weather, there are also mosquitoes. Some parking areas and roads to parking areas are sandy. Stay out of the way of dune buggies.

Getting There

CAR: Island Beach is located in Seaside Park, New Jersey. Take the Garden State Parkway south to Exit 82. Go east on Route 37 toward Island Beach. Cross the bridge over Barnegat Bay and be prepared to bear right toward Seaside Heights and Seaside Park. Proceed south (down the beach) until you get to the park entrance.

Special Note

There are many other great birding day trips to New Jersey. Among the best are the Pequannock Watershed/Clinton Reservoir, Waywayanda State Park, and Ringwood State Park, all located only an hour to an hour and a half from Manhattan. All have an abundance of nesting songbirds that can be accessed via excellent trails. In addition, the New Jersey Audubon Scherman-Hoffman Sanctuaries in Bernardsville (Morris County) are nesting habitat for numerous forest birds. There is also a very complete gift shop.

For Additional Information on Island Beach State Park

Island Beach State Park, 908-793-0506
Island Beach Nature Center, 908-793-1698

Chapter Ten

New York Pelagic Birding Opportunities

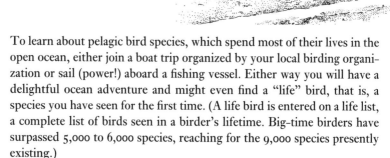

To learn about pelagic bird species, which spend most of their lives in the open ocean, either join a boat trip organized by your local birding organization or sail (power!) aboard a fishing vessel. Either way you will have a delightful ocean adventure and might even find a "life" bird, that is, a species you have seen for the first time. (A life bird is entered on a life list, a complete list of birds seen in a birder's lifetime. Big-time birders have surpassed 5,000 to 6,000 species, reaching for the 9,000 species presently existing.)

Many pelagic species are found in the waters south of Long Island and east of New Jersey. From 6 miles off shore to 100 miles directly south of New York City at the Hudson Canyon of the Continental Shelf, these extraordinary seabirds are found feeding in the upwelling currents as they migrate.

More than 100 fishing boats, called party, open, or head boats, sail from metropolitan area ports. The best known port is Sheepshead Bay in Brooklyn. Boats also leave from Captree on Long Island (90 minutes from Manhattan), Point Lookout (just beyond the Rockaways), Staten Island, Montauk (at the southern tip of Long Island), and smaller ports in New York (Shinnecock) and New Jersey (Brielle and Belmar). From May through October, and sometimes November, these boats sail almost daily. For phone numbers, refer to advertisements in the Friday sports section of the *Daily News* or *Newsday*. *The Fisherman*, a weekly publication, also provides a list of boats from Long Island, Staten Island, and New Jersey.

Trips on a fishing boat vary in price, depending on length of time and distance of the trip. Call and ask how far offshore they go, how long the trip is, and whether they accommodate birdwatchers. Because you will pay the same fee that an angler would, captains usually do not object to birders.

From May through the summer, boats that drift and chum (spread a trail of minced fish, blood, and oil) for bluefish during daylight hours are most likely to reach areas where seabirds are found, especially if the boats go out 6–15 miles. Boats that go more than 10 miles offshore to fish near wrecks may also encounter these birds. In late summer and early autumn, party boats sail as far as 50–100 miles offshore looking for tuna and albacore.

In late spring and into summer, Wilson's Storm-Petrel is the most common seabird in New York waters. Also Cory's, Greater, and Sooty shearwaters may be present along with gulls and terns. Later in the summer, once autumn migration has started, Wilson's Storm-Petrels may still be present along with Leach's Storm-Petrel in very small numbers. Also present may be phalaropes and seabirds, not to mention songbirds that have flown or been blown out from the New England coastline. Warblers, sparrows, and other songbirds often land on fishing boats to rest before taking off again.

In autumn, especially between about October 15 and November 20, when the migration of waterbirds gets going, you may view a procession of loons (Red-throated and Common), Northern Gannet, scoters (all three species), gulls, terns, and other waterfowl from fishing boats that only sail a couple of miles off the coast. If you are lucky you may see feeding frenzies by gannets, gulls, and others. Gannets feed by taking spectacular dives from 100 feet in the air. They enter the water like a spear, becoming completely submerged before reappearing with their catch. Later in the season you may see Razorbill and other alcids.

In late autumn and even winter, being on the water can be a brutal experience for a birder. Winter fishing boats sail out to sea looking for cold-water species such as cod, ling, tautog, and mackerel. If you pick a mild, calm day (an uncommon experience) without fog, you may see such rarities as Northern Fulmar, Black-legged Kittiwake, Dovekie, Common Murre, Thick-billed Murre, Razorbill, and Atlantic Puffin (very rare). There also may be Red-throated and Common loons, scoters, and various species of gulls (including white-winged gull species such as Iceland and Glaucous)

Offshore trips for tuna or cod and other long-distance voyages are not for the fainthearted (or the queasy) because they involve 12–24 hours or more on the water. Some boats even supply bunks for the night cruise out to the fishing grounds, but the ride out and back can be productive if there is enough daylight, so stay outside and be alert. Bring medication for seasickness and be careful on deck. With a boat pitching around and a birder looking through binoculars, accidents can happen, so brace yourself against a rail. Do not fall overboard (no joke). For hard-core pelagic birding, go with an organized birding group. Such trips offer comfortable accommodations at a slightly higher rate. They are designed specifically for finding seabirds, sail at the most productive times of year, and go to the best locations. Some of these charter boats chum to attract the birds (and fish). A special camaraderie prevails on these trips. Experienced birders help identify the common seabirds and also seek out the rarities. For information on such pelagic trips, contact any of the local birding organizations.

Special Notes

If you go out on a fishing boat, take a few minutes to examine the catch. You will be amazed at the beauty of freshly caught fish. The colors can be spectacular while the fish are still alive, rivaling those of birds, butterflies, and flowers.

You will not have a pelagic experience on boats that fish the back bays (e.g., Great South Bay) for fluke, flounder, and weakfish, although the birding can be good (for egrets, gulls, and terns).

Seasickness is common on pelagic trips. If you are susceptible, take medication. If you are uncertain, try a short trip first. Some birders go to sea despite knowing that they will be sick. For them, the birding experience is worth a day of misery.

For cool weather sailing, you will need warm, waterproof clothing and boots. Dress in layers and do not forget a hat and gloves.

Scopes are useful only on calm sea days when mounted on a rifle stock. Leave your tripod at home.

Chapter Eleven

American Kestrel

Hawkwatches near New York City

Looking at a map of the East Coast of North America, you will notice that the New York metropolitan area is situated at an indentation, a place where the Atlantic Ocean juts into the continent. Up the coast from New York City, land extends in an easterly direction, and down the coast the land extends southwest. The city is at the turning point. Many migrating hawks are reluctant to cross open water, so they follow the coast, especially during autumn migration.

Inland from the Atlantic, hawks follow the high ridges of New Jersey and southern New York, just north and west of New York City. Thus the Atlantic coast and the ridges inland act as a giant topographic funnel, concentrating large numbers of fall migrating hawks into a narrow corridor. (For hawkwatches in the city, see chap. 1, "The Bronx/Pelham Bay Park," "Van Cortlandt Park," "New York Botanical Garden," and "Wave Hill"; chap. 2, "Brooklyn/Prospect Park" and "Green-Wood Cemetery"; chap. 3, "Manhattan/Central Park" and "Riverside Park"; and chap. 4, "Queens/Fort Tilden.") The total number of hawks counted at nearby sites is usually about 15,000 per season. For those birdwatchers who wish to see large numbers, often at very close range, the following seven hawkwatch sites, open to the public, can be reached with relative ease. The scenery at all of these sites is superb, especially in autumn. None is a prime site for spring migration.

Raccoon Ridge, Warren County, New Jersey

The top of Raccoon Ridge is one of the best inland places in the east to hawkwatch during fall migration. It compares favorably with the famous Hawk Mountain Sanctuary in Kempton, Pennsylvania, but without the crowds. The hike to the lookout point is about 1 mile, all uphill and relatively steep, but it is worthwhile. Views are magnificent, with the Delaware River to the west and northern New Jersey to the east. Hawks have numbered around 25,000 in a single year, equivalent to or more than the hawk numbers at the best autumn sites in the eastern United States. From mid-September through late October (peaking during the last days of September through the first 10 days of October), Sharp-shinned Hawk, Cooper's Hawk, Broad-winged Hawk, and others stream by; earlier, Bald Eagle, Northern Harrier, and Broad-winged Hawk are common. Many hawkwatching aficionados prefer late season at this site, because this is the time for the big raptors flying just above the treetops. On blustery west and north winds with blue skies, the birds come in at or below eye level. Highlights at this time are Red-tailed Hawk and Golden Eagle (also Bald Eagle). The peak for these species is the last week of October to the first week of November. During this time, also look for Northern Harrier (especially adult males, called Gray Ghosts), Northern Goshawk, and Red-shouldered Hawk. (For directions, refer to Boyle's *A Guide to Bird Finding in New Jersey*.)

The lookout has some additional advantages. Black bear and deer can be seen while you are hiking in. Wild Turkey frequent the fields at the bottom of the mountain. Timber rattlesnakes inhabit the hillsides, especially on the east side of the ridge. The rhododendron groves on the east side of the ridge are beautiful at all times of year and are particularly resplendent during late spring/early summer bloom. Take your time to enjoy the scenery and the wildlife.

Sunrise Mountain, Sussex County, New Jersey

For those who wish to hawkwatch atop the Kittatiny Ridge without a long hike such as the one at Raccoon Ridge, Sunrise Mountain in Stokes State Park is a good choice. From the parking area, the walk is only about 200 yards. Seasonal and avian progressions are similar to those at Raccoon Ridge (see above). (For directions, refer to Boyle's *A Guide to Bird Finding in New Jersey*.)

Montclair Quarry, Essex County, New Jersey

Less than an hour from Manhattan, this hilltop hawkwatch site is located within a suburban neighborhood. In the best of years, Montclair counters tally more than 20,000 hawks. Early in the fall migration season, Broad-winged Hawk are the primary attraction. There are also Osprey, Sharp-shinned Hawk, and a smattering of other species, including Bald Eagle. Later, small numbers of Red-tailed Hawk and a few Golden Eagle are seen each year. Fallouts of songbirds are not uncommon at Montclair.

(For directions, contact the Hawk Migration Association of North America, www.hmana.org, or see Boyle's *A Guide to Bird Finding in New Jersey*.)

Hook Mountain, Rockland County, New York

The Hook is part of the Palisades on the west side of the Hudson River only a few miles north of the Tappan Zee Bridge. It is not, strictly speaking, a ridge or coastal lookout but a combination of these topographic features. The steep hike up the Hook takes about 15–20 minutes and affords panoramic views of the Hudson River from the Croton Peninsula to the Manhattan skyline with the Tappan Zee Bridge very close by. Hawk migration at the Hook is mostly an early season activity. Osprey, Sharp-shinned Hawk, Broad-winged Hawk, and some falcons are the main attractions. Cooper's Hawk are relatively common as are Bald Eagle, which follow along the Hudson River. Large flocks of Broad-winged Hawk, numbering more than 1,000 birds, are seen in the last two weeks of September, with September 16 to 24 being the prime time. The last week of September through the first 10 days of October are prime time for Osprey, Sharp-shinned Hawk, Cooper's Hawk, and falcons, especially American Kestrel. After mid-October, there is a steady though smaller stream of raptors. Red-shouldered and Red-tailed hawks are present in consistent numbers after October 15 until about mid-November. (For directions, see www.hmana.org or Drennan's *Where to Find Birds in New York State*.)

Mount Peter, Orange County, New York

The Mount Peter hawkwatch is situated on a hilltop that is part of a series of ridges leading into northern New Jersey. Good flights of Broad-winged Hawk can be seen here especially from September 10 to 30. More than 10,000 hawks are counted here during some autumn seasons, with Broad-winged Hawk being the most numerous. Sharp-shinned and Red-tailed hawks are also numerous, with smaller numbers of most other species. (For directions, see www.hmana.org or Drennan's *Where to Find Birds in New York State*.)

Butler Sanctuary, Bedford, Westchester County, New York

The Butler Sanctuary is known in the northeast for sightings of record numbers of Broad-winged Hawk in a single day. Each year more than 1,000 Broad-winged Hawk are seen in these one-day flights, but predicting the date is difficult. All of the other migrating hawk species are seen here with regularity but in smaller numbers than those at the other sites listed. (For directions, see www.hmana.org.)

Greenwich Audubon Sanctuary, Greenwich, Connecticut

Sometimes called the Quaker Ridge Hawkwatch, the Greenwich hilltop site is situated within a National Audubon Sanctuary and is similar to the Butler Sanctuary in the kinds of species seen and their flight patterns. Broad-winged Hawk are the predominant species seen in autumn, with virtually all the other species making appearances as well. Sharp-shinned Hawk and Red-tailed Hawk are regular visitors. Small numbers of Northern Harrier, Cooper's Hawk, Red-shouldered Hawk, and American Kestrel are also seen. (For directions, see www.hmana.org.)

Getting There

To reach all of these hawkwatches, an automobile is a necessity. Directions to Sunrise and Raccoon Ridge can be found in Boyle's *A Guide to Bird Finding in New Jersey*. Directions to the other sites can be found at the Hawk Migration Association of North America web site, www.hmana.org. Directions to New York sites can also be found in Drennan's *Where to Find Birds in New York State*. (For additional information on both books, see "Suggested Readings.")

Tips for Hawkwatching

Dress warmly and in layers, with an outer layer that is windproof. Only binoculars are needed. Scopes are of little use for hawkwatching. Learn the shape and movement of the birds to determine the species. Although you may also learn plumage characteristics, distinguishing them in a distant hawk is almost impossible. The best identification guide book is *Hawks in Flight* by Dunne, Sibley, and Sutton (see "Suggested Readings"). With excellent illustrations, it describes species behavior in an easy-to-read format.

Appendix 1

Metropolitan Birding Resources

Clapper Rail

Birding Organizations

Local birding organizations acquaint the novice and advanced birder, newcomer and resident, with metropolitan birding sites. Many people belong to several organizations. By joining their events, programs, and trips, you will enrich your birding experiences and meet knowledgeable birders. You will also be able to participate in significant conservation efforts in your own neighborhood.

There are three major local organizations.

New York City Audubon Society, founded in 1979, is the largest chapter of the National Audubon Society with more than 10,000 members. Its mission is "to protect and conserve wildlife and wildlife habitats in New York City; study and enjoy birds and other wildlife, and foster appreciation of the natural world; and defend and improve the quality of green spaces and the environment in New York City for both wildlife and human beings." The chapter sponsors birding trips and monthly member meetings, open to the public free of charge, and conducts beginning birding classes, all of which are publicized in *The Urban Audubon.* Some of New York City Audubon's projects include yearly surveys of herons nesting on islands in the New York harbor and a breeding bird census of Central Park. Although a comparatively young birding organization, the chapter has become influential in the preservation of bird habitat.

New York City Audubon Society
71 West 23rd Street, Suite 1529
New York, N.Y. 10010
212-691-7483
www.nycaudubon.org

The **Linnaean Society of New York**, founded in 1878 and named for the preeminent Swedish biologist Carolus Linnaeus who invented the system of using Latin binomial names for plant and animal species, holds twice-monthly meetings at the American Museum of Natural History. The meetings are open to the public free of charge. The organization publishes its monthly *News-Letter*, sponsors field trips, and cosponsored the breeding bird census of Central Park.

Linnaean Society of New York
15 West 77th Street
New York, N.Y. 10024
212-252-2668
www.linnaeansociety.org

New Jersey Audubon Society, founded in 1897, is an established environmental force in New Jersey, with more than 20,000 members. As an independent Audubon for the state of New Jersey (it is not affiliated with the National Audubon Society), this organization protects wetlands, open space, and birds throughout the state. It runs numerous sanctuaries, publishes the quarterly *New Jersey Audubon*, and offers a full travel and field trip schedule throughout the year. New Jersey Audubon's birding programs are some of the finest in the country.

New Jersey Audubon Society
9 Hardscrabble Road, P.O. Box 126
Bernardsville, N.J. 07924
908-204-8998
www.njaudubon.org

In addition to these organizations, various chapters of the National Audubon Society provide local focus for birding and conservation.

Audubon chapters in New York State include:

Bedford Audubon, Katonah, N.Y.
Central Westchester Audubon, White Plains, N.Y.
Great South Bay Audubon, Islip, N.Y.
Hudson River Audubon of Westchester, Yonkers, N.Y.
Huntington Audubon
North Shore Audubon, Port Washington, N.Y.
Putnam Highlands Audubon, Garrison, N.Y.
Rockland County Audubon, New City, N.Y.
Saw Mill River Audubon, Chappaqua, N.Y.
Scarsdale Audubon

South Shore Audubon, Freeport, N.Y.
Theodore Roosevelt Sanctuary, Oyster Bay, N.Y.

For information about New York State Audubon chapters, contact

National Audubon Society of New York State
200 Trillium Lane
Albany, N.Y. 12203
516-869-9731

Audubon chapters in New Jersey include

Bergen County Audubon, Paramus, N.J.
Highlands Audubon, Newfoundland, N.J.
Jersey Shore Audubon, Toms River, N.J.
Monmouth County Audubon, Red Bank, N.J.
Morris Highlands Audubon, Denville, N.J.

Audubon chapters in Connecticut include

Greenwich Audubon
Naugatuck Valley Audubon

For information about these out-of-state chapters, contact

National Audubon Society
700 Broadway
New York, N.Y. 10003
212-979-3000
www.audubon.org

Bird clubs within New York City's five boroughs include

Brooklyn Bird Club (see chap. 2, "Brooklyn/Prospect Park")
Queens County Bird Club (see chap. 4, "Queens/Alley Pond Park")

For New York State, the umbrella ornithological society, organized in
1947, is the **Federation of New York State Bird Clubs**. In 1998, the
federation published *Bull's Birds of New York State*, which documents
the status, range, migration patterns, and history of 451 species on the
state checklist at time of publication. It is currently updating *The Atlas of
Breeding Birds in New York State*, which documents the distribution of
the state's breeding birds. Each January, the federation conducts a
statewide waterfowl count of loons, grebes, cormorants, geese, swan,

ducks, and coots. Contact the federation if you wish to take part in this waterfowl count. In addition, the organization publishes two quarterlies, *New York Birders* and *The Kingbird*, and leads numerous field trips throughout the state.

FNYSBC, Inc.
P.O. Box 440
Loch Sheldrake, N.Y. 12759
www.birds.cornell.edu/fnysbc

The federation's web site originates from Cornell University, where the **Cornell Lab of Ornithology** has resided since 1915. This nonprofit, membership organization offers numerous ways in which birders can study birds. BirdSource (partnered with the National Audubon Society) is a web site that not only documents various bird species in North America but allows birders to participate in data gathering. Take a look at the Bird-Source home page, www.birdsource.org, to find out about the Christmas Bird Count, the Irruptive Bird Survey, HawkWatch results, and the Great Backyard Bird Count. Cornell Lab publishes a quarterly, *The Living Bird*.

Cornell Lab of Ornithology
159 Sapsucker Woods Road
Ithaca, N.Y. 14850
607-254-2424
www.birds.cornell.edu

Bird clubs in New Jersey close to New York City include

Fyke Nature Club, Ramsey, N.J.
Montclair Bird Club, Augusta, N.J.
Palisade Nature Association, Greenbrook Sanctuary, Alpine, N.J.
Summit Nature Club, Gillette, N.J.
Tenafly Nature Center Association
Urner Ornithological Club, Netcong, N.J.

Throughout the metropolitan area are many county nature centers, city agencies, and other entities with a focus on wildlife. Among them are the **American Littoral Society**, which runs various educational programs, including birding trips in the city and abroad, and City of New York/Parks and Recreation's **Urban Park Rangers**, which sponsor the Central Park Hawkwatch and lead birdwalks in parks throughout the city.

American Littoral Society
28 West 9th Road
Broad Channel, N.Y. 11693
718-634-6467

Urban Park Rangers
800-201-PARK

The **American Birding Association** (ABA) holds a unique place in the birding world as the largest organization in North America dedicated solely to birding. The benefits of membership include discounts on birding books and other paraphernalia, birding trips, lists of hotlines throughout the country, the monthly newsletter, *Winging It*, and the bimonthly magazine *Birding*. The ABA also publishes *A Birder's Resource Guide*, which includes a complete membership list (for use only by its 22,000 members). ABA membership is for serious birders and birders who wish to improve their identification skills and meet other dedicated birders.

American Birding Association
P.O. Box 6599
Colorado Springs, Colo. 80934-6599
800-850-2473 and 719-578-9703
www.americanbirding.org

Birding Hotlines and Rare Bird Alerts

If you want to know about "rare" birds or about what is happening in the way of migration, call one of the hotlines or rare bird alerts that serve your area or log onto the North American Rare Bird Alert web site at www.narba.org. In New York City, log onto www.borg.com/~vcselem/kirkland/nerba/nyc.txt.

A hotline is simply a recorded message that provides up-to-date information on which birds are around and where they are being seen. For example, the hotline may report a large hawk migration or a fallout of warblers at a particular place. More likely the hotline will provide a narrative of where and when a rare species was seen in the area. "Rare species" usually means vagrants from other parts of the country, not species that are threatened or endangered. For example, the recorded message may report that "on Thursday, December 14, a Snowy Owl was seen on the Jones Beach Causeway. It was perched on a utility pole 4 miles west of the tower." It may also give information about access to an area or warnings about parking or other problems.

Rare bird alerts will help you find birds that you might never find on your own. As you become more experienced, you may find hotline-worthy birds. These need to be reported, both for confirmation and to inform other birders.

In the metropolitan New York area, the most important hotlines are

New York City Rare Bird Alert 212-979-3070
Connecticut (statewide) 203-254-3665
New Jersey (statewide) 908-766-2661
New Jersey (Cape May) 609-861-0466

For additional rare bird alerts or birding hotline numbers, join the ABA. Their *Birder's Resource Guide* lists them all.

Bird-Related Web Sites

Aside from the web sites listed in this and other chapters, you may wish to investigate the following:

www.petersononline.com (information on Peterson Field Guides and the Roger Tory Peterson Institute)

www.learner.org/jnorth (a global study of wildlife migration)

www.PartnersInFlight.org (conservation organization)

www.abcbirds.org (conservation organization)

www.hmana.org (Hawk Migration Association of North America)

www.stokesbirdsathome.com (information on birding and bird behavior)

Christmas Bird Count

In the latter part of the nineteenth century, a Christmastime tradition was to hunt and kill as many birds and other game animals as possible, presumably for the holiday meal. In 1900, the great ornithologist Frank Chapman invited people to "spend a portion of the day with the birds," count the species, and send in the results to *Bird-Lore*, the predecessor of *Audubon*, National Audubon Society's magazine. The count, not the shoot, continues today, sponsored by National Audubon. From just a handful of counts 100 years ago, this scientific enterprise has grown to 1,800 day-long counts. The 100th consecutive Christmas Bird Count, which ran from December 16, 1999, through January 3, 2000, was celebrated with more than 60,000 bird lovers throughout North America counting 75,655,829 birds! This bird count is the longest continuously running citizen science study.

The area covered by each Christmas Bird Count is approximately 177 square miles, within a 7.5-mile radius. More than 100 people comb the fields, forests, beaches, open water, and backyards in some New York City counts. The number of species seen ranges from 85 to 135. The highest numbers are seen in count circles that contain a wide variety of habitat, including ocean, back bays, wetlands, and upland forest and field.

The purpose of the Christmas Bird Count is to monitor changes in bird populations and species status. Less tangible results include what participants learn in the process and how much fun they have taking part. On the designated day, a few die-hard counters start at midnight looking for owls and other night birds. Most people meet at dawn or shortly thereafter and move in teams over preassigned areas. By joining a count group, you will learn about winter birds (identification, behavior, ecology, and so forth) and where to look for them as well as meet other hearty birders. At the end of the count day, participants often gather, hopefully over a bowl of hot soup, to report their tallies and share their experiences. The population data, compared from year to year, contribute to important research and conservation efforts. Look at recent statistics by visiting the web site www.birdsource.org/cbc/index.html.

Christmas Bird Counts in the metropolitan area include the following list. The numbers in parentheses indicate the unofficial count of species seen during the 1999–2000 count day, the 100th Christmas Bird Count.

Metropolitan New York

Brooklyn (129)
Queens (110)
Staten Island (108)
Lower Hudson (90)—listed under New Jersey, but includes Manhattan
Bronx-Westchester (120)

Upstate New York

Peekskill (85)
Rockland County (85)

Long Island

Montauk (135)
Quogue-Watermill (107)
Sagaponack (125)
Smithtown (94)
Orient (119)
Southern Nassau County (130)
Northern Nassau County (107)
Captree (116)
Central Suffolk (130)

Connecticut

Greenwich-Stamford (116)—part in Westchester

New Jersey

Great Swamp-Watchung Ridges (87)
Long Branch (127)—northern New Jersey Shore
Lower Hudson (90)—includes Manhattan, N.Y. (see above)
Sandy Hook (113 in 99th count)—includes nearby Raritan Bay and the
   Atlantic Ocean
Pelagic (16 in 99th count)—20 miles east of Manasquan Inlet

Anyone, novice or expert, can participate in a Christmas Bird Count. Call the National Audubon Society or your local chapter to find out who the compiler is for your area. A small fee of $5.00 is collected on the day of the count to cover National Audubon's costs for inputting the data onto BirdSource and publishing the results.

Important Bird Areas in New York State

The Important Bird Area (IBA) concept—to identify sites that are essential for sustaining naturally occurring bird populations—was initiated in 1985 by Great Britain's BirdLife International. More than 65,000 square kilometers have been so designated in Europe, and the program has spread to Asia, Africa, the Americas, and the Middle East. The National Audubon Society brought the idea to this country. To date in New York State alone, 127 sites have been granted IBA status. They include the following sites in this guidebook:

Pelham Bay Park (chap. 1, "The Bronx")
Van Cortlandt Park (chap. 1, "The Bronx")
Prospect Park (chap. 2, "Brooklyn")
Central Park (chap. 3, "Manhattan")
North Brother/South Brother Islands (chap. 3, "Manhattan/Central
   Park")
Jamaica Bay complex (chap. 4, "Queens")
Harbor Herons complex (chap. 5, "Staten Island")
Jones Beach State Park (chap. 6, "Nassau County")
Hempstead Lake State Park (chap. 6, "Nassau County")
Edith G. Read Wildlife Sanctuary (chap. 7, "Westchester County")
Marshlands Conservancy (chap. 7, "Westchester County")
Montauk Point (chap. 9, "Great Birding Day Trips")
Doodletown Road/Iona Island (chap. 9, "Great Birding Day Trips")
Shawangunk Grasslands National Wildlife Refuge (chap. 9, "Great
   Birding Day Trips")
Butler Sanctuary (chap. 11, "Hawkwatches near New York City")
Hook Mountain (chap. 11, "Hawkwatches near New York City")

To learn about the criteria and the process for Important Bird Area designation, contact the National Audubon Society of New York State at www.ny.audubon.org/iba/ or read *Important Bird Areas in New York State* compiled by Jeffrey V. Wells (see "Suggested Readings"). If you are interested in which other states have initiated Important Bird Area programs, contact the National Audubon Society.

Appendix 2

Management of Birding Sites in New York City

Common Yellowthroat

Knowing the management agency and ownership of New York City's parklands is essential if you want to be effective in protecting wildlife and habitat. Some parks encourage residents to participate in management issues through such affiliates as the Central Park Conservancy, the Prospect Park Alliance, and the Mariners Marsh Conservancy. For other city parks, citizens have to take the initiative. No matter how small or how vast the parkland, pay attention to how well it is managed. Are trees and bushes pruned during nesting season? Are nutrient-rich dead trees (snags) removed? Is pesticide used? Are recreational facilities or other developments proposed that would encroach on the natural areas? If there is a concern, call your local environmental organizations. You may have hit on an issue that requires their experience and clout. It is equally important to support park owners for good management practices. Get involved.

United States—U.S. Department of the Interior/National Park Service

Floyd Bennett Field (1,500 acres), Brooklyn
Dead Horse Bay (138.8 acres), Brooklyn
Jamaica Bay Wildlife Refuge (9,000 acres), Queens
Jacob Riis Park (27.5 acres), Queens
Fort Tilden (317 acres), Queens
Breezy Point (1,059 acres), Queens
Great Kills Park (1,200 acres, with an additional 250 acres managed by the City of New York/Parks and Recreation), Staten Island

New York State—New York State Department of Environmental Conservation

Mount Loretto Nature Preserve (194 acres), Staten Island
Saw Mill Creek Park (5 acres, with an additional 111 acres managed by the City of New York/Parks and Recreation), Staten Island
Goethals Pond (67 acres), Staten Island

New York City—City of New York/Parks and Recreation

Pelham Bay Park (2,764 acres), Bronx
Van Cortlandt Park (1,146 acres), Bronx
Spuyten Duyvil Shorefront Park (0.187 acre), Bronx
Riverdale Park (97 acres), Bronx
Prospect Park (526 acres), Brooklyn
Central Park (843 acres), Manhattan
Inwood Hill Park (196 acres), Manhattan
Riverside Park (324 acres), Manhattan
Forest Park (538 acres), Queens
Alley Pond Park (635 acres), Queens
Great Kills Park (250 acres, with an additional 1,200 acres managed by the National Park Service), Staten Island
Wolfe's Pond Park (336 acres), Staten Island
Long Pond Park (140 acres), Staten Island
Conference House Park (254 acres), Staten Island
Saw Mill Creek Park (111 acres, with an additional 5 acres owned by New York State), Staten Island
Mariners Marsh Preserve (107 acres), Staten Island
Clove Lakes Park (198 acres), Staten Island

New York City—Economic Development Corporation

Arlington Marsh (no distinct boundaries), Staten Island

Semipublic/Private Ownership

Wave Hill (28 acres), Bronx
New York Botanical Garden (250 acres), Bronx
Brooklyn Botanic Garden (52 acres), Brooklyn
Green-Wood Cemetery (478 acres), Brooklyn
Point Lookout (no distinct boundaries), Nassau County

Appendix 3

Checklist of the Birds of New York City

Brant

This checklist includes species that can be seen in the five boroughs and adjoining waters. Meant as a tool for birders, it provides a relative measure of seeing a specific species when birding in an appropriate habitat in New York City. Assessing relative abundance is tricky: some species are common in one location because their preferred habitat is available, but they are not found nearby because that habitat is not present. For example, a species that may be common in Jamaica Bay because it prefers saltmarsh, may not be found in the uplands of Prospect Park.

Species not included in the list because they have been seen only once or twice include Pacific Loon, Magnificent Frigatebird, Wood Stork, Sandhill Crane, Reddish Egret, Roseate Spoonbill, Fulvous Whistling-Duck, Cinnamon Teal, Wilson's Plover, Sharp-tailed Sandpiper, Broad-billed Sandpiper, Spotted Redshank, Sooty Tern, Cave Swallow, Sage Thrasher, Townsend's Solitaire, Townsend's Warbler, Black-throated Gray Warbler, Swainson's Warbler, Lark Bunting, and Painted Bunting. Nesting indicators are not provided for species that have not nested since the 1970s.

Seasonal Occurrence

Winter	December–February (nonbreeding season, including some fall and spring migrants)
Spring	March–May (breeding and migration)
Summer	June–mid-July (breeding and postbreeding, including dispersal)
Early fall	mid-July–mid-September (southbound, postbreeding migration)
Late fall	mid-September–November (migration)

Relative Abundance and Status

c	common—easily seen; more than 12 individuals per day in season in habitat

f	fairly common—usually seen; 3–12 individuals per day in season in habitat
u	uncommon—seen, but in small numbers; 1–3 per day in season in habitat
s	scarce—seen in habitat, but not daily
r	rare—seen, but only a few times per season
vr	very rare—not seen every season
i	introduced—not native to North America/an alien species
p	pelagic—Atlantic Ocean off of New York City, not normally or only rarely seen from shore
?	nesting unconfirmed
*	nests within city limits
**	formerly nested within city limits

Species	Winter	Spring	Summer	Early Fall	Late Fall
Loons to Cormorants					
Red-throated Loon	u				f
Common Loon	u	u		r	f
Pied-billed Grebe*	u	s	r	f	u
Horned Grebe	u	s			u
Red-necked Grebe	vr	vr			
Eared Grebe		vr		vr	vr
Northern Fulmar (p)					
Cory's Shearwater (p)					
Greater Shearwater (p)					
Sooty Shearwater (p)					
Wilson's Storm-Petrel (p)			vr		
Leach's Storm-Petrel (p)					
Northern Gannet (p)	u	c		s	f–c
American White Pelican		vr			
Brown Pelican			vr	vr	
Double-crested Cormorant*	f	c	c	c	c
Great Cormorant	f–u	u–s			u
Bitterns to Vultures					
American Bittern**	r	r		vr	r
Least Bittern*			vr		
Great Blue Heron	s	u	u	f	f
Great Egret*	r	c	c	f	u
Snowy Egret*	vr	c	c	c	u
Little Blue Heron*		r	r	r	vr
Tricolored Heron*		r	s	r	
Cattle Egret*		u	u	u	
Green Heron*		u	u	u	
Black-crowned Night-Heron*	s	c	c	f	s
Yellow-crowned Night-Heron*		u	u	u	
Glossy Ibis*		f	c	c	
White-faced Ibis		vr	vr		

Species	Winter	Spring	Summer	Early Fall	Late Fall
Black Vulture		vr			vr
Turkey Vulture	s	u	u	s	u
Waterfowl					
Greater White-fronted Goose	vr				
Snow Goose	s				f
Canada Goose*	c	c	c	c	c
Brant	c	c			c
Mute Swan* (i)	c	c	c	c	c
Tundra Swan	r				r
Wood Duck*	s	u	u	u	s
Gadwall*	f	f	f	f	f
Eurasian Wigeon	vr				vr
American Wigeon**	f	u	vr	c	f
American Black Duck*	c	c	u	u	c
Mallard*	c	c	c	c	c
Blue-winged Teal*	r	r	r	u	s
Northern Shoveler*	f	u	s	f	c
Northern Pintail**	u			u	c
Green-winged Teal**	f	f	s	u	c
Canvasback	f	r		o	u
Redhead	r			r	r
Ring-necked Duck	s	s	vr	r	u
Tufted Duck	vr				vr
Greater Scaup	c	f		u	f
Lesser Scaup	f	s		f	f
King Eider	vr				vr
Common Eider	vr				r
Harlequin Duck	r				r
Surf Scoter	u			u	u
White-winged Scoter	o				u
Black Scoter	r			r	f
Oldsquaw	f	u		u	f
Bufflehead	c	c		s	c
Common Goldeneye	f	s		s	u
Barrow's Goldeneye	vr				vr
Hooded Merganser	f	f		u	f
Common Merganser	u	r		s	u
Red-breasted Merganser	c	f			c
Ruddy Duck*	c	c	u	u	c
Diurnal Raptors					
Osprey*		u	u	f	u
Swallow-tailed Kite		vr			
Mississippi Kite		vr		vr	
Bald Eagle	r	r		u	s
Northern Harrier*	u	u	s	u	f
Sharp-shinned Hawk	u	u		u	f
Cooper's Hawk*?	s	u		s	u

Species	Winter	Spring	Summer	Early Fall	Late Fall
Northern Goshawk	vr			vr	vr
Red-shouldered Hawk**	r	s		s	u
Broad-winged Hawk*		u	s	f	u
Red-tailed Hawk*	f	f	u	f	f
Rough-legged Hawk	s	r			r
Golden Eagle					vr
American Kestrel*	f	u	s	f	f
Merlin	r	r		s	u
Peregrine Falcon*	s	s	s	s	u
Gyrfalcon	vr				vr
Pheasant to Rails					
Ring-necked Pheasant* (i)	s	s	s	s	s
Wild Turkey*	s	s	s	s	s
Northern Bobwhite*	r	r	r	r	r
Clapper Rail*	r	u	f	u	r
King Rail**					
Virginia Rail*	r	u	u	s	r
Sora	vr	s	s	s	vr
Purple Gallinule				vr	
Common Moorhen*		u	f		
American Coot*	u	f	f	f	f
Shorebirds					
Black-bellied Plover	r	c	s	c	f
American Golden-Plover	vr	vr	vr	s	vr
Semipalmated Plover		c		c	s
Piping Plover*		u	u	u	
Killdeer*	s	u	f	f	s
American Oystercatcher*	r	f	f	f	f
Black-necked Stilt		vr	vr		
American Avocet			vr	vr	
Greater Yellowlegs	r	f	f	c	f
Lesser Yellowlegs		f	u	c	u
Solitary Sandpiper		s	r	s	
Willet*	vr	c	c	f	r
Spotted Sandpiper*		f	f	f	s
Upland Sandpiper*		r	r	s	
Whimbrel		u	s	u	
Hudsonian Godwit		s		u	
Marbled Godwit		s		u	
Ruddy Turnstone	s	c	f	c	f
Red Knot	r	f		f	s
Sanderling	c	c	s	c	c
Semipalmated Sandpiper		c	s	c	r
Western Sandpiper		u		f	r
Red-necked Stint				vr	
Little Stint				vr	
Least Sandpiper		c	s	c	

Species	Winter	Spring	Summer	Early Fall	Late Fall
White-rumped Sandpiper		u		u	
Baird's Sandpiper		r		r	
Pectoral Sandpiper		u		u	r
Purple Sandpiper	f			f	
Dunlin	c	c		f	c
Curlew Sandpiper		vr		vr	
Stilt Sandpiper		u		u	
Buff-breasted Sandpiper		r		r	
Ruff		vr		vr	
Short-billed Dowitcher		f		c	u
Long-billed Dowitcher	vr	r		s	r
Common Snipe		u		u	u
American Woodcock*	r	f	s	f	u
Wilson's Phalarope		r		r	
Red-necked Phalarope				vr	
Red Phalarope (p)					
Jaegers to Alcids					
Pomarine Jaeger (p)		r		r	r
Parasitic Jaeger (p)					
Laughing Gull*	r	c	c	c	u
Little Gull	r				
Black-headed Gull	r				
Bonaparte's Gull	c	f			f
Ring-billed Gull	c	c	c	c	c
Herring Gull*	c	c	c	c	c
Iceland Gull	r				
Lesser Black-backed Gull	r			r	
Glaucous Gull	vr				
Great Black-backed Gull*	c	c	c	c	c
Sabine's Gull(p)					vr
Black-legged Kittiwake (p)	r	r			r
Gull-billed Tern		s	r		
Caspian Tern		r		s	s
Royal Tern				s	s
Sandwich Tern			vr		
Roseate Tern		r	s	s	
Common Tern*		c	c	c	s
Arctic Tern			vr	vr	
Forster's Tern*		c	c	c	s
Least Tern*		u	f	f	s
Black Tern			r	r	
Black Skimmer**		f	c	c	
Dovekie (p)					
Common Murre (p)					
Thick-billed Murre (p)					
Razorbill (p)					
Atlantic Puffin (p)					

Species	Winter	Spring	Summer	Early Fall	Late Fall
Pigeons to Owls to Woodpeckers					
Rock Dove* (i)	c	c	c	c	c
Mourning Dove*	c	c	c	c	c
Monk Parakeet*(i)	u	u	u	u	u
Black-billed Cuckoo*			s	s	r
Yellow-billed Cuckoo*			s	vr	s
Barn Owl*	s	s	s	s	s
Eastern Screech-Owl*	s	s	s	s	s
Great Horned Owl*	u	u	u	u	u
Snowy Owl	r				r
Barred Owl	vr	r		r	r
Long-eared Owl	r				vr
Short-eared Owl**	r	r		r	r
Northern Saw-whet Owl	r			r	
Common Nighthawk*		s	f	f	r
Chuck-will's-widow		r			
Whip-poor-will		r			
Chimney Swift*		f	c	f	s
Ruby-throated Hummingbird		u	u	u	r
Belted Kingfisher*?	s	u	u	u	u
Red-headed Woodpecker	r	r		r	
Red-bellied Woodpecker*	u	u	u	u	u
Yellow-bellied Sapsucker	s	u		u	u
Downy Woodpecker*	f	f	f	f	f
Hairy Woodpecker*	s	s	s	s	s
Northern Flicker*	u	f	f	f	f
Pileated Woodpecker	r	vr			
Flycatchers					
Olive-sided Flycatcher		s		s	
Eastern Wood-Pewee*		u	s	f	
Yellow-bellied Flycatcher		s		s	
Acadian Flycatcher		s			
Alder Flycatcher		s		s	
Willow Flycatcher*		f	f	f	
Least Flycatcher		u		u	
Eastern Phoebe*		f	r	f	f
Ash-throated Flycatcher					vr
Great Crested Flycatcher*		s	s	s	
Western Kingbird	vr	vr		vr	r
Eastern Kingbird*		f	f	c	
Shrikes to Vireos to Wrens					
Loggerhead Shrike	vr				vr
Northern Shrike	vr				
White-eyed Vireo*	vr	u	u	u	s
Yellow-throated Vireo		s		s	
Blue-headed Vireo	vr	u			u
Warbling Vireo*		u	u	u	

Species	Winter	Spring	Summer	Early Fall	Late Fall
Philadelphia Vireo		r		r	
Red-eyed Vireo*		c	r	f	s
Blue Jay*	c	c	c	c	c
American Crow*	c	c	c	c	c
Fish Crow*	u	c	c	c	f
Horned Lark*	u	f	s	s	u
Purple Martin*		s	s		
Tree Swallow*	s	c	c	c	c
Northern Rough-winged Swallow*		u	f	f	
Bank Swallow		s			s
Cliff Swallow		s		s	
Barn Swallow*		c	c	c	s
Black-capped Chickadee*	f	f	f	f	f
Tufted Titmouse*	f	f	f	f	f
Red-breasted Nuthatch	f	f			f
White-breasted Nuthatch*	f	f	f	f	f
Brown Creeper		s			s
Carolina Wren*	u	u	u	u	u
House Wren*		f	u	f	r
Winter Wren	r	s			s
Sedge Wren					r
Marsh Wren*	s	f	f	f	s
Kinglets to Thrushes to Waxwings					
Golden-crowned Kinglet	s	f		s	c
Ruby-crowned Kinglet	s	f		c	c
Blue-gray Gnatcatcher*		u	r	u	
Eastern Bluebird**		r		r	r
Veery*?		u	r	u	
Gray-cheeked Thrush		r		r	
Bicknell's Thrush		r		vr	
Swainson's Thrush		u		r	
Hermit Thrush	u	u		u	u
Wood Thrush*	vr	u	s	u	r
American Robin*	u	c	c	c	c
Varied Thrush	vr				
Gray Catbird*	r	c	c	c	u
Northern Mockingbird*	f	f	f	f	f
Brown Thrasher*	r	u	u	u	u
European Starling*(i)	c	c	c	c	c
American Pipit	vr			s	u
Cedar Waxwing*	u	f	f	f	f
Warblers					
Blue-winged Warbler*?		u	s	u	
Golden-winged Warbler		r	r		
Tennessee Warbler		u		u	r
Orange-crowned Warbler	r	r		r	r
Nashville Warbler	vr	u		u	s

Species	Winter	Spring	Summer	Early Fall	Late Fall
Northern Parula		f		f	
Yellow Warbler*		f	f	f	
Chestnut-sided Warbler		u		u	s
Magnolia Warbler		u		u	s
Cape May Warbler		u		u	s
Black-throated Blue Warbler		f		f	u
Yellow-rumped Warbler	u	c		c	c
Black-throated Green Warbler		f		f	s
Blackburnian Warbler		u		u	s
Yellow-throated Warbler		r		r	
Pine Warbler		u			u
Prairie Warbler	vr	u		u	
Palm Warbler	r	f		u	f
Bay-breasted Warbler		s		s	
Blackpoll Warbler		f		u	s
Cerulean Warbler		r			
Black-and-white Warbler		f	f		
American Redstart*		c	r	c	u
Prothonotary Warbler		r			
Worm-eating Warbler		r		r	
Ovenbird**		f		u	
Northern Waterthrush		u		u	
Louisiana Waterthrush		r		r	
Kentucky Warbler		r		vr	
Connecticut Warbler		r		r	r
Mourning Warbler		r		s	
Common Yellowthroat*		f	f	c	u
Hooded Warbler		s		r	
Wilson's Warbler		u	u	s	
Canada Warbler		f		f	
Yellow-breasted Chat*	vr	r	r	r	r
Tanagers to Sparrows to Grosbeaks					
Summer Tanager		r			
Scarlet Tanager*		u	s	u	
Eastern Towhee*	s	f	c	c	f
American Tree Sparrow	f	u			u
Chipping Sparrow*	r	u	u	f	f
Clay-colored Sparrow					r
Field Sparrow*	s	u	u	u	u
Vesper Sparrow		r	vr	vr	r
Lark Sparrow	r				vr
Savannah Sparrow*	u	f	u	f	c
Grasshopper Sparrow**		r	r	r	r
Henslow's Sparrow					
LeConte's Sparrow					
Saltmarsh Sharp-tailed Sparrow*	u	u	u	u	f
Seaside Sparrow*	r	s	s	s	s

Species	Winter	Spring	Summer	Early Fall	Late Fall
Fox Sparrow	s	u			
Song Sparrow*	c	c	c	c	c
Lincoln's Sparrow		r			r
Swamp Sparrow*	u	f	f	f	c
White-throated Sparrow	c	c			c
White-crowned Sparrow	r	u			u
Dark-eyed Junco	c			s	c
Lapland Longspur	vr				
Snow Bunting	u				u
Northern Cardinal*	f	f	f	f	f
Rose-breasted Grosbeak*		u	r	u	s
Blue Grosbeak*		r	r	r	r
Indigo Bunting*		s	u	u	s
Dickcissel	vr	r			r
Blackbirds and Grackles to Orioles, Finches, and Old World Sparrows					
Bobolink		u		u	s
Red-winged Blackbird*	u	c	c	c	c
Eastern Meadowlark*	s	f	s	f	f
Yellow-headed Blackbird					vr
Rusty Blackbird	f	f			u
Brewer's Blackbird		u		u	u
Common Grackle*	u	c	c	c	c
Boat-tailed Grackle*	f	f	f	f	f
Brown-headed Cowbird*	f	c	f	c	c
Orchard Oriole*		r	r	r	
Baltimore Oriole*	vr	f	f	f	r
Purple Finch	r	s		s	
House Finch*	c	c	c	c	c
Red Crossbill	r			r	
White-winged Crossbill	r			r	
Common Redpoll	r			r	
Pine Siskin	s			s	
American Goldfinch*	u	f	f	f	f
Evening Grosbeak	r			r	
House Sparrow*(i)	c	c	c	c	c

Checklist reviewers: Ronald V. Bourque, Peter Joost, David S. Künstler, Peter Rhoades Mott, Norman I. Stotz, Don Riepe, and Steve Walter

Suggested Readings

Identification Guides

American Bird Conservancy. *All the Birds of North America: A Revolutionary System Based on Feeding Behaviors and Field-Recognizable Features.* New York: HarperCollins, 1997.

Kaufman, Kenn. *Focus Guide to the Birds of North America.* Boston: Houghton Mifflin Co., 2000.

National Audubon Society. *Field Guide to North American Birds (Eastern Region).* New York: Alfred A. Knopf, 1994.

National Geographic Society. *Field Guide to the Birds of North America.* 3rd ed. Washington, D.C.: National Geographic Society, 1999.

Peterson, Roger T. *A Field Guide to the Birds: A Completely New Guide to All the Birds of Eastern and Central North America.* 4th ed. Boston: Houghton Mifflin Co., 1980. (Also available in large format.)

Robbins, Chandler S., Bertel Bruun, and Herbert S. Zim. *A Guide to Field Identification: Birds of North America.* Rev. ed. New York: Golden Press, 1983.

Sibley, David Allen. *National Audubon Society Sibley Guide to Birds.* New York: Knopf, 2000.

Stokes, Donald, and Lillian Stokes. *Field Guide to the Birds: Eastern Region.* New York: Little, Brown and Co., 1996.

General Birding and Bird Finding

Bird, David M. *The Bird Almanac: The Ultimate Guide to Essential Facts and Figures of the World's Birds.* Buffalo, N.Y.: Firefly Press, 1999.

Connor, Jack. *The Complete Birder: A Guide to Better Birding.* Boston: Houghton Mifflin Co., 1987.

Dunne, Pete, David Sibley, and Clay Sutton. *Hawks in Flight: Flight Identification of North American Migrant Raptors.* Boston: Houghton Mifflin Co., 1988.

Ehrlich, Paul R., David S. Dobkin, and Darryl Wheye. *The Birder's Handbook: A Field Guide to the Natural History of North American Birds.* New York: Fireside, Simon and Schuster, 1988.

Gill, Frank B. *Ornithology.* 2nd ed. New York: W. H. Freeman and Co., 1995.

Pasquier, Roger. *Watching Birds: An Introduction to Ornithology.* Boston: Houghton Mifflin Co., 1977.

Stokes Nature Guides. *A Guide to Bird Behavior.* 3 vols. New York: Little, Brown and Co., 1989.

Sutton, Clay, and Patricia Sutton. *How to Spot Hawks and Eagles.* Sherburne, Vt.: Chapters, 1996.

Sutton, Patricia, and Clay Sutton. *How to Spot an Owl.* Sherburne, Vt.: Chapters, 1994.

Migration Books

Able, Kenneth P., ed. *Gatherings of Angels: Migrating Birds and Their Ecology.* Ithaca, N.Y.: Cornell University Press, a Comstock Book, 1999.

Dunne, Pete, Richard Kane, and Paul Kerlinger. *New Jersey at the Crossroads of Migration.* Franklin Lakes, N.J.: New Jersey Audubon Society, 1989.

Kerlinger, Paul. *Flight Strategies of Migrating Hawks.* Chicago: University of Chicago Press, 1989.

———. *How Birds Migrate.* Mechanicsburg, Pa.: Stackpole Books, 1995.

Weidensaul, Scott. *Living on the Wind: Across the Hemisphere with Migratory Birds.* New York: North Point Press, Farrar, Straus and Giroux, 1999.

Area Guides—Birding

Andrle, Robert F., and Janet R. Carroll. *The Atlas of Breeding Birds in New York State.* Ithaca, N.Y.: Cornell University Press, 1988.

Arbib, Robert S., Jr., Olin Sewall Pettingill, Jr., and Sally Hoyt Spofford. *Enjoying Birds around New York City.* Boston: Houghton Mifflin Co., 1966.

Barton, Howard, and Patricia I. Pelkowski. *A Seasonal Guide to Bird Finding on Long Island.* Smithtown, N.Y.: ECCS, Sweetbriar Nature Center, 1999.

Boyle, William J. *A Guide to Bird Finding in New Jersey.* New Brunswick, N.J.: Rutgers University Press, 1986.

Bull, John. *Birds of the New York Area*. New York: Harper and Row, 1964.

Drennan, Susan Roney. *Where to Find Birds in New York State: The Top 500 Sites*. Syracuse, N.Y.: Syracuse University Press. 1981.

Levine, Emanuel, ed. *Bull's Birds of New York State*. Ithaca, N.Y.: Cornell University Press, a Comstock Book, 1998.

Rosgen, Dave, and Gene Billings. *Finding Birds in Connecticut: A Habitat Guide to 450 Sites*. Torrington, Conn.: Rainbow Press, 1996.

Walsh, J., V. Elia, R. Kane, and T. Halliwell. *Birds of New Jersey*. Bernardsville, N.J.: New Jersey Audubon Society, 1999.

Wells, Jeffrey V., compiler. *Important Bird Areas in New York State*. Albany, N.Y.: National Audubon Society, 1998.

Area Guides—Natural History and Hiking

Barlow, Elizabeth. *The Forest and Wetlands of New York City*. New York: Little, Brown and Co., 1971.

Boyle, Robert H. *The Hudson River: A Natural and Unnatural History*. New York: W. W. Norton, 1979.

Buff, Sheila. *Nature Walks in and around New York City: The Forests and Wetlands of New York City*. Boston: Appalachian Mountain Club, 1996.

Burton, Dennis. *Nature Walks of Central Park*. New York: Henry Holt and Co., 1997.

Davis, William T. *Days Afield on Staten Island*. Reprint of 1892 ed. New York: Staten Island Institute of Arts and Sciences, 1992.

Glassberg, Jeffrey. *Butterflies through Binoculars: A Field Guide to Butterflies in the Boston–New York–Washington Region*. New York: Oxford University Press, 1999.

Kershner, Bruce. *Secret Places of Staten Island: A Visitor's Guide to Scenic and Historic Treasures of Staten Island*. Dubuque, Iowa: Kendall/Hunt Publishing Co., 1998.

Kieran, John. *A Natural History of New York City*. Boston: Houghton Mifflin Co., 1959.

Mittelbach, Margaret, and Michael Crewdson. *Wild New York: A Guide to the Wildlife, Wild Places, and Natural Phenomena of New York City*. New York: Crown Publishers, 1997.

Pettigrew, L. *New Jersey Wildlife Viewing Guide*. Helena, Mont.: Falcon Press, 1998.

Sullivan, Robert. *The Meadowlands: Wilderness Adventures at the Edge of a City*. New York: Scribner, 1998.

Tanacredi, John T. *Gateway: A Visitor's Companion*. Mechanicsburg, Pa.: Stackpole Books, 1995.

Villani, Robert. *Long Island: A Natural History*. New York: Harry N. Abrams, Inc., 1997.

Waldman, John. *Heartbeats in the Muck: A Dramatic Look at the History, Sea Life, and Environment of New York Harbor*. New York: Lyons Press, 2000.

Winn, Marie. *Red-Tails in Love: A Wildlife Drama in Central Park*. New York: Vintage, 1999.

Local Periodicals

American Littoral Society, *Littorally Speaking*

Brooklyn Bird Club newsletter, *The Clapper Rail*

Brooklyn Center for the Urban Environment, *CityGreen*

Linnaean Society of New York, *News-Letter*

Mariners Marsh Conservancy, *The Marsh Messenger*

New Jersey Audubon Society; *Records of New Jersey Birds*

New York City Audubon Society newsletter, *The Urban Audubon*

Protectors of Pine Oak Woods newsletter

Queens County Bird Club newsletter, *News and Notes*

Staten Island Institute of Arts and Sciences newsletter

Index

New York City Audubon Society

With more than 10,000 members, the New York City Audubon Society is the largest Audubon chapter in the United States. New York City Audubon members in the five boroughs protect and restore wildlife habitat through grassroots advocacy, scientific research, and public programs.

The key element in these stewardship efforts is citizen monitoring. Working under the direction of ornithologists, chapter volunteers have studied the nesting success of wading birds on the islands in New York Harbor since 1985. Each year, the results of the Harbor Herons Project are shared with affiliated nonprofit organizations and government agencies to ensure the protection of the entire Harbor Herons complex.

From 1994 to 1996, New York City Audubon conducted a research and restoration outreach project at Bayswater Point and Dubos Point, two parklands on Jamaica Bay. Scientists, naturalists, and chapter members engaged local residents and students of all ages in the study of birds, insects, marine life, and plants. More than 200 people took part in the three-year project that resulted in an extensive report, *Jamaica Bay Coastal Habitat Restoration Project at Bayswater Point State Park and Dubos Point Wetlands Sanctuary, Queens*.

In 1998, New York City Audubon members completed the first comprehensive breeding bird census of Central Park. The survey, following the protocols of the Cornell Lab of Ornithology, revealed that in one season, 31 species nested in Central Park.

New York City Audubon conducts beginning birding classes, leads birding field trips, holds monthly programs on natural science topics, and publishes a newsletter, *The Urban Audubon*. Members organize and take part in these activities as well as in education and research projects.

Join New York City Audubon so that you can take part in important citywide conservation work. Members of New York City Audubon also become members of the National Audubon Society, one of the oldest conservation organizations in the United States.

For detailed information about becoming a member, contact the New York City Audubon Society at 212-691-7483, 71 West 23rd Street, Suite 1529, New York, N.Y. 10010 or log on to www.nycaudubon.org.